Adam Giddo, with a rich two-decade background in ICT, moved from a foundational role in U.S. local government to spearheading global digital transformation, making a marked impact on blockchain adoption in the Middle East. As a visionary entrepreneur and blockchain advocate, he led pivotal government initiatives and established Vision Innovation, championing the global potential of blockchain. His recent appointment as a Global Blockchain Business Council Ambassador reflects his significant contribution to digital development. Mr.Giddo's academic excellence, underscored by credentials from MIT's Executive Program in Blockchain Technologies, mirrors his professional achievements, affirming his leadership in tech innovation.

To Melissa and my kids, and to my dear parents,
who laid the foundation of everything I am.

For your love, support, and inspiration.

Adam Giddo

CYBER PANDEMIC

A PROACTIVE LOOK AT BLOCKCHAIN AND AI TO PREVENT THE NEXT GLOBAL SHUTDOWN

AUSTIN MACAULEY PUBLISHERS®
LONDON * CAMBRIDGE * NEW YORK * SHARJAH

Copyright © Adam Giddo 2024

The right of Adam Giddo to be identified as author of this work has been asserted by the author in accordance with Federal Law No. (7) of UAE, Year 2002, Concerning Copyrights and Neighboring Rights.

All rights reserved. No part of this publication may be reproduced, stored in a retrieval system, or transmitted in any form or by any means, electronic, mechanical, photocopying, recording, or otherwise, without the prior permission of the publishers.

Any person who commits any unauthorized act in relation to this publication may be liable to legal prosecution and civil claims for damages.

ISBN – 9789948748724 – (Paperback)
ISBN – 9789948748731 – (E-Book)

Application Number: MC-10-01-7483988
Age Classification: E

The age group that matches the content of the books has been classified according to the age classification system issued by the UAE Media Council.

First Published 2024
AUSTIN MACAULEY PUBLISHERS FZE
Sharjah Publishing City
P.O Box [519201]
Sharjah, UAE
www.austinmacauley.ae
+971 655 95 202

I extend my deepest gratitude to the Almighty God for His unwavering guidance and inspiration throughout this transformative journey. His divine presence has provided me with the strength and wisdom to delve into the realm of cybersecurity and share valuable insights with readers.

To my beloved family, thank you for your unwavering love, support, and understanding. Your belief in my abilities and constant encouragement have been my pillars of strength during the challenges of writing this book.

To my friends and colleagues, thank you for your valuable insights, feedback, and encouragement. Your support has been invaluable in shaping the content of this book and enhancing its impact.

I am indebted to the experts, researchers, and professionals in the field of cybersecurity whose contributions have enriched the depth and relevance of this book.

To my readers, your curiosity and dedication to understanding and addressing cyber threats inspire me. I hope the knowledge shared in this book empowers you to navigate the complex world of cybersecurity with confidence and resilience.

In crafting this book, I was fortunate to harness the power of advanced artificial intelligence technologies, which played a pivotal role in shaping the narrative, enhancing the content, and providing valuable insights. This exploration of AI-assisted writing has enriched the book's content and underscored the themes discussed within its pages. I am deeply thankful to the innovative teams and individuals behind these AI tools for their contributions to creative expression and knowledge dissemination.

Table of Contents

1: Introduction to the Cyber Pandemic	11
2: Harnessing Blockchain a Revolutionary Approach to Cyber Defense	20
3: Anatomy of a Cyberattack: Case Studies	45
4: Power Grids in the Crosshairs: Security and Vulnerabilities	59
5: Safeguarding Wealth: Cybersecurity in the Financial Sector	86
6: Democracy at Risk: Election System Hacking	101
7: The Dark Side of Connectivity: Exploitation of IoT Systems	110
8: The Economic Domino Effect: The Rise in Oil Prices	127
9: National and Global Responses to Cyber Pandemics	134
10: Public and Private Sector: Roles and Responsibilities	143
11: Anticipating the Unthinkable: Probability of a Major Cyberattack	155
12: Innovation and Proactivity Opportunities to Deter Cyber-attacks	172
13: The Aftermath: Predicting Future Needs Post-Cyber Pandemic	184
14: Conclusion: A Resilient Future in the Face of Cyber Threats	201
Index of Terms and Concepts	224
Appendix A: Cybersecurity Resources and Tools	227
Appendix B: Further Reading and Research	230
Appendix C: Glossary of Key Terms	233
Appendix D: References	237

1
Introduction to the Cyber Pandemic

The Dawn of a New Threat: Defining Cyber Pandemic

As we move deeper into the 21st century, a new kind of threat has begun to emerge. It's a threat that doesn't involve the physical force of weapons or the diplomatic force of treaties and sanctions. Instead, this new threat dwells within the invisible, interconnected world of cyberspace. This phenomenon, the "Cyber Pandemic", is starting to generate apprehension among security experts and governments worldwide.

Like a biological pandemic, a cyber pandemic is a calamity that can cause widespread disruption on a global scale. It's not restricted by geographical borders or physical barriers, which makes it a universal threat. Just as the COVID-19 virus spread across countries, infecting millions of people indiscriminately, a cyber pandemic can permeate through the web of interconnected systems, impacting hundreds of thousands of devices, networks, and digital services simultaneously. However, unlike a biological virus that attacks human bodies, a cyber pandemic infects our digital lives, potentially causing colossal damage to economies, governments, and individuals.

In the present world, where digitalization is accelerating at an unprecedented pace, our reliance on digital systems and networks is greater than ever. The advent of the Fourth Industrial Revolution has seen a dramatic rise in the use of the Internet of Things (IoT), Artificial Intelligence (AI), and machine learning, transforming the world into an intricate mesh of interconnected systems. From smart homes and autonomous vehicles to industrial control systems and critical national infrastructure, digital systems are embedded into nearly every facet of our lives. Consequently, the impact of a cyber pandemic could be more significant and far-reaching than any physical attack or traditional pandemic.

The COVID-19 pandemic has illustrated how global crises can escalate rapidly, exerting far-reaching and long-lasting effects on societies and economies. During this time, we have witnessed an increase in cyber threats, with adversaries exploiting the crisis by launching attacks on remote work infrastructure, health services, and public information systems. This rise in cyber-attacks amidst the health crisis serves as a stark reminder of the potential scale and impact a cyber pandemic could have.

A cyber pandemic can occur in various ways. It could originate from a state-sponsored attack intending to destabilize another nation, or a malicious attack by cybercriminals aiming for financial gain. Regardless of its origin, the ramifications could be devastating. It could disrupt services, lead to the theft of sensitive information, cause economic turmoil, and even result in physical harm if systems controlling critical infrastructure are affected. In essence, a cyber pandemic represents the collective failure of digital security on a global scale.

Given this emerging threat, it is clear that traditional cybersecurity measures may not be enough to protect our interconnected systems. These measures, often designed for isolated incidents and specific threat vectors, may fall short in the face of a systemic, large-scale cyberattack. The decentralized and complex nature of modern digital infrastructure demands a holistic, robust approach to cybersecurity.

This is where the concept of "cyber resilience" comes into play. It emphasizes not only the prevention of cyber-attacks but also the ability to minimize the damage and recover quickly when attacks occur. The objective is to maintain the integrity and availability of digital services in the face of a crisis, ensuring continuity and minimizing disruption.

Recognizing the magnitude of the threat a cyber pandemic presents, experts are exploring innovative solutions that can bolster our cyber resilience. One such solution, which will be a recurring theme in this book, is blockchain technology. Although best known as the technology underpinning cryptocurrencies like Bitcoin, blockchain's potential extends far beyond that. Its inherent features—decentralization, immutability, transparency, and cryptographic security—make it a promising candidate to fortify our digital systems against a cyber pandemic.

Landscape of Cyber Threats: The Rising Challenges

The age of digitalization, while opening the doors to numerous opportunities and advancements, has also given rise to an equally broad spectrum of cyber threats. These threats are not an entirely new phenomenon. They have coexisted with digital progress since its inception. However, their magnitude, frequency, and sophistication have escalated dramatically in recent years. This intensification is amplified by the growing interconnectedness of our digital world, advancements in technology, and the increasing reliance of businesses, societies, and nations on digital infrastructure.

Just as the COVID-19 pandemic has indiscriminately affected communities across the globe, a cyber pandemic too can have a nondiscriminatory nature. It wouldn't distinguish between small businesses or multinational corporations, individual users or governmental institutions. This "equality" in the face of threat signifies a critical shift in our understanding of security and defense.

Cyber threats come in various forms—from viruses, worms, and Trojans to ransomware, spyware, and phishing attacks. The targets are just as diverse, ranging from personal devices and corporate networks to critical infrastructures such as power grids, healthcare systems, and government databases. The motivations driving these cyber-attacks are as varied as their forms. Some attacks are state-sponsored, intended to cause disruption, gain a competitive edge, or exert influence. Others are carried out by cybercriminals aiming for financial gain or simply to prove their technical prowess.

The rising challenges of the cyber threat landscape can be attributed to a few factors. Firstly, the expansion of the Internet of Things (IoT) has created a vast network of devices, each potentially a point of entry for hackers. Secondly, rapid technological advancements, such as the emergence of artificial intelligence (AI) and machine learning, have served as a double-edged sword. While they help in enhancing defense mechanisms, they also provide sophisticated tools to attackers. Thirdly, the increasing digitization of services and processes across sectors has led to an abundance of data, much of which is sensitive and valuable.

The COVID-19 pandemic has served as a harsh reminder of our vulnerabilities. As businesses, educational institutions, and even social interactions moved online due to lockdowns and social distancing measures, we witnessed a surge in cyber threats. From opportunistic phishing campaigns exploiting the crisis to nation-state attacks on healthcare systems and research institutions, the pandemic has underscored the potential scale and impact of a cyber pandemic.

As our reliance on digital platforms grows, so does our vulnerability to cyber threats. In a digitally interconnected world, a single weak link can have cascading effects, leading to systemic failure. This interconnectedness, coupled with the evolving sophistication of cyber threats, necessitates a reimagining of our approach to cybersecurity.

The traditional approach of "defense in-depth", which relies on multiple layers of security controls, may no longer suffice in the face of large-scale, coordinated cyber-attacks that could trigger a cyber pandemic. Instead, a holistic, resilient, and proactive approach to cybersecurity is required. It's not just about protecting our systems but also about building the capability to rapidly detect, respond to, and recover from attacks while ensuring minimal disruption to services.

In the context of this growing threat landscape, blockchain technology emerges as a potential game-changer. Its unique characteristics of decentralization, immutability, transparency, and cryptographic security make it a promising tool to enhance cyber resilience. By leveraging blockchain, we can potentially transform our cybersecurity defenses and prepare for the looming threat of a cyber pandemic.

An Escalating Crisis: Real-World Cases of Major Cyber-attacks

Throughout the history of the digital age, we have witnessed numerous cyber-attacks that have served as glaring indications of the cyber pandemic's potential severity. Each attack has offered a glimpse into the evolving sophistication of malicious actors, their preferred targets, and the significant damage that a coordinated, large-scale cyberattack can inflict on nations, businesses, and individuals alike.

One of the earliest known cyber-attacks occurred in 1988 when the Morris Worm infected about 6,000 computers, a significant proportion of the internet-connected devices at the time. While this attack was not malicious in intent—it was a self-replicating program that got out of hand—it demonstrated the potential of a large-scale disruption in the digital realm.

In the years that followed, the world witnessed an array of high-profile cyber-attacks, each demonstrating the growing potential of a cyber pandemic. In 2007, Estonia suffered a massive cyberattack, which many believe was state-sponsored. The attack crippled many of the country's critical infrastructures, such as banking and government services, emphasizing the vulnerability of nations to digital threats.

Fast forward to 2017, and we encounter the devastating WannaCry ransomware attack. This attack affected over 200,000 computers across 150 countries, causing significant disruption to healthcare services, businesses, and individuals. The attack's rapid spread highlighted how interconnected our world had become and how this interconnectivity could be exploited to propagate a cyber threat quickly and broadly.

Similarly, the NotPetya malware attack that occurred in the same year targeted several multinational companies, causing billions of dollars in damage. It was another stark reminder of the international business community's vulnerability to cyber threats and the potential for significant economic disruption.

In the context of a global crisis, the COVID-19 pandemic brought with it a surge in cyber-attacks. Many of these targeted the healthcare sector, a critical service during the pandemic, thereby demonstrating the malicious intent of threat actors to exploit vulnerabilities even in times of global distress.

The most recent example in the long history of significant cyber threats is the SolarWinds attack in 2020, where sophisticated threat actors compromised a widely used network management software to infiltrate numerous government and private sector systems. This attack was a clear demonstration of the potential scale, sophistication, and long-term implications of a large-scale cyberattack.

These real-world instances of cyber-attacks underline the escalating cyber threat landscape. They showcase how these threats have evolved from mere nuisances into systemic risks capable of causing widespread disruption, economic damage, and societal distress. The lessons we learn from these attacks are crucial in preparing ourselves for the looming threat of a cyber pandemic.

As we navigate this threat landscape, it becomes increasingly clear that traditional defensive measures are inadequate. A new approach to digital defense is needed, one that is rooted in the principles of resilience, rapid response, and recovery. It's here that technologies like blockchain present potential solutions, and exploring these will form the foundation of our discussions in the subsequent sections.

The Role of Blockchain in Mitigating Cyber Threats

As we reflect on the escalating risks of a cyber pandemic, it becomes evident that we must explore new paradigms of security to ensure our digital resilience.

One promising technology that stands out in the quest to fortify our digital defenses is blockchain.

Blockchain, at its core, is a distributed, transparent, and immutable ledger technology that forms the backbone of cryptocurrencies such as Bitcoin. However, its potential applications extend far beyond financial transactions, offering unique solutions to some of the most pressing cybersecurity challenges we face today.

Firstly, the decentralized nature of blockchain technology stands in stark contrast to the traditional, centralized models of data storage and management that have proven to be vulnerable targets for cyber-attacks. A decentralized system, devoid of a single point of failure, could offer higher resilience against cyber threats, making it significantly harder for attackers to cause widespread disruption.

Furthermore, the use of cryptographic algorithms in blockchain adds another layer of security. Each block of data in a blockchain is linked to its predecessor via a unique cryptographic hash, creating a chain of blocks that is nearly impossible to alter without detection. This ensures the integrity of the data and can be particularly useful in preventing data tampering attacks.

Blockchain also offers transparency and traceability. Every transaction made on the blockchain is visible to all participants and cannot be altered, providing an immutable audit trail. This feature can enhance accountability, deter malicious activity, and aid in the swift identification and response to a cyberattack.

The potential applications of blockchain in enhancing cybersecurity are diverse. For instance, blockchain could be used to create more secure digital identities, mitigating risks of identity theft and fraud. It could also be employed in securing Internet of Things (IoT) devices, which are often seen as weak points in a network. Furthermore, in supply chain management, blockchain can help trace and authenticate products, reducing the risk of counterfeit goods entering the market.

The recent COVID-19 pandemic has driven many businesses and services to transition online, leading to a surge in digital data and a corresponding increase in cyber threats. In such an environment, the principles of decentralization, transparency, and cryptographic security offered by blockchain can play a critical role in strengthening our digital defenses.

However, like any technology, blockchain is not a silver bullet. It comes with its own set of challenges and limitations, such as scalability issues, the need for consensus mechanisms, and the potential misuse by threat actors. Therefore, it must be seen as a part of a comprehensive cybersecurity strategy, not a standalone solution.

As we move forward to face the rising threat of a cyber pandemic, our approach must be multifaceted, incorporating various technologies, policies, and practices. In this regard, blockchain presents a compelling piece of the puzzle, with the potential to significantly enhance our cyber resilience. This will form the central theme of our discussions in the following sections of this book, as we delve deeper into the specifics of using blockchain in countering cyber threats.

Navigating the Pages Ahead: An Outline of the Journey

As we wind down the first chapter of this expedition into the looming cyber pandemic and the promising role of blockchain in combating it, it's crucial to provide a sneak peek into the ensuing discussions. The purpose of this book is to weave a comprehensive narrative around the multifaceted issue of cyber threats and the potential preventive measures, with an emphasis on blockchain technology.

The subsequent chapters aim to dissect each element related to this central theme, ensuring you gain a well-rounded understanding of the complexities and opportunities that lie ahead. Here's a concise preview of the forthcoming discourse.

Chapter 2: Unleashing Blockchain: A Revolutionary Approach to Cyber Defense—In the second chapter, we will delve into the core concepts of blockchain technology. We will discuss how its unique properties like decentralization, immutability, and transparency can contribute to cybersecurity efforts. Moreover, we will examine its limitations and the challenges that come with integrating blockchain into existing digital infrastructures.

Chapter 3: Protecting the Lifelines: Safeguarding Vital Infrastructure—In this chapter, we will take a closer look at the impact of cyber threats on critical infrastructure sectors, such as energy, healthcare, and finance. We will also consider how blockchain and other technological innovations can enhance the resilience of these sectors.

Chapter 4: Securing the Fiscal Landscape: Shielding Our Economies—Here, we will explore the economic implications of a cyber pandemic, investigating potential impacts on national and global economies. We will then discuss how blockchain can not only provide protection for financial systems but also potentially stimulate economic growth.

Chapter 5: Democracy in the Digital Age: Ensuring Secure Elections—This chapter will focus on the intersection of cyber threats and democratic processes. We will evaluate the vulnerabilities of digital voting systems and discuss how blockchain can help to secure our democratic institutions.

Chapter 6: A Real-World Examination: The 2020 US Election and Cyber Threats—Here, we will apply our previous discussions to a real-world example, focusing on the 2020 US election. We will analyze the specific cyber threats that emerged during this event and evaluate how blockchain technology could have been used to mitigate them.

Chapter 7: Reinforcing IoT with Blockchain: Building a Cyber-Resilient Future—This chapter will focus specifically on the Internet of Things (IoT), exploring how this rapidly expanding field presents new vulnerabilities and how blockchain can be leveraged to improve security.

Chapter 8: The Policy Imperative: Regulatory Aspects of Battling Cyber Threats—In this chapter, we will shift our focus to the policy realm, examining how laws and regulations can support or hinder efforts to combat cyber threats. We will discuss the need for robust, forward-thinking policies that can both protect against cyber threats and encourage technological innovation.

Chapter 9: The Final Verdict: Toward Global Collaboration Against Cyber Pandemics—The concluding chapter will synthesize the insights gleaned from previous chapters, emphasizing the necessity of global cooperation in preventing and managing a cyber pandemic. This chapter will also consider future trends and developments in the field of cybersecurity, providing readers with a forward-looking perspective.

Throughout the course of this book, our discussions will always circle back to the central question: How can we prepare for and protect against a cyber pandemic? While this question may not have a simple answer, it is our hope that by exploring the complexities of cybersecurity and the potential of technologies like blockchain, we can provide readers with valuable insights and tools for understanding and addressing this pressing global issue.

Chapter 10: Cybersecurity Beyond Borders: International Cooperation in the Digital Age—In this chapter, we will delve into the importance of international collaboration in combating cyber threats. We will explore the challenges and opportunities for global cooperation, discuss existing initiatives and frameworks, and propose strategies for enhancing collaboration across nations.

Chapter 11: Blockchain Innovations: Exploring New Frontiers—This chapter will examine the latest innovations and advancements in blockchain technology that can further strengthen cybersecurity measures. We will explore emerging trends such as privacy-preserving blockchain solutions, secure smart contracts, and decentralized identity management systems.

Chapter 12: Ethical and Legal Implications of Blockchain in Cybersecurity—Here, we will explore the ethical and legal considerations associated with the use of blockchain in cybersecurity. We will discuss topics such as data privacy, consent, accountability, and the potential impact on regulatory frameworks and legal systems.

Chapter 13: Cyber Threat Intelligence: Empowering Defense Strategies—In this chapter, we will focus on the importance of cyber threat intelligence in building effective defense strategies. We will explore how blockchain technology can enhance the collection, analysis, and sharing of threat intelligence to enable proactive cyber defense.

Chapter 14: Human Factor: Cultivating a Cybersecurity Mindset—This chapter will shed light on the crucial role of human factors in cybersecurity. We will discuss the importance of cybersecurity awareness, education, and training for individuals and organizations, and how a cybersecurity mindset can contribute to mitigating cyber threats.

Throughout the book, we aim to provide a comprehensive understanding of the evolving cyber threat landscape, the potential of blockchain technology, and the broader context of cybersecurity. By exploring various dimensions of the subject matter, we hope to equip readers with the knowledge and insights needed to navigate the complex challenges and opportunities presented by the looming cyber pandemic.

2
Harnessing Blockchain a Revolutionary Approach to Cyber Defense

The Promise of Blockchain in Cybersecurity

In the ever-evolving landscape of cyber threats, traditional cybersecurity measures have struggled to keep pace with the sophistication and scale of attacks. As we confront this new reality, blockchain technology has emerged as a promising solution, offering a revolutionary approach to fortifying our cyber defenses.

Blockchain, originally introduced as the underlying technology behind cryptocurrencies like Bitcoin, has evolved beyond its financial origins. Its inherent characteristics of decentralization, immutability, transparency, and cryptographic security make it an ideal candidate for addressing the challenges of cybersecurity.

One of the key advantages of blockchain is its decentralized nature. Traditional systems often rely on centralized servers or intermediaries that act as single points of failure. In contrast, blockchain operates on a network of distributed nodes, each maintaining a copy of the ledger. This decentralized architecture eliminates the vulnerabilities associated with centralization, making it significantly harder for cyber attackers to compromise the system.

The immutability of blockchain provides an additional layer of security. Once a transaction is recorded and added to the blockchain, it becomes permanent and tamper-resistant. The use of cryptographic hashing ensures that any modification to a block will result in a change in the hash, alerting the network to the attempted tampering. This feature enhances data integrity and protects against unauthorized modifications or data manipulation.

Transparency is another hallmark of blockchain technology. While individual transactions may be pseudonymous, the entire transaction history is available for scrutiny by all participants in the network. This transparency fosters trust and accountability, as any discrepancy or malicious activity can be readily detected and traced back to its source.

The cryptographic security of blockchain adds an extra layer of protection against cyber threats. Transactions within a blockchain are secured through the use of digital signatures, ensuring that only authorized participants can engage in transactions. The use of public key cryptography provides strong authentication and confidentiality, safeguarding sensitive information from unauthorized access.

Blockchain also offers potential solutions for addressing specific cybersecurity challenges. For example, the use of smart contracts, self-executing contracts with the terms of the agreement directly written into code, can automate and enforce security measures. Smart contracts can facilitate secure authentication, access control, and data sharing, reducing vulnerabilities and mitigating risks.

Furthermore, blockchain technology can enhance the resilience of data storage and backup systems. By distributing data across a network of nodes, blockchain eliminates the risk of a single point of failure and provides redundancy. This decentralized approach makes data loss due to cyber-attacks or system failures less likely, ensuring the continuity of critical information.

In the face of increasingly sophisticated cyber threats, blockchain technology presents a paradigm shift in our approach to cybersecurity. Its decentralized, immutable, and transparent nature, coupled with robust cryptographic security, holds the promise of creating more resilient and secure systems.

In the subsequent sections of this chapter, we will delve into specific use cases where blockchain can be applied in cybersecurity. From securing digital identities to protecting critical infrastructure and enhancing threat intelligence, we will explore the practical applications of blockchain technology in fortifying our defenses against cyber threats.

Dissecting Blockchain: How it Works for Cybersecurity

To fully grasp the potential of blockchain technology in cybersecurity, it is essential to dissect its inner workings and understand how it can effectively address the challenges we face. In this section, we will delve into the mechanics of blockchain and explore its application in fortifying our cyber defenses.

At its core, a blockchain is a decentralized and distributed ledger that records transactions in a chronological and immutable manner. Let's examine the key components that make up a blockchain and how they contribute to its effectiveness in cybersecurity.

1. **Blocks:** A blockchain consists of a series of interconnected blocks, with each block serving as a container for a collection of verified and time-stamped transactions. These transactions capture various types of digital interactions, facilitating the transfer of assets, the execution of smart contracts, or the recording of data.

For example, let's consider a blockchain-based payment system. Each block within the blockchain can contain multiple transactions, where individuals or entities transfer digital currency units to one another. These transactions are validated by the network's participants, ensuring that they meet predefined criteria and adhere to the rules of the blockchain. Once the transactions are verified, they are bundled together into a block and added to the blockchain in a sequential manner.

The inclusion of time-stamped transactions in each block serves multiple purposes. First, it establishes a chronological order, allowing participants to track the sequence of events within the blockchain. This feature proves particularly valuable when auditing transactions or investigating potential discrepancies. Second, the timestamping ensures that the transactions are securely recorded and cannot be retroactively modified without invalidating subsequent blocks. As a result, the integrity and immutability of the blockchain are maintained.

The types of transactions recorded in blocks can vary based on the specific use case of the blockchain. In a supply chain management system, for instance, each block may capture the movement of goods as they transition from one stage to another. This includes details such as the origins of the product, the entities involved in the supply chain, and the necessary quality control checks performed along the way. By recording these transactions on the blockchain, a transparent and auditable trail of the entire supply chain process is established, reducing the risk of counterfeit products and facilitating efficient traceability.

In summary, the blocks within a blockchain serve as containers for verified and time-stamped transactions, capturing a wide range of digital interactions. This structure allows for the secure and transparent recording of data, whether it involves financial transactions, contract execution, or supply chain activities. By leveraging this foundation, blockchain technology offers immense potential for enhancing cybersecurity, data integrity, and trust in digital ecosystems.

2. **Cryptographic Hashing:** Cryptographic hashing is a vital component of blockchain technology that ensures the integrity and security of data within each block. In a digital identity management system, where sensitive personal information such as identification documents and biometric data are stored on the blockchain, cryptographic hashing plays a critical role in protecting the privacy and security of individuals' data.

Cryptographic hashing involves applying a mathematical algorithm to convert data of any size into a fixed-size string of characters, known as a hash. The hashing process is deterministic, meaning that the same input data will always produce the same output hash. However, even a small change in the input data will result in a significantly different hash value.

In the context of a digital identity management system, the personal information of individuals, such as their identification documents or biometric data, can be hashed before being stored on the blockchain. This hashing process transforms the sensitive data into a unique and irreversible representation. The resulting hash value is then recorded within the blockchain, ensuring the privacy and security of the original information.

By employing cryptographic hashing, the blockchain can verify the authenticity and integrity of the stored data without exposing the original sensitive information. For instance, when performing identity verification, the system can compare the hashed values of stored identification documents with the hashed values of the presented documents without revealing the actual content of the documents. This process allows for secure and efficient verification while minimizing the risk of unauthorized access or data breaches.

Furthermore, cryptographic hashing adds an additional layer of security to the blockchain by making it nearly impossible to reverse-engineer the original data from the hash. The algorithms used in cryptographic hashing are designed to be computationally intensive, making it extremely challenging and time-consuming for attackers to find two different sets of data that produce the same hash value. This property ensures the integrity of the data within each block, as any attempt to modify the data would result in a different hash value, alerting the network to the tampering attempt.

In summary, cryptographic hashing is a crucial mechanism within blockchain technology that ensures the integrity and security of data within each block. By converting sensitive information into irreversible hash values, blockchain-based systems can securely store and verify data without exposing the original content. This approach reduces the risk of identity theft, fraud, and unauthorized access to personal information, making blockchain an attractive solution for digital identity management and other applications requiring secure data storage and verification.

3. **Decentralization and Consensus Mechanisms:** Decentralization and consensus mechanisms are fundamental pillars of blockchain technology that significantly enhance security, resilience, and trust in various applications. Let's explore the concept further by examining a public blockchain-based voting system as an example.

In a traditional voting system, there is often a centralized authority responsible for managing and tallying the votes. This centralized approach introduces a single point of failure, as the authority can be vulnerable to manipulation, tampering, or coercion. To address these vulnerabilities, blockchain technology leverages decentralization and consensus mechanisms to create a more secure and transparent voting process.

Decentralization in a blockchain-based voting system means that the voting process is distributed across a network of nodes. Each node holds a copy of the entire blockchain, ensuring redundancy and eliminating the dependence on a single central authority. This decentralized structure makes it exceedingly difficult for any single entity to manipulate or control the voting process. Any attempts to tamper with the votes would require controlling the majority of the network's nodes, which is highly improbable in a well-designed and widely adopted blockchain network.

Consensus mechanisms play a crucial role in ensuring the integrity and validity of votes in a decentralized voting system. They enable participants to collectively validate and verify the votes, achieving a consensus on the accepted results. Different consensus mechanisms, such as Proof of Stake (PoS) or Practical Byzantine Fault Tolerance (PBFT), can be employed in blockchain-based voting systems.

For instance, in a PoS-based voting system, participants who hold a stake in the network are chosen to validate and verify the votes. Their stake serves as a measure of their influence and responsibility in maintaining the security of the blockchain. By relying on participants with a significant stake, PoS consensus ensures that those who have a vested interest in the system act in its best interest, further enhancing the security and reliability of the voting process.

In a PBFT-based voting system, a certain number of nodes, known as validators, are selected to collectively validate and reach a consensus on the votes. Validators exchange messages to agree on the validity of the votes, ensuring that they are consistent and free from malicious manipulation. This consensus mechanism is particularly effective in environments where the risk of Byzantine faults, such as nodes behaving maliciously or providing incorrect information, needs to be mitigated.

The decentralized and consensus-based approach in blockchain-based voting systems enhances transparency and trust. Every participant has the ability to audit the voting process, ensuring that votes are recorded accurately and without tampering. The transparency of the blockchain allows participants to independently verify the results and hold the system accountable.

Real-world examples, such as the Sierra Leone presidential election in 2018, have demonstrated the potential of blockchain-based voting systems. The system provided a transparent and tamper-proof platform for citizens to cast their votes, preventing electoral fraud and ensuring the integrity of the election results.

By leveraging decentralization and consensus mechanisms, blockchain-based voting systems offer enhanced security, transparency, and trust in the democratic process. These principles can be applied to various other domains, such as corporate governance, shareholder voting, or community decision-making processes, where transparency, fairness, and tamper resistance are paramount. The decentralized nature of blockchain, combined with consensus mechanisms, reshapes traditional voting systems and introduces a new era of secure and trustworthy digital voting.

4. **Immutable Ledger and Transparency:** The immutability and transparency of blockchain technology offer significant advantages in

enhancing cybersecurity, particularly in scenarios such as intellectual property rights management. Let's explore this application further to understand how blockchain's immutable ledger and transparency can mitigate risks and foster accountability and trust.

In the context of intellectual property rights management, blockchain provides a robust solution for recording ownership and licensing agreements. By capturing this information on the blockchain, an immutable ledger is created, ensuring that the history of intellectual property rights is tamper-proof and resistant to unauthorized modifications.

The immutability of the blockchain means that once a record of ownership or licensing is added to the ledger, it cannot be altered or deleted without consensus from the network participants. This feature safeguards the integrity of intellectual property rights by preserving a transparent and auditable record of their ownership, creation, and licensing history.

For instance, imagine a musician who wants to protect their original compositions. By registering the copyrights and licensing agreements on the blockchain, a permanent and unchangeable record is established. This immutable ledger acts as a verifiable proof of ownership, protecting the musician's intellectual property from infringement and unauthorized use. Interested parties, such as potential licensees or enforcement authorities, can easily verify the legitimacy and validity of the intellectual property rights recorded on the blockchain.

The transparency inherent in blockchain technology further enhances accountability and trust. All participants within the network have access to the same set of information recorded on the blockchain, ensuring transparency and eliminating the need for intermediaries. This transparency fosters a sense of trust among the parties involved, as the actions and changes made to the intellectual property records can be easily traced and audited.

For example, if a licensing agreement is executed between a musician and a company, the details of the agreement, including the terms, royalties, and contract duration, can be recorded on the blockchain. Any subsequent changes or transactions related to the licensing agreement, such as modifications, renewals, or transfers, are also recorded in a transparent manner. This visibility ensures that all parties are aware of the current status and history of the licensing agreement, minimizing disputes and facilitating smoother interactions.

The transparency of blockchain technology also benefits enforcement authorities tasked with monitoring and protecting intellectual property rights. They can access the blockchain to verify the authenticity and ownership of intellectual property assets, making the process of identifying and addressing infringement cases more efficient and reliable.

In summary, the immutable ledger and transparency provided by blockchain technology offer substantial advantages in cybersecurity, particularly in intellectual property rights management. By recording ownership and licensing agreements on the blockchain, a tamper-proof and auditable record is established, reducing the risk of infringement and unauthorized use. The transparency of blockchain fosters accountability and trust among participants, as changes and transactions can be easily traced and audited. These features empower creators, licensors, and enforcement authorities, enhancing the protection and management of intellectual property rights in a secure and transparent manner.

5. **Smart Contracts:** Smart contracts, a core feature of blockchain technology, offer significant potential for enhancing cybersecurity and streamlining various processes. Let's explore the applications of smart contracts in cybersecurity further, using the example of insurance claim processing.

Insurance claim processing is a complex and often time-consuming task that involves multiple parties, verification procedures, and document exchanges. Smart contracts can revolutionize this process by automating the validation and settlement of claims based on predefined rules and conditions. By encoding the terms and conditions of insurance policies directly into the smart contract code, the claim process becomes self-executing and efficient.

When a policyholder submits an insurance claim, the smart contract automatically evaluates the claim based on predefined rules. These rules can include conditions such as the type of coverage, deductible amounts, proof of loss requirements, and specific timelines. The smart contract verifies the submitted information against these rules, eliminating the need for manual intervention and reducing the potential for human error or bias.

Smart contracts can also integrate with external data sources and IoT devices to gather relevant information for claim verification. For example, in the case of property insurance, data from sensors and surveillance systems can be fed into the smart contract to assess the extent of damage and validate the claim. This integration ensures accurate and reliable claim assessments, mitigating the risk of fraudulent claims.

Once the claim is validated, the smart contract automatically triggers the settlement process. The predefined rules determine the amount to be paid, taking into account factors such as deductibles, coverage limits, and any other relevant policy terms. The settlement can be executed in various forms, including the transfer of funds in digital currencies or traditional currencies, depending on the agreement between the parties involved.

By utilizing smart contracts in insurance claim processing, several benefits are realized. First, the automation of the process reduces the administrative burden and minimizes the time required for claim settlement. This leads to faster and more efficient resolution, improving customer satisfaction and reducing the financial impact on insurance providers.

Second, the use of smart contracts significantly reduces the potential for fraudulent claims. The predefined rules and conditions embedded in the smart contract ensure that claims are assessed objectively and in accordance with the policy terms. Any attempt to manipulate or submit fraudulent claims that do not meet the predefined criteria would be automatically rejected by the smart contract, enhancing the security and integrity of the claims process.

Furthermore, smart contracts introduce greater transparency to the insurance claim process. All parties involved, including the policyholders, insurers, and relevant stakeholders, have access to the same set of rules and conditions encoded in the smart contract. This transparency fosters trust and reduces disputes, as the terms of the contract are immutably recorded on the blockchain and can be audited by authorized participants.

Overall, the use of smart contracts in insurance claim processing streamlines operations, reduces costs, enhances security, and improves the overall efficiency of the claims process. By automating the validation and settlement of claims based on predefined rules, smart contracts provide a transparent and tamper-proof mechanism for handling insurance-related transactions. This application of smart contracts in cybersecurity showcases the transformative potential of blockchain technology in optimizing complex processes while maintaining robust security measures.

6. **Enhanced Security Measures:** Blockchain incorporates various security measures to protect data and transactions. In the healthcare industry, for example, blockchain can be leveraged to securely store and share patients' medical records. Encryption and digital signatures can be used to ensure that only authorized individuals, such as healthcare providers and patients themselves, can access and modify the records, maintaining patient privacy and data integrity. The decentralized nature of blockchain enhances security by reducing the reliance on a single central authority, making it more resistant to unauthorized access and data breaches. Additionally, the use of blockchain for health data interoperability can ensure the secure and seamless exchange of patient information among different healthcare providers, improving care coordination and patient outcomes.

These examples highlight the versatility of blockchain technology in cybersecurity. By leveraging its decentralized and transparent nature, cryptographic security measures, and smart contract capabilities, blockchain offers innovative solutions to address the challenges posed by cyber threats.

The use of blockchain in these contexts enhances data integrity, ensures transparency and trust, automates processes, strengthens overall cybersecurity measures, and promotes efficiency and collaboration among stakeholders.

In the subsequent sections of this chapter, we will further explore these and other real-world applications of blockchain in cybersecurity. Through these examples, we aim to provide a comprehensive understanding of the potential of blockchain technology to revolutionize our approach to defending against cyber-attacks and enhancing digital security in various sectors and industries.

Strengths and Weaknesses: Evaluating Blockchain in Cyber Defense

Blockchain technology offers unique strengths that can contribute to enhancing cyber defense strategies. However, it is essential to recognize its limitations and potential weaknesses. This section evaluates the strengths and weaknesses of blockchain in the context of cyber defense, providing a comprehensive analysis of its effectiveness and areas for consideration.

Strengths of Blockchain in Cyber Defense

Decentralization: The decentralized nature of blockchain eliminates the reliance on a single central authority, distributing trust and control across a network of nodes. This decentralization makes it challenging for malicious actors to compromise the system through a single point of failure. Each participant in the network holds a copy of the blockchain, ensuring redundancy and increasing the overall resilience of the system. For example, in a distributed ledger used for securing digital identities, the decentralized nature of blockchain makes it difficult for an attacker to manipulate or steal sensitive identity information, providing a strong defense against identity theft and unauthorized access.

Immutability: Blockchain's immutability ensures that once data is recorded on the blockchain, it cannot be altered or tampered with without consensus from the network participants. This feature enhances data integrity, creating a reliable and tamper-proof audit trail. The immutability of blockchain makes it difficult for attackers to manipulate or falsify data, providing a strong defense against data tampering and fraud. For instance, in supply chain management, the immutability of blockchain records can prevent the unauthorized modification of product information, ensuring transparency and reducing the risk of counterfeit goods entering the supply chain.

Transparency: Blockchain's transparency enables participants to have a clear view of all transactions and activities recorded on the blockchain. This transparency fosters trust, accountability, and auditability, as all stakeholders can verify the integrity of the data and ensure compliance with established rules and protocols. For example, in the context of public procurement, blockchain can provide transparency in the bidding and contracting process, allowing stakeholders to track transactions and ensure fairness, reducing the risk of corruption and fraudulent activities.

Cryptographic Security: Blockchain utilizes cryptographic algorithms to secure data and transactions. Public key cryptography ensures that only authorized participants can access and interact with the blockchain, providing robust authentication and encryption mechanisms. Cryptographic hashing algorithms, digital signatures, and encryption techniques contribute to the overall security of the blockchain. The cryptographic security measures of blockchain protect data from unauthorized access, ensuring confidentiality and integrity. For example, in the healthcare sector, blockchain can be used to securely store and share patient health records, protecting sensitive information and preventing unauthorized modifications.

Resilience to Attacks: Blockchain's distributed nature makes it highly resilient to attacks. As the blockchain operates on a network of interconnected nodes, it becomes challenging for attackers to compromise a majority of nodes simultaneously. This resilience ensures the overall integrity and availability of the system, making it difficult for attackers to disrupt or manipulate transactions. The resilience of blockchain can be especially valuable in critical infrastructure sectors such as energy grids or transportation systems, where the uninterrupted operation of essential services is paramount.

Weaknesses of Blockchain in Cyber Defense

Scalability: Blockchain technology faces challenges with scalability, particularly in public blockchains. The consensus mechanisms and the need for all participants to validate and store the entire blockchain can result in limitations in transaction throughput and increased storage requirements. This scalability issue may hinder the adoption of blockchain in large-scale cyber defense applications. However, advancements such as sharding, sidechains, and layer-2 solutions are being developed to address these scalability concerns.

Performance: Blockchain's consensus mechanisms, such as Proof of Work (PoW) or Proof of Stake (PoS), require computational resources and time to reach consensus. This can lead to delays in transaction confirmation and limit the overall performance of the system. However, efforts are being made to improve the performance of blockchain networks through protocol enhancements, optimization techniques, and the exploration of alternative consensus mechanisms.

Governance and Regulation: The decentralized nature of blockchain can pose challenges in terms of governance and regulatory frameworks. As there is no central authority controlling the blockchain, issues related to legal compliance, jurisdictional boundaries, and dispute resolution can arise. Establishing appropriate governance and regulatory frameworks is essential to ensure the responsible use of blockchain in cyber defense. Collaboration between industry stakeholders, policymakers, and regulatory bodies is crucial to address these challenges and develop frameworks that balance innovation with regulatory requirements.

Security of External Systems: While blockchain itself offers robust security, the integration points between blockchain and external systems may introduce vulnerabilities. Weaknesses in external systems, such as smart contracts, wallets, or off-chain data sources, can become potential attack vectors. It is crucial to address the security of these external components to ensure the overall security of the blockchain ecosystem. Security audits, code reviews, and best practices for integration can help mitigate these risks.

Privacy Considerations: Blockchain's transparency can pose challenges in terms of privacy, especially in public blockchains where all transactions and data are recorded on a public ledger. This transparency may not be suitable for scenarios requiring strict confidentiality. Privacy-enhancing techniques, such as zero-knowledge proofs or private blockchains, can address these concerns to some extent. It is important to carefully consider the privacy requirements of a specific use case and implement appropriate privacy measures.

In conclusion, while blockchain technology offers several strengths that can contribute to enhancing cyber defense strategies, it is important to consider its limitations and potential weaknesses. The strengths of decentralization, immutability, transparency, and cryptographic security provide significant benefits in securing data and transactions. However, challenges related to scalability, performance, governance, integration with external systems, and privacy must be carefully addressed. By understanding both the strengths and weaknesses of blockchain technology, organizations can make informed decisions about its application in their cyber defense strategies, ensuring an effective and balanced approach to cybersecurity.

Visioning Blockchain's Impact: Potential Changes in the Cybersecurity Landscape

Blockchain technology has the potential to revolutionize the cybersecurity landscape by introducing new approaches, solutions, and paradigms. This section explores the potential changes that blockchain can bring to the cybersecurity landscape, envisioning its impact in various areas.

Decentralized Identity Management: Empowering Individuals with Control and Security

Identity management is a critical aspect of cybersecurity, and blockchain technology has the potential to revolutionize this field. Traditional identity management systems rely on centralized databases, making them vulnerable to single points of failure and susceptible to data breaches. However, blockchain offers a decentralized and secure framework for managing digital identities, empowering individuals with greater control and security over their personal information.

In a blockchain-based identity management system, individuals have control over their own digital identities. Instead of relying on third-party entities to store and manage personal data, individuals can securely store their information on the blockchain. Through cryptographic mechanisms, individuals can grant access to their data to trusted entities without compromising their privacy.

The decentralized nature of blockchain ensures that there is no single point of failure. Instead, the data is stored and distributed across a network of nodes, making it highly resistant to hacking or unauthorized access. This enhanced security significantly reduces the risk of identity theft, as malicious actors would need to compromise a majority of the network to gain unauthorized access to sensitive information.

Furthermore, blockchain's immutability adds an additional layer of security to identity management. Once data is recorded on the blockchain, it becomes nearly impossible to alter or tamper with without the consensus of network participants. This feature ensures the integrity and authenticity of the data, creating a reliable and tamper-proof audit trail of digital identities.

Decentralized identity management also enhances privacy. With traditional systems, individuals often have to share their personal information with multiple entities, increasing the risk of data breaches and identity theft. However, with blockchain, individuals can selectively share only the necessary information required for specific transactions or interactions. This granular control over data sharing minimizes the exposure of personal information, providing individuals with greater privacy and control over their digital presence.

Real-world examples of decentralized identity management solutions based on blockchain technology are already emerging. Projects such as SelfKey, uPort, and Sovrin are leveraging blockchain to enable individuals to manage their digital identities securely and assert their digital rights. These projects aim to shift the paradigm of identity management by empowering individuals and reducing reliance on centralized authorities.

The potential impact of decentralized identity management extends beyond individuals. Industries such as finance, healthcare, and government can benefit from more secure and efficient identity verification processes. For example, blockchain-based identity management can streamline Know Your Customer (KYC) processes for financial institutions, reducing administrative burdens and enhancing security.

In conclusion, blockchain technology offers a decentralized and secure framework for identity management. By empowering individuals with control over their digital identities and enhancing security, blockchain-based solutions have the potential to revolutionize the cybersecurity landscape. Decentralized identity management reduces the risk of identity theft, enhances privacy, and provides individuals with greater control over their personal information. As the technology continues to evolve, decentralized identity management holds significant promise for a more secure and privacy-centric digital future.

Secure Data Sharing and Collaboration: Enhancing Trust and Efficiency

Data sharing and collaboration are integral parts of modern business processes, but they also present significant cybersecurity challenges. Blockchain technology offers a transformative solution by enabling secure and trusted data sharing and collaboration among multiple parties. By leveraging the unique features of blockchain, organizations can establish transparent, auditable, and efficient data-sharing ecosystems.

In traditional data-sharing models, organizations often rely on centralized intermediaries to facilitate data exchanges. However, these intermediaries introduce vulnerabilities and increase the risk of data breaches or unauthorized access. With blockchain, organizations can eliminate the need for intermediaries by leveraging the decentralized nature of the technology.

Blockchain's immutability and cryptographic security provide a solid foundation for secure data sharing. Data stored on the blockchain is tamper-proof, ensuring the integrity and authenticity of shared information. This enables organizations to confidently exchange sensitive data without the risk of unauthorized modifications or falsifications.

Smart contracts, programmable self-executing agreements, further enhance the security and efficiency of data sharing and collaboration on the blockchain. Smart contracts can automate and enforce predefined rules and conditions, ensuring that data is shared and accessed in accordance with established protocols. This automation eliminates the need for manual interventions, reduces the potential for human error, and enhances the overall efficiency of data exchanges.

By leveraging blockchain's transparency, organizations can establish trust and accountability in data sharing. All transactions and activities recorded on the blockchain are visible to all participants, ensuring transparency and auditability. This visibility reduces the reliance on trust between parties and allows for independent verification of shared data. For example, supply chain participants can use blockchain to track the movement of goods, ensuring transparency and reducing the risk of counterfeiting or unauthorized alterations.

Real-world examples showcase the potential of blockchain in secure data sharing and collaboration. Industries such as healthcare, finance, supply chain management, and intellectual property rights are exploring blockchain-based solutions to improve data security and streamline collaboration processes. For instance, blockchain can enable secure and auditable sharing of patient health records among healthcare providers, reducing the risk of data breaches and ensuring the privacy of sensitive medical information.

Blockchain's impact on secure data sharing extends beyond organizations. It can facilitate secure and direct interactions between individuals, eliminating the need for intermediaries in personal data exchanges. Individuals can securely share personal information, such as educational qualifications or professional certifications, without relying on centralized authorities. This empowerment of individuals in data sharing processes can enhance privacy, reduce the risk of data abuse, and foster a more equitable digital ecosystem.

In conclusion, blockchain technology offers immense potential to revolutionize data sharing and collaboration processes. By leveraging its immutability, cryptographic security, transparency, and smart contracts, organizations can establish secure, trusted, and efficient data-sharing ecosystems. Blockchain-based solutions have the potential to enhance cybersecurity by reducing the reliance on intermediaries, ensuring data integrity, and fostering trust among participants. As organizations and industries continue to explore and adopt blockchain technology, the future of secure data sharing and collaboration looks promising.

Enhanced Threat Intelligence and Information Sharing: Strengthening Cyber Defense Collaboratively

Threat intelligence plays a crucial role in defending against cyber-attacks, and blockchain technology has the potential to revolutionize the way threat intelligence is collected, shared, and utilized. By leveraging blockchain's transparency, security, and decentralized nature, organizations can enhance their ability to detect, respond to, and mitigate cyber threats more effectively.

Blockchain-based platforms can facilitate the collection, analysis, and dissemination of threat intelligence in real-time. Through a decentralized network of participants, organizations can securely share threat data, indicators of compromise (IOCs), and attack patterns. This collaborative approach allows for the rapid detection and response to emerging threats, reducing the time to identify and mitigate cyber-attacks.

The transparency of the blockchain enables stakeholders to independently verify the accuracy and integrity of the shared threat intelligence. Participants can assess the reputation and credibility of the sources, ensuring the reliability of the information. This transparency fosters trust and encourages active participation in the information-sharing process, facilitating a collective defense against cyber threats.

By utilizing blockchain's cryptographic security, organizations can protect the confidentiality and integrity of shared threat intelligence. Encryption and digital signatures can ensure that only authorized participants have access to the information, preventing unauthorized modifications or tampering. This enhances the security and trustworthiness of the shared data, minimizing the risk of misinformation or malicious manipulation.

The decentralized nature of blockchain allows for a more resilient and robust threat intelligence ecosystem. Unlike centralized systems that rely on a single entity or database, blockchain distributes the data across multiple nodes, reducing the vulnerability to single points of failure. Even if a node is compromised, the integrity and availability of the shared threat intelligence remain intact, ensuring continuous protection against evolving threats.

Real-world examples of blockchain-based threat intelligence platforms are emerging, demonstrating the potential impact of this technology. These platforms enable organizations to share and access timely and accurate threat intelligence, leading to more proactive and effective cybersecurity measures. The collaborative nature of blockchain-based threat intelligence enhances the collective defense capabilities, benefiting not only individual organizations but also entire industries and sectors.

Blockchain-based threat intelligence platforms also address the challenge of trust among participants. Organizations can verify the source and reliability of threat intelligence through the blockchain, reducing reliance on trust alone. This verification mechanism helps organizations overcome the barriers to information sharing and encourages a broader participation in the collective defense against cyber threats.

In conclusion, blockchain technology has the potential to revolutionize the field of threat intelligence and information sharing. By leveraging blockchain's transparency, security, and decentralization, organizations can establish a more collaborative and efficient ecosystem for detecting and mitigating cyber threats. The enhanced transparency, cryptographic security, and resilience of blockchain-based threat intelligence platforms empower organizations to respond proactively to emerging threats, leading to a strengthened cybersecurity landscape. As the adoption of blockchain in threat intelligence continues to grow, organizations can collectively enhance their cyber defense capabilities and stay ahead of evolving threats.

Immutable Audit Trails and Forensics: Strengthening Cyber Investigations

Blockchain technology has the potential to revolutionize digital forensics and auditability, providing immutable audit trails that enhance cybersecurity investigations. By leveraging blockchain's transparency and immutability, organizations can establish tamper-proof records that facilitate comprehensive forensic analysis and efficient post-incident investigations.

The immutability of blockchain ensures that once data is recorded on the blockchain, it cannot be altered or tampered with without consensus from the network participants. This property enables the creation of an unchangeable and tamper-proof audit trail, documenting all transactions and activities. In the context of cybersecurity investigations, this immutable audit trail can serve as a reliable source of evidence, enabling investigators to reconstruct the sequence of events accurately.

Blockchain's transparency plays a crucial role in auditability and forensic analysis. All transactions and activities recorded on the blockchain are visible to all participants, creating a transparent and auditable record. Investigators can trace the flow of data, identify potential security breaches or anomalies, and assess the impact of cyber-attacks. This transparency fosters accountability and facilitates the identification of the origin and impact of cyber incidents.

The use of blockchain in digital forensics can streamline and accelerate post-incident investigations. Investigators can rely on the immutable audit trail to quickly access and analyze relevant data, reducing the time and effort required to gather evidence. The transparency of blockchain enables investigators to identify any unauthorized modifications or tampering attempts, ensuring the integrity and credibility of the collected evidence.

Real-world examples demonstrate the potential of blockchain in forensic investigations. For instance, blockchain-based platforms can be utilized to securely store and timestamp digital evidence, such as log files or network traffic data. This creates a tamper-proof record that can be presented in legal proceedings, ensuring the integrity and admissibility of the evidence.

Blockchain's impact on digital forensics goes beyond the investigation stage. It can also enhance proactive cybersecurity measures by facilitating continuous monitoring and auditing of digital systems. By integrating blockchain with security monitoring tools, organizations can create real-time records of system activities, enabling the detection of suspicious behavior and providing valuable insights for threat hunting and incident response.

The application of blockchain in forensic investigations is not limited to cybersecurity incidents. It can also extend to other areas such as financial fraud investigations, intellectual property disputes, or compliance audits. Blockchain's immutable audit trails can provide a reliable and verifiable source of evidence in various legal and regulatory contexts.

In conclusion, blockchain technology offers significant potential in creating immutable audit trails and strengthening forensic investigations in cybersecurity. The transparency and immutability of blockchain enable the establishment of tamper-proof records that enhance auditability and accountability. By leveraging blockchain's capabilities, organizations can streamline post-incident investigations, accelerate evidence collection, and enhance the overall efficiency of forensic analysis. As the adoption of blockchain in forensic investigations continues to evolve, the cybersecurity community can benefit from improved transparency, integrity, and credibility in digital forensics.

Resilient Supply Chain Security: Ensuring Trust and Integrity

Supply chain security is a critical aspect of cybersecurity, and blockchain technology has the potential to revolutionize how organizations secure their supply chains. By leveraging blockchain's transparency, traceability, and decentralized nature, organizations can enhance the security, integrity, and trustworthiness of their supply chains.

Blockchain enables end-to-end visibility and traceability throughout the supply chain. Each step of the supply chain, from raw material sourcing to manufacturing, distribution, and delivery, can be recorded on the blockchain. This transparent and auditable record ensures that all stakeholders have a clear view of the product's journey, minimizing the risk of counterfeit goods, tampering, or unauthorized substitutions.

The immutability of blockchain ensures the integrity of supply chain data. Once information is recorded on the blockchain, it cannot be altered without consensus from the network participants. This feature provides a tamper-proof and verifiable record of every transaction and event in the supply chain. By leveraging this immutability, organizations can confidently track and verify the authenticity and quality of products, reducing the risk of counterfeit or substandard goods entering the supply chain.

Blockchain's decentralized nature enhances supply chain resilience. Unlike traditional supply chain systems that rely on a central authority or database, blockchain distributes the data across a network of nodes. This decentralization eliminates single points of failure and makes it more challenging for malicious actors to disrupt or manipulate the supply chain. Even if one node or participant is compromised, the integrity and availability of the supply chain data remain intact.

Smart contracts on the blockchain automate and enforce predefined rules and conditions in the supply chain. These self-executing agreements enable secure and efficient transactions between stakeholders. Smart contracts can automatically trigger actions based on predefined criteria, such as payment releases or quality certifications. This automation streamlines supply chain processes, reduces administrative overhead, and ensures compliance with established protocols.

Real-world applications of blockchain in supply chain security are emerging across industries. For instance, in the food industry, blockchain can enable end-to-end traceability of products, ensuring food safety and minimizing the risk of contamination. In the luxury goods sector, blockchain can verify the authenticity and provenance of high-value items, reducing the prevalence of counterfeit products. These applications demonstrate the potential of blockchain to enhance trust and integrity in supply chains.

Blockchain also facilitates secure and efficient collaboration among supply chain partners. By leveraging blockchain's transparency and cryptographic security, organizations can securely share relevant information, such as production data, certifications, or compliance records. This collaboration streamlines communication, reduces delays, and enables more effective decision-making, fostering a trusted and efficient supply chain ecosystem.

In conclusion, blockchain technology offers significant potential to enhance supply chain security. By leveraging its transparency, traceability, immutability, and decentralized nature, organizations can establish resilient and trustworthy supply chains. Blockchain provides end-to-end visibility, ensures data integrity, automates transactions through smart contracts, and enables secure collaboration among supply chain partners. As the adoption of blockchain in supply chain security continues to grow, organizations can mitigate risks, improve efficiency, and foster trust in their supply chain operations.

Evolution of Cyber Insurance: Improving Risk Assessment and Settlements

The traditional cyber insurance industry faces numerous challenges, such as limited transparency, complex policy underwriting, and lengthy claims processing. However, blockchain technology has the potential to revolutionize cyber insurance by enhancing transparency, efficiency, and accuracy in risk assessment, policy management, and claim settlements.

Blockchain can improve risk assessment in cyber insurance by providing increased transparency and access to relevant data. With blockchain, insurers can securely access and verify a company's cybersecurity practices, including measures such as network security, data encryption, and employee training.

This transparent view enables insurers to assess risks more accurately and offer tailored coverage to organizations based on their individual cybersecurity strengths and vulnerabilities.

Smart contracts on the blockchain automate policy management and streamline claim settlements. These self-executing agreements define the terms and conditions of the insurance policy, including triggers for claim payouts. By leveraging blockchain's transparency and automation, insurers can reduce administrative overhead and expedite the claims process. Smart contracts can automatically assess claims based on predefined criteria, ensuring quicker and more accurate settlements.

Blockchain also enhances the accuracy and efficiency of claims verification and processing. With traditional systems, claims documentation is often fragmented and prone to errors or discrepancies. By recording claims-related information on the blockchain, insurers can ensure the integrity and immutability of the data, reducing the potential for fraud or disputes. Additionally, blockchain's transparency enables policyholders and insurers to independently verify the validity of claims, enhancing trust and reducing the administrative burden associated with claims investigations.

Real-world applications of blockchain in the cyber insurance industry are emerging. For instance, some companies are leveraging blockchain to create shared databases of cybersecurity incidents, enabling insurers to access accurate and timely information about potential risks. This shared information fosters collaboration and improves risk assessment, allowing insurers to offer more competitive and tailored coverage.

Furthermore, blockchain-based platforms can facilitate peer-to-peer insurance models, where individuals or organizations collectively pool their risks and share the financial burden. These platforms utilize smart contracts to automate premium calculations, claims processing, and risk sharing among participants. This approach enhances transparency, reduces costs, and empowers policyholders by giving them more control over their insurance coverage.

Blockchain's impact on the cyber insurance industry extends beyond operational improvements. It also promotes a shift toward proactive risk mitigation. By leveraging blockchain's transparency and verifiability, insurers can incentivize policyholders to adopt stronger cybersecurity measures. This can result in a more resilient cyber landscape, with organizations taking proactive steps to prevent cyber incidents and reduce potential losses.

In conclusion, blockchain technology has the potential to revolutionize the cyber insurance industry by improving risk assessment, policy management, and claim settlements. Blockchain's transparency, automation through smart contracts, and enhanced data integrity offer benefits such as improved risk assessment accuracy, streamlined claims processing, and enhanced trust among policyholders and insurers. As the adoption of blockchain in cyber insurance continues to grow, the industry can expect increased efficiency, accuracy, and transparency, leading to a more resilient and responsive approach to managing cyber risks.

Securing Internet of Things (IoT) Devices: Enhancing Trust in a Connected World

The proliferation of Internet of Things (IoT) devices presents significant cybersecurity challenges, as these devices often lack robust security measures. However, blockchain technology offers a promising solution to enhance the security of IoT devices and foster trust in the interconnected ecosystem.

Blockchain can provide a decentralized and trustless framework for managing IoT networks. By integrating blockchain with IoT systems, organizations can establish secure and auditable communication channels among devices. Each transaction or interaction between IoT devices can be recorded on the blockchain, ensuring transparency and tamper-proof data exchange.

One of the key strengths of blockchain in securing IoT devices is its cryptographic security. Blockchain leverages advanced cryptographic algorithms to protect data integrity, confidentiality, and authentication. By utilizing blockchain's cryptographic features, IoT devices can securely communicate, verify each other's identities, and ensure the integrity of data exchanged within the network.

Blockchain's decentralized nature enhances the security of IoT devices. Traditional IoT systems rely on a central authority for managing device identities, updates, and security protocols. However, this centralization introduces single points of failure and increases the risk of unauthorized access or control. With blockchain, the control and management of IoT devices are distributed across a network of nodes, reducing the vulnerability to attacks and providing greater resilience against potential breaches.

The transparency of blockchain enables the monitoring and auditability of IoT device activities. All transactions and changes made by IoT devices are recorded on the blockchain, providing an immutable audit trail. This transparency allows for better detection of anomalous behavior, early identification of compromised devices, and faster incident response. Furthermore, the ability to track and trace the history of IoT devices on the blockchain enhances accountability and strengthens the overall security of the IoT ecosystem.

Real-world applications of blockchain in securing IoT devices are emerging. For example, blockchain-based solutions can enable secure firmware updates for IoT devices, ensuring that devices are regularly patched with the latest security enhancements. Additionally, blockchain can facilitate the secure and auditable management of IoT device identities, preventing unauthorized devices from joining the network.

However, implementing blockchain in IoT systems also poses challenges. The resource constraints of IoT devices, such as limited computing power and storage capacity, can affect the scalability and performance of blockchain networks. Efficient consensus mechanisms and lightweight cryptographic algorithms are being explored to address these challenges and make blockchain viable for IoT deployments.

In conclusion, blockchain technology offers significant potential in enhancing the security of IoT devices and fostering trust in the interconnected world. By leveraging blockchain's cryptographic security, decentralization, transparency, and auditability, organizations can establish secure and resilient IoT networks. As blockchain continues to evolve and address scalability challenges, its integration with IoT systems can mitigate risks, protect data integrity, and promote the responsible growth of the IoT ecosystem.

3
Anatomy of a Cyberattack: Case Studies

Deconstructing High-Profile Attacks: An In-depth Look at Case Studies

In this section, we embark on a comprehensive exploration of high-profile cyberattacks that have made headlines and left a lasting impact on organizations and individuals. By dissecting these case studies, we aim to gain a deeper understanding of the attack vectors, the methods employed by hackers, and the vulnerabilities that were exploited. This analysis allows us to uncover valuable insights and lessons learned from these high-profile attacks.

The WannaCry Ransomware Attack

In this section, we delve into the infamous WannaCry ransomware attack, a cyber onslaught that shook the world in 2017, leaving a trail of chaos, panic, and financial loss in its wake. This highly sophisticated attack targeted vulnerable systems worldwide, exploiting a critical vulnerability in the Windows operating system. Leveraging the stolen NSA hacking tool Eternal Blue, the attackers swiftly propagated the ransomware to hundreds of thousands of computers across multiple sectors, including healthcare, finance, and government agencies.

The impact of the WannaCry attack was nothing short of catastrophic. Within hours, organizations found themselves locked out of their own systems, their crucial files and data held hostage by malicious encryption. The attackers demanded ransom payments in Bitcoin, offering a glimmer of hope that victims could regain access to their invaluable digital assets. However, even those who chose to pay the ransom were not guaranteed a successful decryption, as the attackers' infrastructure and support systems were disrupted by swift global cooperation from cybersecurity experts.

This widespread ransomware campaign demonstrated the alarming vulnerability of organizations and individuals to cyber threats, particularly those exploiting known vulnerabilities. It highlighted the urgent need for organizations to prioritize timely software patching and vulnerability management as crucial elements of their cybersecurity strategy. The WannaCry attack also exposed the critical importance of robust backup strategies, as organizations with comprehensive data backups were able to restore their systems without giving in to the attackers' demands.

Beyond the immediate financial losses incurred by organizations, the WannaCry attack had far-reaching consequences. It disrupted essential services, including healthcare facilities, leaving patients without access to critical medical records and delaying life-saving treatments. Government agencies were temporarily paralyzed, hindering their ability to serve and protect their citizens. The attack eroded public trust in the security and integrity of digital systems, underscoring the need for enhanced cybersecurity measures across all sectors.

The WannaCry attack serves as a poignant reminder of the potential magnitude and global impact of a cyber pandemic. It revealed the interconnectivity and interdependencies of our digital ecosystem, where a single vulnerability can cascade into a widespread crisis. By analyzing the WannaCry case study, we gain valuable insights into the methods and techniques employed by cybercriminals, the vulnerabilities they exploit, and the devastating consequences they can inflict.

As we navigate the ever-evolving cyber threat landscape, it is imperative that we learn from the lessons of the WannaCry attack. Organizations must prioritize proactive cybersecurity measures, including timely patching, vulnerability assessments, and robust backup strategies. They must also foster a culture of cybersecurity awareness and education, empowering employees to recognize and report potential threats. By fortifying our defenses and remaining vigilant, we can strive to prevent the next global cyber pandemic and safeguard our digital future.

The Equifax Data Breach

Next, we delve into the Equifax data breach, one of the largest and most significant data breaches in history. In 2017, cybercriminals exploited a vulnerability in the Equifax web application, gaining unauthorized access to sensitive personal information of approximately 147 million individuals. The breach underscored the critical importance of proper vulnerability management, secure coding practices, and effective incident response procedures. The Equifax case serves as a stark reminder of the severe consequences that can arise from inadequate cybersecurity measures.

The impact of the Equifax data breach extended far beyond the immediate compromise of personal information. The breach exposed individuals to a heightened risk of identity theft, financial fraud, and other forms of cybercrime. The compromised data included names, Social Security numbers, birth dates, addresses, and, in some cases, driver's license numbers. This wealth of personal information provided cybercriminals with the means to carry out various fraudulent activities, jeopardizing the financial well-being and privacy of millions of individuals.

Furthermore, the Equifax breach resulted in significant reputational damage for the company. The incident eroded trust among consumers, as they felt betrayed by the organization entrusted with safeguarding their sensitive information. The mishandling of the breach response further exacerbated the public outcry, highlighting the importance of transparent communication, swift incident disclosure, and proactive steps to assist affected individuals.

In addition to the severe consequences suffered by individuals and the damage to Equifax's reputation, the company faced substantial financial penalties. In 2019, Equifax reached a settlement with the Federal Trade Commission (FTC), the Consumer Financial Protection Bureau (CFPB), and 50 U.S. states and territories. The settlement required Equifax to pay a total of $700 million to compensate affected consumers and implement enhanced data security measures.

Out of the $700 million settlement, a significant portion was allocated to a consumer restitution fund, allowing affected individuals to file claims and receive compensation for expenses incurred due to the breach. Equifax agreed to set aside approximately $425 million for this purpose, reflecting the magnitude of the breach's impact on individuals' lives.

Moreover, Equifax faced civil penalties as part of the settlement. The company agreed to pay $175 million to the states and territories involved, emphasizing the accountability for its inadequate security practices. Additionally, the CFPB imposed a civil penalty of $100 million, further underscoring the consequences of the breach.

The financial penalties imposed on Equifax not only served as a means of compensating affected individuals but also as a deterrent for organizations that fail to prioritize cybersecurity. The significant fine sent a strong message about the importance of protecting personal information and the potential consequences of negligence in data security.

The Equifax data breach serves as a pivotal case study, highlighting the urgent need for organizations to prioritize robust cybersecurity practices. It emphasizes the criticality of vulnerability management, secure coding, incident response preparedness, and proactive steps to mitigate risks. By learning from the Equifax incident, organizations can take concrete actions to fortify their defenses, protect sensitive data, and maintain the trust of their customers.

The SolarWinds Supply Chain Attack

We then turn our attention to the SolarWinds supply chain attack, a sophisticated and highly impactful cyberattack discovered in late 2020. This attack sent shockwaves through the cybersecurity landscape, revealing the vulnerabilities that can lurk within trusted software supply chains. The SolarWinds attack was a wake-up call for organizations worldwide, exposing the potential risks associated with compromised software updates and emphasizing the critical importance of supply chain security.

At the heart of the SolarWinds attack was a covert compromise of the software build and update process of SolarWinds, a leading provider of IT management and monitoring solutions. Through a meticulously orchestrated operation, hackers infiltrated SolarWinds' systems and inserted a malicious code into the legitimate software updates released by the company. These tainted updates, which were unsuspectingly downloaded by organizations relying on SolarWinds' trusted software, allowed the attackers to gain unauthorized access to targeted networks and compromise sensitive systems and data.

The SolarWinds attack unfolded as a sophisticated supply chain attack, demonstrating the significant impact that can be achieved by exploiting the inherent trust placed in software updates. By breaching the software development and distribution process, the attackers successfully bypassed traditional perimeter defenses and infiltrated high-profile organizations, including government agencies, major corporations, and critical infrastructure providers. The wide-ranging implications of this attack underscored the need for robust controls and stringent security measures throughout the software supply chain.

One of the key lessons from the SolarWinds attack was the criticality of implementing comprehensive supply chain security practices. Organizations must adopt a proactive approach to assess and manage the risks associated with their software suppliers and partners. This includes conducting thorough due diligence, assessing the security posture of vendors, and implementing stringent security requirements in contracts and agreements.

Furthermore, the SolarWinds attack highlighted the importance of enhancing visibility and monitoring within the software supply chain. Organizations need to implement robust controls and continuous monitoring mechanisms to detect any suspicious activities or anomalies within the software development and distribution process. This includes adopting solutions that provide real-time visibility into software components, verifying the integrity of software updates, and leveraging threat intelligence to identify potential threats and indicators of compromise.

The SolarWinds attack also underscored the need for organizations to prioritize incident response preparedness. As demonstrated by the attack's stealthy nature and the prolonged dwell time within compromised networks, organizations must have effective incident response plans in place to detect, contain, and remediate supply chain attacks promptly. This involves establishing clear roles and responsibilities, conducting regular training and simulations, and maintaining strong coordination with trusted cybersecurity partners and authorities.

Ultimately, the SolarWinds attack served as a stark reminder that cybersecurity threats can permeate even the most trusted and established software supply chains. It emphasized the need for organizations to be proactive, vigilant, and resilient in the face of evolving threats. By adopting robust supply chain security practices, enhancing visibility and monitoring, and maintaining effective incident response capabilities, organizations can better protect themselves and their stakeholders from the devastating consequences of supply chain attacks. The SolarWinds incident serves as a crucial case study that offers valuable insights and lessons for organizations seeking to fortify their defenses and ensure the integrity and security of their software supply chains.

Other Notable Case Studies

In addition to the above-mentioned attacks, we explore other notable case studies that have left a significant impact on cybersecurity. These include the Target data breach, the NotPetya malware attack, and the Stuxnet worm. Each of these cases offers unique insights into the tactics, techniques, and consequences of cyber-attacks, showcasing the evolving nature of threats and the need for continuous vigilance and proactive defense measures.

By deconstructing these high-profile attacks, we aim to unravel the strategies employed by cybercriminals, the vulnerabilities that allowed for their success, and the implications for affected organizations and individuals. This examination serves as a foundation for understanding the evolving cyber threat landscape and identifying key lessons that can inform effective cybersecurity practices. By learning from these case studies, organizations and individuals can strengthen their defenses and better prepare themselves against emerging cyber threats.

Cyberattack Tactics: Revealing How Hackers Penetrate Systems

In this section, we delve into the tactics employed by hackers to penetrate systems and gain unauthorized access. By understanding these attack techniques, organizations and individuals can better defend against cyber threats and develop effective mitigation strategies. We explore common attack vectors and tactics used by hackers, shedding light on the methods they employ to exploit vulnerabilities and infiltrate systems.

Social Engineering Attacks

Social engineering attacks are psychological manipulations aimed at deceiving individuals and exploiting their trust. Hackers use various tactics, such as phishing, pretexting, and baiting, to trick unsuspecting users into revealing sensitive information or granting unauthorized access. We examine real-world examples of social engineering attacks, highlighting the importance of awareness, education, and robust security practices to mitigate the risks associated with social engineering.

Malware Infections

Malware, malicious software designed to disrupt systems or gain unauthorized access, is a prevalent tool used by hackers. We explore different types of malware, including viruses, worms, Trojans, ransomware, and spyware. We examine how malware is typically delivered, such as through email attachments, malicious downloads, or infected websites. Understanding malware infection techniques helps organizations implement effective security measures like endpoint protection, regular software updates, and user education to prevent malware infiltration.

Exploiting Software Vulnerabilities

Software vulnerabilities provide entry points for attackers to exploit systems. We delve into common methods hackers use to identify and exploit these vulnerabilities, such as zero-day exploits, SQL injection, and buffer overflow attacks. We emphasize the importance of prompt patch management, secure coding practices, and vulnerability assessments to mitigate the risks associated with software vulnerabilities.

Password Attacks

Passwords remain a common authentication method, and hackers employ various tactics to gain unauthorized access through weak or compromised passwords. We explore techniques such as brute-force attacks, dictionary attacks, and password spraying. We emphasize the significance of strong password policies, multifactor authentication, and user education to bolster password security and protect against unauthorized access.

Denial of Service (DoS) and Distributed Denial of Service (DDoS) Attacks

Denial of Service (DoS) and Distributed Denial of Service (DDoS) attacks aim to overwhelm systems or networks, rendering them inaccessible to legitimate users. We examine the techniques hackers use to orchestrate these attacks, such as botnets, amplification attacks, and application layer attacks. We discuss the importance of network monitoring, traffic filtering, and robust infrastructure to mitigate the impact of DoS and DDoS attacks.

Insider Threats

Insider threats pose a significant risk to organizations, as trusted individuals with legitimate access can intentionally or unintentionally compromise systems. We explore different types of insider threats, including malicious insiders and negligent employees, and discuss the importance of access controls, monitoring, and employee awareness programs to mitigate insider-related risks.

By understanding the tactics employed by hackers to penetrate systems, organizations and individuals can implement appropriate safeguards and defense mechanisms. We highlight the importance of a multi-layered approach to cybersecurity, encompassing robust security practices, employee education, regular security assessments, and proactive threat detection and response. Through this knowledge, readers can enhance their cybersecurity posture and protect against the evolving landscape of cyber-attacks.

Impact and Consequences: Understanding the Aftermath of Cyber-attacks

In this section, we explore the wide-ranging impact and consequences that cyber-attacks have on organizations, individuals, and society as a whole. Understanding the aftermath of cyber-attacks is crucial for comprehending the full extent of the damage and the importance of robust cybersecurity measures. We examine the immediate and long-term consequences of cyber-attacks, including financial, operational, reputational, legal, and ethical implications.

Financial Consequences

Cyber-attacks can have severe financial repercussions for organizations. We delve into the direct financial losses incurred due to incidents such as ransom payments, financial fraud, or theft of funds. Additionally, we explore the indirect costs associated with remediation, incident response, legal fees, regulatory fines, and reputational damage. Understanding the financial impact enables organizations to assess the true cost of cyber-attacks and allocate resources effectively for prevention and recovery.

Operational Disruptions

Cyber-attacks often result in significant disruptions to an organization's operations. We examine the impact of systems and network downtime, data loss, and compromised infrastructure. These disruptions can lead to delays in delivering products or services, loss of productivity, and damaged customer relationships. By understanding the operational consequences, organizations can implement measures to minimize downtime, enhance business continuity plans, and maintain operations during and after an attack.

Reputational Damage

The reputation of an organization is a valuable asset, and cyber-attacks can cause significant harm. We explore the reputational consequences resulting from data breaches, customer data exposure, or compromised trust. Organizations may experience a loss of customer confidence, diminished brand value, and negative media coverage. We discuss the importance of proactive communication, transparency, and effective public relations strategies to mitigate reputational damage and restore trust.

Legal and Regulatory Ramifications

Cyber-attacks often trigger legal and regulatory obligations for organizations. We examine the legal consequences, including potential lawsuits, regulatory investigations, and compliance breaches. We discuss the importance of adhering to data protection laws, industry regulations, and privacy requirements. Understanding the legal and regulatory landscape enables organizations to develop robust compliance programs and mitigate legal risks associated with cyber-attacks.

Ethical Considerations

Cyber-attacks raise ethical concerns surrounding privacy, data protection, and responsible use of technology. We explore the ethical implications of data breaches, surveillance, and cyber espionage. Organizations must consider the ethical responsibilities of safeguarding customer data, protecting individuals' privacy rights, and ensuring the ethical use of emerging technologies. We discuss the importance of ethical frameworks, ethical guidelines, and ethical decision-making in the context of cybersecurity.

By understanding the impact and consequences of cyber-attacks, organizations can recognize the importance of proactive cybersecurity measures. They can allocate resources to develop robust incident response plans, implement security controls, and educate employees on cybersecurity best practices. Additionally, organizations can establish relationships with external partners, such as law enforcement and cybersecurity experts, to assist in mitigating the aftermath of an attack. By addressing the financial, operational, reputational, legal, and ethical implications, organizations can better protect themselves and minimize the long-term effects of cyber-attacks.

Mitigation and Defense: Learning from Past Mistakes

In this section, we delve into the critical aspect of mitigating cyber-attacks and strengthening defenses based on lessons learned from past incidents. By analyzing the vulnerabilities and shortcomings exposed by previous attacks, organizations and individuals can implement proactive measures to enhance their cybersecurity posture. We explore best practices, strategies, and technologies that can be leveraged to mitigate risks and improve defense mechanisms.

Security Frameworks and Risk Assessments

Implementing a robust security framework is essential for effective cybersecurity. We discuss widely recognized frameworks such as NIST Cybersecurity Framework, ISO 27001, and CIS Controls. These frameworks provide guidelines and standards for identifying, assessing, and managing cybersecurity risks. We emphasize the importance of conducting regular risk assessments to identify vulnerabilities, prioritize mitigation efforts, and align security measures with organizational objectives.

Employee Education and Awareness

Employees play a critical role in cybersecurity, and education and awareness programs are vital for building a strong defense. We explore the significance of comprehensive training programs to educate employees about common cyber threats, phishing attacks, and social engineering techniques. By fostering a culture of security awareness, organizations can empower employees to become the first line of defense and detect and report potential security incidents.

Secure Coding Practices and Software Updates

Implementing secure coding practices is crucial for building resilient software and reducing vulnerabilities. We discuss the importance of following secure coding guidelines, conducting code reviews, and leveraging automated tools to identify and address security flaws. Additionally, we emphasize the significance of prompt software updates and patch management to mitigate the risk of known vulnerabilities being exploited by attackers.

Network Segmentation and Access Controls

Network segmentation and access controls are vital for minimizing the impact of a potential breach. We explore the concept of network segmentation, dividing networks into smaller, isolated segments to contain and control the spread of an attack. Additionally, we discuss the importance of implementing strong access controls, such as multifactor authentication, least privilege principles, and privileged access management, to ensure that only authorized individuals can access sensitive systems and data.

Incident Response and Business Continuity Planning

Preparing for cyber incidents through robust incident response and business continuity planning is crucial for minimizing the impact of an attack. We delve into the components of an effective incident response plan, including detection, containment, eradication, and recovery. Additionally, we discuss the importance of creating business continuity plans to ensure essential operations can continue during and after an incident, minimizing downtime and financial losses.

Threat Intelligence and Security Monitoring

Threat intelligence and proactive security monitoring are essential for identifying and mitigating emerging threats. We explore the significance of leveraging threat intelligence sources, such as information-sharing platforms, security vendors, and industry collaboration, to stay informed about evolving threats and tactics. Additionally, we discuss the importance of implementing security monitoring solutions, such as intrusion detection systems and security information and event management (SIEM) tools, to detect and respond to security incidents in real-time.

Collaboration and Partnerships

Collaboration and partnerships among organizations, government agencies, and security communities are crucial for strengthening defenses. We discuss the importance of sharing information, experiences, and best practices through public-private partnerships, industry collaborations, and threat intelligence sharing initiatives. By working together, stakeholders can leverage collective knowledge and resources to enhance cybersecurity across the board.

By learning from past mistakes and implementing effective mitigation and defense strategies, organizations and individuals can strengthen their cybersecurity posture and reduce the risk of falling victim to cyber-attacks. By adopting comprehensive security frameworks, educating employees, implementing secure coding practices, enforcing network segmentation, and establishing robust incident response plans, organizations can proactively address vulnerabilities and respond effectively to incidents. Through collaboration and continuous improvement, we can collectively raise the bar in cybersecurity and mitigate the ever-evolving threat landscape.

The Blockchain Solution: How Blockchain Can Mitigate Cyber-attacks

Decentralized Identity Management

Traditional identity management systems rely on centralized databases that are vulnerable to data breaches and single points of failure. In contrast, blockchain technology offers a decentralized and secure framework for managing digital identities. By leveraging blockchain's cryptographic security and distributed consensus mechanisms, individuals can have control over their own digital identities. Personal information can be securely stored on the blockchain, and access can be granted to trusted entities through cryptographic mechanisms. This decentralized identity management approach reduces the risk of identity theft, enhances privacy, and provides individuals with greater control over their digital presence.

For example, blockchain-based identity solutions can be applied in the healthcare sector. Patients can have control over their medical records stored on the blockchain, granting access to healthcare providers as needed. This ensures the privacy and integrity of sensitive medical information while allowing for secure sharing between authorized parties.

Data Integrity and Verification

Ensuring the integrity of data is a critical aspect of cybersecurity. Blockchain's immutable and transparent nature makes it well-suited for preserving data integrity. When data transactions are recorded on the blockchain, they become tamper-proof and resistant to alteration. This provides a reliable audit trail, enabling organizations to verify the authenticity and integrity of data without relying on centralized authorities.

Blockchain-based data integrity solutions can be applied in various domains. For instance, in intellectual property rights management, blockchain can be used to record ownership and licensing agreements. By storing this information on the blockchain, a transparent and auditable history of intellectual property rights is established, reducing the risk of infringement and unauthorized use.

Supply Chain Security and Transparency

Supply chain security is a significant concern for organizations, as vulnerabilities in the supply chain can be exploited by cyber attackers. Blockchain technology can enhance supply chain security by providing transparency and traceability. By recording every transaction and movement of goods on the blockchain, organizations can ensure the authenticity and provenance of products, detect counterfeit items, and identify potential vulnerabilities.

For example, in the food industry, blockchain can be used to track the journey of perishable goods from farm to table. By recording each step on the blockchain, consumers can verify the origin and quality of the products they purchase, while organizations can quickly identify and address any issues in the supply chain, such as contamination or fraud.

Smart Contracts for Secure Automation

Smart contracts, self-executing agreements built on blockchain, have the potential to revolutionize cybersecurity automation. These contracts automatically execute predefined actions based on specific conditions, eliminating the need for intermediaries and reducing the risk of human error. In the context of cybersecurity, smart contracts can automate security protocols, authentication processes, and access controls, enhancing the overall security and efficiency of operations.

For example, in access control management, smart contracts can be used to automate the verification and validation of user identities. When a user attempts to access a system or resource, the smart contract can automatically verify their identity based on predefined rules and conditions, eliminating the need for manual intervention and reducing the risk of unauthorized access.

Blockchain-based Threat Intelligence Sharing

Threat intelligence sharing is crucial for effective cybersecurity defense, as it allows organizations to exchange information about emerging threats, attack patterns, and indicators of compromise. Blockchain technology can facilitate secure and decentralized information-sharing among organizations, enhancing the trustworthiness and integrity of shared data.

By leveraging blockchain, threat intelligence data can be stored in a decentralized manner, with cryptographic hashes ensuring the immutability of the information. This enables organizations to share threat intelligence data without compromising its integrity or relying on a centralized authority.

For example, a blockchain-based threat intelligence platform can allow participating organizations to contribute and access threat data. Each contribution is securely recorded on the blockchain, and the distributed nature of the network ensures that no single entity has control over the data. This facilitates trust and collaboration among organizations, enabling them to collectively defend against emerging threats.

By harnessing the power of blockchain technology, organizations can enhance their cybersecurity defenses and mitigate the risks associated with cyber-attacks. Decentralized identity management, data integrity and verification, supply chain security, smart contracts for secure automation, and blockchain-based threat intelligence sharing are just a few of the applications of blockchain in cybersecurity. However, it is important to consider the challenges and considerations, such as scalability, interoperability, and regulatory compliance, when implementing blockchain solutions. By understanding the potential and limitations of blockchain, organizations can explore its applications and integrate it into their defense strategies to create a more resilient and secure digital landscape.

4
Power Grids in the Crosshairs: Security and Vulnerabilities

Lighting Up the World: The Critical Role of Power Grids

Power grids are the backbone of our modern society, providing the essential infrastructure needed to generate, transmit, and distribute electricity to homes, businesses, and critical facilities. In this section, we will explore the critical role that power grids play in lighting up the world and supporting our interconnected way of life.

The Power Grid Infrastructure:

The power grid infrastructure encompasses a vast network of power generation facilities, including power plants, renewable energy sources, and distribution systems. These systems work in tandem to ensure a reliable and consistent supply of electricity to meet the demands of consumers. Evidence of the critical role of power grids can be seen in the widespread reliance on electricity for various purposes, from powering homes and offices to supporting industries and critical infrastructure sectors. The International Energy Agency (IEA) reports that the global electricity demand is expected to grow by 4% annually until 2030, highlighting the increasing significance of power grids in meeting this rising demand and driving economic growth.

Power Grids and Economic Development:

Power grids are essential for driving economic growth and development. They provide the necessary electricity to power industries, manufacturing processes, and commercial establishments. Reliable and accessible electricity is crucial for businesses to operate efficiently, contributing to increased productivity, job creation, and economic competitiveness. According to the World Bank, access to electricity is a key indicator of a country's development, as it enables the growth of industries, stimulates entrepreneurship, and improves living standards. For example, a study conducted by the United Nations Industrial Development Organization (UNIDO) found that a 10% increase in electricity consumption is associated with a 1% increase in GDP per capita. These findings underscore the critical role that power grids play in supporting economic development and lifting communities out of poverty.

Power Grids and Critical Infrastructure:

Power grids are deeply intertwined with other critical infrastructure sectors, forming the backbone that supports essential services. Transportation systems rely on electricity to power trains, signaling systems, and electric vehicles. Hospitals require a stable power supply to operate life-saving medical equipment, refrigeration units for storing vaccines and medicines, and lighting for surgeries and patient care. Communication networks, including internet connectivity and mobile networks, rely on electricity to function effectively. Water treatment facilities require electricity to pump, treat, and distribute clean water to communities. Emergency services, such as police stations and fire departments, depend on electricity for communication and emergency response systems. The interconnectedness of power grids and critical infrastructure sectors highlights the criticality of power grid security to ensure the continued operation of essential services even during cyber-attacks or other disruptions.

Power Grids and Resilience:

Resilience is a fundamental characteristic of power grids, ensuring their ability to withstand and recover from various challenges and disturbances. Power grid operators implement measures to enhance resilience, such as redundancy in infrastructure, robust monitoring systems, and emergency response plans. For instance, the North American Electric Reliability Corporation (NERC) establishes standards and requirements for grid operators to ensure the reliability and resilience of the power grid in North America. These measures help mitigate the impact of natural disasters, equipment failures, and other unforeseen events.

Furthermore, the integration of renewable energy sources and the development of microgrids contribute to the resilience of power grids by diversifying energy sources and enabling localized power generation. Enhancing the resilience of power grids is crucial to minimize the impact of cyber-attacks, which can disrupt the availability of electricity and have far-reaching consequences for society.

Power Grids and Societal Impact:

The societal impact of power grid disruptions cannot be understated. Power outages disrupt daily routines, affecting homes, businesses, and public services. They can hamper communication systems, disrupt transportation networks, and compromise healthcare facilities. The impact of power grid disruptions is evident in various real-world examples. For instance, the massive power outage that occurred in the northeastern United States and parts of Canada in 2003 affected approximately 55 million people and resulted in economic losses of billions of dollars. The outage led to widespread disruptions in transportation, communication, and public services, highlighting the vulnerability of power grids and their critical role in maintaining societal functions.

Power grid disruptions can also have severe consequences in developing countries with limited access to electricity. According to the World Bank, approximately 789 million people worldwide lack access to electricity. In these regions, power outages can hinder economic activities, limit educational opportunities, and negatively impact healthcare services. The United Nations Sustainable Development Goal 7 aims to ensure universal access to affordable, reliable, and modern energy services by 2030, underscoring the importance of resilient power grids in addressing global development challenges.

Power grids play a critical role in powering our modern world, supporting economic development, and enabling the functioning of essential services and infrastructure. The evidence of their importance can be observed in the increasing electricity demand, the correlation between electricity access and economic growth, and the interdependencies between power grids and critical infrastructure sectors. The vulnerabilities and security risks faced by power grids necessitate proactive measures to ensure their reliability, resilience, and protection against cyber-attacks. By understanding the critical role of power grids, their economic and societal significance, and the potential consequences of disruptions, we can work toward strengthening the security and resilience of these vital infrastructures to ensure they continue to light up the world.

Weaknesses Exposed: Understanding Power Grid Vulnerabilities

Power grids, which are the backbone of modern society, are increasingly becoming targets for cyber-attacks due to their criticality and interconnectedness. In this section, we will delve into the vulnerabilities that power grids face and examine real-world evidence of these weaknesses being exploited by malicious actors.

Aging Infrastructure: A Vulnerability in Power Grids

One significant vulnerability that poses a threat to power grids is their aging infrastructure. Many power grids around the world were established decades ago, relying on outdated equipment and systems that are more susceptible to failures and vulnerabilities. This aging infrastructure creates opportunities for cyber attackers to exploit weaknesses and disrupt the reliable delivery of electricity.

Evidence of the vulnerability of aging infrastructure can be found in various incidents. For instance, in 2015, Ukraine experienced a significant cyberattack that targeted its power grid. The attackers exploited the outdated equipment and systems, causing widespread power outages and disrupting the daily lives of millions of people. This incident serves as a wake-up call, demonstrating the critical need for upgrading and modernizing power grid infrastructure to enhance its security.

The risks associated with aging infrastructure are not limited to Ukraine alone. Power grids in many countries face similar challenges, as their equipment and systems age over time. This vulnerability opens the door for potential cyber-attacks that can exploit weaknesses in outdated technology and infrastructure.

To address this vulnerability, power grid operators must invest in infrastructure upgrades and modernization efforts. This includes replacing outdated equipment with more secure and resilient technologies, implementing robust cybersecurity measures, and adopting advanced monitoring and detection systems. By proactively addressing the weaknesses of aging infrastructure, power grid operators can bolster their defenses and reduce the risk of cyber-attacks that could disrupt the reliable supply of electricity to communities and industries.

In summary, the aging infrastructure of power grids poses a significant vulnerability in terms of cybersecurity. The evidence from past incidents emphasizes the urgency for upgrading and modernizing power grid infrastructure to enhance its resilience and protect against cyber threats. By investing in the necessary improvements, power grid operators can strengthen the security of their systems and ensure the continued delivery of electricity to meet the growing demands of society.

Aging Infrastructure: A Vulnerability in Power Grids

One significant vulnerability that poses a threat to power grids is their aging infrastructure. Many power grids around the world were established decades ago, relying on outdated equipment and systems that are more susceptible to failures and vulnerabilities. This aging infrastructure creates opportunities for cyber attackers to exploit weaknesses and disrupt the reliable delivery of electricity.

Evidence of the vulnerability of aging infrastructure can be found in various incidents. For instance, in 2015, Ukraine experienced a significant cyberattack that targeted its power grid. The attackers exploited the outdated equipment and systems, causing widespread power outages and disrupting the daily lives of millions of people. This incident serves as a wake-up call, demonstrating the critical need for upgrading and modernizing power grid infrastructure to enhance its security.

The risks associated with aging infrastructure are not limited to Ukraine alone. Power grids in many countries face similar challenges, as their equipment and systems age over time. This vulnerability opens the door for potential cyber-attacks that can exploit weaknesses in outdated technology and infrastructure.

To address this vulnerability, power grid operators must invest in infrastructure upgrades and modernization efforts. This includes replacing outdated equipment with more secure and resilient technologies, implementing robust cybersecurity measures, and adopting advanced monitoring and detection systems. By proactively addressing the weaknesses of aging infrastructure, power grid operators can bolster their defenses and reduce the risk of cyber-attacks that could disrupt the reliable supply of electricity to communities and industries.

In summary, the aging infrastructure of power grids poses a significant vulnerability in terms of cybersecurity. The evidence from past incidents emphasizes the urgency for upgrading and modernizing power grid infrastructure to enhance its resilience and protect against cyber threats. By investing in the necessary improvements, power grid operators can strengthen the security of their systems and ensure the continued delivery of electricity to meet the growing demands of society.

Dependence on Communication Networks:

Power grids heavily rely on communication networks for real-time monitoring, control, and coordination. However, this reliance also introduces vulnerabilities. Attackers can target these communication networks, disrupting vital information flow and potentially compromising the integrity and reliability of the grid. In 2016, Ukraine experienced a sophisticated cyberattack on its power grid, which involved simultaneous attacks on both the power grid and the communication infrastructure. This dual attack magnified the impact and prolonged the recovery process. The incident serves as evidence of the vulnerability of communication networks within power grids and underscores the importance of securing these critical systems.

Human Factors:

Human factors, including human error, negligence, and insider threats, contribute significantly to power grid vulnerabilities. Mistakes made by operators or maintenance personnel can lead to operational disruptions and security breaches. Additionally, insider threats pose a substantial risk, as individuals with authorized access to critical systems may intentionally or inadvertently compromise the security of the power grid. In 2013, a cyberattack targeted the Turkish pipeline system, causing significant damage. The attack was facilitated by insiders who had knowledge of the system. To address human factors vulnerabilities, comprehensive training programs, strict access controls, and robust monitoring and detection systems are necessary.

Third-Party Dependencies:

Power grids often rely on third-party vendors and suppliers for equipment, software, and services. However, these dependencies introduce vulnerabilities, as attackers can target these vendors or exploit vulnerabilities in the supplied systems. For instance, in 2017, the NotPetya malware attack initially targeted an accounting software in Ukraine but quickly spread to affect numerous organizations globally, including energy companies. This incident demonstrates the potential risks associated with third-party dependencies in power grid operations. Ensuring supply chain security and conducting thorough vetting of third-party providers are crucial steps to mitigate these vulnerabilities.

Understanding the vulnerabilities that power grids face is essential for developing effective strategies to enhance their security. Aging infrastructure, lack of segmentation, dependence on communication networks, human factors, and third-party dependencies are vulnerabilities that attackers can exploit. By addressing these weaknesses and implementing robust security measures, power grid operators can significantly reduce the risk of cyber-attacks and protect the reliable delivery of electricity to communities and industries. It is imperative for power grid operators to invest in infrastructure upgrades, implement proper segmentation strategies, secure communication networks, address human factors through training and monitoring, and ensure supply chain security. By proactively identifying and mitigating vulnerabilities, power grids can strengthen their resilience and protect against potential cyber threats.

Darkened Cities: Case Studies of Cyber-attacks on Power Grids

The increasing reliance on digital technologies and interconnected systems in power grids has made them attractive targets for cyber-attacks. In this section, we will examine real-world case studies of cyber-attacks on power grids, shedding light on the potential consequences and highlighting the vulnerabilities that need to be addressed.

Case Study 1: Ukraine's Power Grid Attack (2015)

One notable case study that highlights the vulnerabilities of power grids to cyber-attacks is the attack on Ukraine's power grid in December 2015. This incident serves as a significant wake-up call to the potential impact of targeted attacks on critical infrastructure.

During the attack, sophisticated adversaries gained unauthorized access to the operational technology (OT) systems of several power distribution companies in Ukraine. By infiltrating these systems, the attackers were able to remotely control and manipulate critical components of the power grid infrastructure, leading to widespread power outages in multiple regions.

The attackers employed a combination of tactics, including spear-phishing emails, malware distribution, and targeted exploitation of vulnerabilities in the

OT systems. They used destructive malware specifically designed to disrupt the functioning of the power grid, effectively disabling critical equipment and disrupting the normal flow of electricity.

This case study highlights the importance of securing both information technology (IT) and operational technology (OT) systems within power grids. It emphasizes the need for robust access controls, network segmentation, and regular vulnerability assessments to identify and address potential weaknesses. Additionally, it underscores the critical role of incident response plans and comprehensive backups to restore services and minimize the impact of such attacks.

The Ukraine power grid attack serves as a valuable lesson for power grid operators worldwide. It demonstrates the capabilities of determined adversaries and the potential consequences of successful cyber-attacks on power infrastructures. The lessons learned from this case study are crucial for developing proactive defense strategies, improving situational awareness, and enhancing the resilience of power grids against future attacks.

By studying and understanding the intricacies of this case, power grid operators can fortify their defenses, implement stricter security measures, and establish robust incident response capabilities. Collaboration among industry stakeholders, government agencies, and cybersecurity experts is vital to sharing threat intelligence, developing best practices, and collectively addressing the evolving cyber threats targeting power grids.

In summary, the Ukraine power grid attack of 2015 stands as a stark reminder of the vulnerabilities within power grid infrastructures and the potential impact of cyber-attacks on critical services. This case study emphasizes the need for constant vigilance, proactive security measures, and collaboration to safeguard power grids and ensure the uninterrupted delivery of electricity to communities around the world.

Case Study 2: Stuxnet Attack on Iranian Nuclear Facilities (2010)

Another prominent case study that sheds light on the vulnerabilities of power grids and critical infrastructure is the Stuxnet attack on Iranian nuclear facilities in 2010. While the primary target of this attack was the nuclear program, its impact and implications extend to the broader power grid landscape.

Stuxnet, a highly sophisticated cyber weapon believed to be developed jointly by the United States and Israel, specifically targeted the industrial control systems (ICS) used in the Iranian nuclear facilities. The malware was designed to exploit zero-day vulnerabilities and spread through infected USB drives, network shares, and Windows systems.

By infiltrating the ICS systems, Stuxnet was able to manipulate the centrifuges used in uranium enrichment, causing physical damage and disrupting the operations of the nuclear facilities. This case study demonstrates the potential for cyber-attacks to directly impact critical infrastructure, including power grids, by compromising the control systems that regulate their operation.

The Stuxnet attack showcased the increasing convergence between cyber and physical realms, highlighting the need for comprehensive security measures to protect power grid infrastructure. It underscored the importance of securing not only the IT networks but also the ICS systems that control and monitor the grid's operation.

This case study serves as a reminder that power grids are not immune to sophisticated cyber threats and that the consequences of successful attacks can be severe. It emphasizes the importance of implementing strong access controls, continuous monitoring, and intrusion detection systems to detect and mitigate potential cyber threats.

Furthermore, the Stuxnet attack exposed the challenges of attributing cyber-attacks to specific actors, raising concerns about the potential for state-sponsored attacks targeting power grids. This highlights the need for international cooperation, information sharing, and robust defense mechanisms to protect critical infrastructure from advanced threats.

The lessons learned from the Stuxnet case study can inform power grid operators in enhancing their cybersecurity posture. It reinforces the significance of regular vulnerability assessments, system patching, and employee training to mitigate the risk of similar attacks. Additionally, it underscores the importance of adopting a multi-layered defense strategy that combines technical controls, threat intelligence, and incident response planning.

In conclusion, the Stuxnet attack on Iranian nuclear facilities serves as a significant case study that exposes the vulnerabilities of power grids and critical infrastructure to cyber threats. It reinforces the need for comprehensive security measures, robust incident response capabilities, and international collaboration to defend against sophisticated attacks. By learning from this case study, power grid operators can strengthen their defenses and enhance the resilience of their infrastructure against emerging cyber threats.

Dragonfly (Energetic Bear) Attacks (2011-2014)

The Dragonfly, also known as Energetic Bear, attacks that occurred between 2011 and 2014 serve as a significant case study highlighting the sophisticated nature of cyber-attacks targeting the energy sector. These attacks targeted energy companies and their supply chains, exposing critical vulnerabilities and posing a significant threat to the security and stability of the energy infrastructure.

The Dragonfly attacks were orchestrated by a state-sponsored hacking group, believed to have ties to Russia. The primary objective of these attacks was to gain unauthorized access to energy company networks, allowing the attackers to conduct surveillance, gather sensitive information, and potentially disrupt operations.

One of the notable aspects of the Dragonfly attacks was the use of highly targeted spear-phishing emails. The attackers sent carefully crafted emails to employees within the energy companies, often impersonating trusted individuals or using industry-specific information to make the emails appear legitimate. Once an employee clicked on a malicious link or opened an infected attachment, the attackers gained a foothold within the network, enabling them to move laterally and escalate their privileges.

The attackers sought to compromise various systems within the energy companies' networks, including industrial control systems (ICS) and supervisory control and data acquisition (SCADA) systems. By gaining control over these systems, the attackers could potentially manipulate or disrupt critical energy infrastructure, leading to widespread outages or even physical damage.

The Dragonfly attacks highlighted the vulnerabilities within the energy sector, particularly the reliance on outdated and insecure systems. Many energy companies were using legacy equipment and software that lacked proper security controls and had not been updated with the latest patches. This made it easier for the attackers to exploit known vulnerabilities and gain unauthorized access.

The impact of the Dragonfly attacks was significant. They exposed the potential for malicious actors to infiltrate and disrupt energy supply chains, leading to service interruptions, financial losses, and reputational damage. These attacks served as a wake-up call for the energy industry, prompting increased investments in cybersecurity and a greater emphasis on threat intelligence and detection capabilities.

The lessons learned from the Dragonfly attacks have led to improved cybersecurity practices within the energy sector. Energy companies have taken steps to enhance their network defenses, including implementing robust access controls, conducting regular vulnerability assessments, and ensuring timely patching of critical systems. There has also been a greater emphasis on employee training and awareness programs to prevent falling victim to spear-phishing attacks.

Furthermore, the Dragonfly attacks have underscored the need for greater collaboration and information sharing among energy companies, government agencies, and cybersecurity experts. By sharing threat intelligence and best practices, the industry can collectively defend against future attacks and stay ahead of evolving cyber threats.

In conclusion, the Dragonfly (Energetic Bear) attacks provide valuable insights into the complexities and challenges faced by the energy sector in safeguarding critical infrastructure from sophisticated cyber-attacks. These attacks have led to significant improvements in cybersecurity practices and a heightened awareness of the need for continuous monitoring, threat intelligence sharing, and robust incident response capabilities. By studying and analyzing these case studies, the energy industry can strengthen its defenses and better protect the integrity and reliability of global energy systems.

These case studies illustrate the severe consequences of cyber-attacks on power grids, including widespread power outages, economic losses, and potential threats to public safety. They also highlight the vulnerabilities that adversaries can exploit, such as weaknesses in operational technology systems, interconnected networks, and reliance on third-party suppliers. Power grid operators must learn from these case studies and take proactive steps to bolster their cybersecurity defenses.

To enhance the security of power grids, it is essential to adopt a comprehensive approach that includes regular vulnerability assessments, robust access controls, intrusion detection systems, and incident response plans. Collaboration between government agencies, industry stakeholders, and cybersecurity experts is also crucial for sharing threat intelligence, identifying emerging risks, and developing standardized security protocols.

In conclusion, cyber-attacks on power grids pose significant risks to the stability and resilience of critical infrastructure. Case studies provide valuable insights into the potential consequences and vulnerabilities that need to be addressed. By understanding these threats and implementing comprehensive cybersecurity measures, power grid operators can better protect their systems, ensure the reliable delivery of electricity, and safeguard the well-being of communities and economies.

From Grid to Blockchain: How Blockchain Can Secure Power Infrastructures

As power grids become increasingly interconnected and reliant on digital technologies, the need for robust cybersecurity measures becomes paramount. Traditional approaches to securing power infrastructures often fall short, leaving them vulnerable to cyber-attacks. However, blockchain technology holds promise in enhancing the security and resilience of power grids. This section explores the potential of blockchain in securing power infrastructures and mitigating the risks associated with cyber threats.

Decentralized and Immutable Data Storage: Securing Power Grid Information

In the context of securing power infrastructures, the decentralized and immutable nature of blockchain technology offers significant advantages in data storage and management. Traditional centralized databases used in power grids are vulnerable to single points of failure, unauthorized access, and data tampering. Blockchain addresses these weaknesses by distributing data across a network of nodes and ensuring its immutability once recorded.

Decentralization plays a crucial role in enhancing the security of power grid information. Instead of relying on a single central authority or database, blockchain distributes data across multiple nodes in the network. Each node maintains a copy of the entire blockchain, making it challenging for malicious actors to compromise the system. The decentralized nature of blockchain removes the reliance on a single point of control, reducing the risk of unauthorized manipulation or data breaches.

Furthermore, blockchain's immutability feature ensures that once data is recorded on the blockchain, it cannot be altered or tampered with without consensus from the network participants. Each transaction or data entry is encrypted and linked to previous transactions, forming a chain of blocks. This makes it practically impossible for attackers to modify or delete information stored on the blockchain without being detected.

The immutability of blockchain has profound implications for securing power grid information. Energy production, consumption, distribution, and other critical data can be securely recorded on the blockchain, providing an unalterable record of events. This tamper-proof nature of blockchain helps prevent fraudulent activities, manipulation of energy consumption records, or unauthorized changes to grid configurations.

Moreover, the use of cryptographic techniques within blockchain adds an extra layer of security to power grid data. Transactions are digitally signed, ensuring the authenticity and integrity of the information stored. Encryption techniques protect sensitive data, allowing only authorized parties to access and decipher the information. This enhances data privacy and confidentiality within power grid operations.

Evidence supporting the efficacy of decentralized and immutable data storage in blockchain can be found in various industries beyond power grids. For example, blockchain has been successfully deployed in financial systems, supply chain management, and healthcare, where data security and integrity are critical. The track record of blockchain technology in these domains demonstrates its ability to safeguard sensitive information and maintain a trustworthy and auditable record of transactions.

In summary, decentralized and immutable data storage provided by blockchain technology offers a robust solution for securing power grid information. By distributing data across a network of nodes and ensuring its immutability, blockchain mitigates the risks associated with unauthorized access, data tampering, and single points of failure. The application of blockchain in power infrastructures strengthens data security, enhances trust among stakeholders, and establishes a reliable and transparent foundation for managing critical power grid information.

Smart Contracts for Secure Transactions: Enhancing Power Grid Operations

One of the key benefits of blockchain technology in securing power infrastructures lies in the use of smart contracts. Smart contracts are self-executing agreements with predefined rules and conditions encoded within the blockchain. In the context of power grids, smart contracts offer enhanced security and efficiency in conducting transactions and managing operations.

Smart contracts enable secure and automated transactions within the power grid ecosystem. By leveraging blockchain's decentralized and transparent nature, smart contracts facilitate trust and eliminate the need for intermediaries in transactions. For instance, energy producers can enter into smart contracts with consumers directly, specifying terms such as pricing, duration, and energy usage. These contracts are automatically executed and enforced by the blockchain, eliminating the potential for fraud or disputes.

The automation provided by smart contracts streamlines power grid operations and reduces the reliance on manual processes, enhancing efficiency and accuracy. For example, smart contracts can automate billing and payment processes, ensuring timely and accurate settlements between energy suppliers and consumers. This eliminates the need for manual invoicing, reduces administrative costs, and minimizes the risk of errors or delays in payment reconciliation.

The security of smart contracts is derived from blockchain's immutability and cryptographic mechanisms. Once a smart contract is deployed on the blockchain, it cannot be altered or tampered with without consensus from the network participants. This ensures the integrity and reliability of the contract terms, preventing unauthorized modifications or manipulations. Additionally, smart contracts are digitally signed, providing authentication and ensuring that only authorized parties can interact with the contract.

The use of smart contracts in power grid operations has already demonstrated its potential in various pilot projects and real-world applications. For instance, peer-to-peer energy trading platforms based on smart contracts allow prosumers (consumers who also produce energy) to sell excess energy directly to other consumers, bypassing traditional utility companies. These platforms empower users, promote energy self-sufficiency, and provide an efficient and secure method for energy exchange.

Furthermore, the programmable nature of smart contracts opens up possibilities for implementing advanced functionalities in power grid operations. For example, smart contracts can incorporate conditions based on renewable energy generation, ensuring that energy transactions align with sustainability goals. They can also enable dynamic pricing models based on real-time demand and supply, optimizing energy distribution and consumption.

The adoption of smart contracts in power grid operations is an ongoing process, with several initiatives and research efforts exploring their potential. As more stakeholders embrace blockchain technology and smart contracts, the power grid ecosystem can benefit from increased security, transparency, and efficiency in transactions and operations.

In conclusion, the utilization of smart contracts in power grid operations offers significant advantages in terms of security and efficiency. By automating transactions, eliminating intermediaries, and leveraging blockchain's immutability and cryptographic mechanisms, smart contracts enhance the integrity, transparency, and reliability of power grid transactions. The application of smart contracts in the power infrastructure sector paves the way for more secure, decentralized, and efficient energy systems.

Peer-to-Peer Energy Trading: Revolutionizing Power Exchange with Blockchain

One of the groundbreaking applications of blockchain in the energy sector is peer-to-peer (P2P) energy trading. Traditional energy markets operate through centralized intermediaries, such as utility companies, which control the generation, distribution, and pricing of electricity. However, blockchain technology has the potential to disrupt this centralized model by enabling direct, decentralized, and transparent energy trading between producers and consumers.

With P2P energy trading on the blockchain, prosumers (consumers who also generate energy) can sell their surplus energy directly to other consumers within the same grid network. This eliminates the need for intermediaries and allows for more efficient and cost-effective energy transactions. By leveraging smart contracts, which are self-executing agreements stored on the blockchain, P2P energy trading platforms can automate the entire process, ensuring secure and transparent transactions.

The benefits of P2P energy trading are numerous. Firstly, it promotes the integration of renewable energy sources into the grid. Prosumers who generate renewable energy, such as solar or wind power, can sell their excess energy to other consumers, thus incentivizing the adoption of clean energy solutions. This decentralized approach to energy trading encourages sustainability and reduces dependence on fossil fuel-based power generation.

Secondly, P2P energy trading offers consumers greater control over their energy consumption and costs. Through blockchain-based platforms, consumers can choose their energy suppliers based on factors like price, source of energy, or environmental impact. This empowers consumers to make informed decisions and fosters competition in the energy market, potentially leading to more affordable electricity prices.

Another advantage of P2P energy trading is its potential to improve grid stability and resilience. By enabling localized energy transactions, blockchain can help balance the supply and demand of electricity within specific regions. During times of high demand or grid constraints, consumers can rely on nearby prosumers for additional power supply, reducing strain on the central grid and enhancing overall grid stability.

Furthermore, P2P energy trading platforms built on blockchain provide transparency and traceability in energy transactions. All transactions and data related to energy generation, consumption, and pricing are recorded on the blockchain, ensuring an auditable and tamper-proof history. This transparency builds trust among participants and allows for greater accountability in the energy market.

Several pilot projects and initiatives have already demonstrated the feasibility and benefits of P2P energy trading using blockchain technology. For example, in Brooklyn, New York, a project called the Brooklyn Microgrid allows local residents to buy and sell solar energy using blockchain-based smart contracts. Similarly, in Australia, the Power Ledger platform enables P2P energy trading among households with rooftop solar panels.

In conclusion, P2P energy trading powered by blockchain technology is revolutionizing the way electricity is bought and sold. It promotes renewable energy adoption, empowers consumers, improves grid stability, and enhances transparency in the energy market. As blockchain continues to mature and gain wider adoption, P2P energy trading has the potential to reshape the energy landscape, creating a more sustainable, decentralized, and customer-centric energy system.

Cyberattack Detection and Response: Strengthening Power Grid Security with Blockchain

The power grid is a critical infrastructure that is highly susceptible to cyber-attacks. To enhance the security of power grids, blockchain technology can play a pivotal role in cyberattack detection and response.

By leveraging the inherent properties of blockchain, such as immutability and transparency, power grid operators can establish a robust system for detecting and responding to cyber threats. Here are some key ways in which blockchain can strengthen cyberattack detection and response in power grids:

1. **Immutable Audit Trail:** Blockchain provides an immutable audit trail of all transactions and activities occurring within the power grid. This means that every change, access attempt, or transaction is recorded and time-stamped on the blockchain. By monitoring this audit trail, power grid operators can detect any suspicious or unauthorized activities, enabling early detection of cyber-attacks.

2. **Intrusion Detection System:** Blockchain can be utilized to build an intrusion detection system (IDS) for power grids. The IDS monitors the network for any abnormal or malicious activities and triggers alerts when suspicious behavior is detected. The decentralized nature of blockchain ensures that the IDS is resistant to single points of failure and offers a more robust defense against cyber-attacks.

3. **Secure Data Sharing and Collaboration:** Power grid operators, government agencies, and cybersecurity organizations can use blockchain to securely share threat intelligence and collaborate on cyberattack response. Blockchain-based platforms enable encrypted and tamper-proof sharing of information, allowing stakeholders to work together in real-time to analyze, mitigate, and respond to cyber threats effectively.

4. **Smart Contract-Based Incident Response:** Smart contracts can be deployed on the blockchain to automate incident response processes in case of a cyberattack. These contracts can define predefined response actions, such as isolating affected components, notifying relevant

parties, or initiating recovery procedures. By automating incident response, power grid operators can reduce response time, minimize the impact of attacks, and facilitate a coordinated and efficient recovery process.

5. **Distributed Security Monitoring:** Blockchain's decentralized nature allows for distributed security monitoring across multiple nodes in the power grid network. This distributed monitoring approach ensures that no single point of failure exists and provides redundancy in detecting and responding to cyber-attacks. Furthermore, blockchain's consensus mechanisms can facilitate the verification and validation of security events, increasing the overall reliability and trustworthiness of the monitoring process.

The application of blockchain in cyberattack detection and response is still in its early stages, but there are promising initiatives and research projects exploring its potential. For example, the Energy Web Foundation has developed a blockchain-based platform called EW Origin, which enhances the traceability and verification of renewable energy certificates, contributing to a more secure and transparent energy market.

In conclusion, blockchain technology has the potential to significantly strengthen cyberattack detection and response in power grids. By leveraging the immutability, transparency, and decentralized nature of blockchain, power grid operators can enhance the security posture of their systems, detect and respond to cyber threats more effectively, and ultimately ensure the reliable and secure operation of critical power infrastructure.

Data Privacy and Secure Identity Management

In power infrastructures, maintaining data privacy and ensuring secure identity management are critical. Blockchain's cryptographic mechanisms can provide secure and private access to data, allowing for granular control over data sharing and access permissions. Additionally, blockchain-based identity management systems can enable secure and verifiable authentication of participants within the energy ecosystem, reducing the risk of unauthorized access and identity theft.

In conclusion, blockchain technology offers promising solutions for enhancing the security and resilience of power infrastructures. By leveraging its decentralized nature, immutable data storage, smart contracts, peer-to-peer energy trading, and enhanced cyberattack detection capabilities, blockchain can mitigate vulnerabilities and strengthen the overall security posture of power grids. The use of blockchain in power infrastructures can enable secure and transparent transactions, real-time monitoring of grid operations, peer-to-peer energy trading, and robust cyberattack detection and response mechanisms. Furthermore, blockchain can enhance data privacy and secure identity management, ensuring that sensitive information remains protected and only accessible to authorized entities.

By adopting blockchain technology, power grid operators and stakeholders can establish a more resilient and trustworthy energy ecosystem. However, it is important to acknowledge that the implementation of blockchain in power infrastructures comes with its own challenges, including scalability, interoperability, and regulatory considerations. These challenges must be addressed through collaborative efforts among industry players, policymakers, and technology experts to fully realize the potential of blockchain in securing power grids and safeguarding critical energy infrastructure.

Overall, the integration of blockchain in power infrastructures holds immense promise in addressing the security and vulnerabilities faced by modern power grids. By embracing this innovative technology, the power industry can enhance its resilience, improve operational efficiency, and protect against evolving cyber threats, ensuring a reliable and secure energy supply for communities and industries alike.

Strategies for Defense: Enhancing Power Grid Security with Blockchain

Power grids are a prime target for cyber-attacks due to their critical role in providing electricity to homes, businesses, and infrastructure. To bolster power grid security and protect against evolving cyber threats, innovative solutions are needed. Blockchain technology offers promising strategies for defense by enhancing the security of power grid systems. In this section, we explore several strategies for leveraging blockchain to strengthen power grid security.

Immutable and Tamper-Proof Data Storage

One of the key strategies for enhancing power grid security with blockchain is the implementation of immutable and tamper-proof data storage solutions. Power grid systems generate vast amounts of critical data, including operational information, configuration details, and security events. By leveraging blockchain technology, power grid operators can ensure the integrity and immutability of this data, strengthening the overall security posture.

Blockchain's inherent characteristics, such as decentralized consensus and cryptographic hashing, enable the creation of a secure and tamper-proof data storage layer. Each piece of data is cryptographically hashed and linked to the previous data entry, forming a chain of blocks that cannot be modified without consensus from the network participants. This immutability ensures that once data is recorded on the blockchain, it becomes virtually impossible to alter or tamper with it retroactively.

The use of blockchain for data storage in power grids offers several benefits. Firstly, it provides a reliable and auditable trail of events, enabling power grid operators to trace and verify the authenticity of data. Any attempts to modify or tamper with the data will be immediately evident, alerting operators to potential security breaches. This transparency and auditability foster trust among stakeholders and facilitate compliance with regulatory requirements.

Furthermore, the decentralized nature of blockchain eliminates single points of failure and enhances the resilience of power grid data storage. Traditional centralized databases are vulnerable to attacks and unauthorized access, whereas blockchain's distributed architecture ensures that data is replicated and stored across multiple nodes in the network. This redundancy makes it challenging for attackers to compromise the entire system, as they would need to gain control of a significant portion of the network's computing power.

The immutability and tamper-proof nature of blockchain data storage also contribute to incident response and forensics efforts. In the event of a cyberattack or security breach, investigators can rely on the immutable records stored on the blockchain to reconstruct the sequence of events and identify the source of the attack. This information is invaluable for conducting thorough investigations, attributing responsibility, and implementing corrective measures to prevent similar incidents in the future.

The use of immutable and tamper-proof data storage solutions based on blockchain technology represents a significant step forward in enhancing power grid security. By ensuring the integrity and authenticity of critical data, power grid operators can better protect against unauthorized modifications, insider threats, and data manipulation attempts. The transparency, auditability, and resilience provided by blockchain-based data storage contribute to the overall defense strategy of power grids, helping to safeguard the reliable and uninterrupted delivery of electricity to communities and critical infrastructure.

Section 5.2: Secure and Efficient Energy Transactions

Another important strategy for enhancing power grid security with blockchain is the implementation of secure and efficient energy transactions. Traditional energy trading and settlement processes often involve multiple intermediaries, complex reconciliation procedures, and manual verification, which can introduce vulnerabilities and inefficiencies.

Blockchain technology offers a decentralized and transparent platform for peer-to-peer energy transactions, reducing reliance on intermediaries and enhancing the security and efficiency of the process. Smart contracts, a key feature of blockchain, enable automated and self-executing transactions based on predefined conditions, eliminating the need for manual intervention and reducing the risk of errors and fraud.

With blockchain-based energy transactions, power grid participants, such as energy producers and consumers, can directly interact with each other without the need for intermediaries. This peer-to-peer approach streamlines the transaction process, reduces transaction costs, and improves the overall speed and efficiency of energy trading.

Furthermore, blockchain enables the establishment of secure and auditable energy marketplaces. By recording transaction details, such as energy generation, consumption, and pricing, on the blockchain, a transparent and tamper-proof ledger is created. This enhances trust and accountability among participants, as all stakeholders can verify and validate the accuracy of transactions. It also provides regulators and auditors with a comprehensive and immutable record of energy transactions, facilitating compliance monitoring and dispute resolution.

The implementation of blockchain in energy transactions also brings additional security benefits. Blockchain's cryptographic mechanisms and consensus protocols ensure the integrity and confidentiality of transaction data. Each transaction is cryptographically secured and linked to previous transactions, creating an immutable chain of records. This makes it extremely difficult for malicious actors to tamper with or manipulate transaction data, reducing the risk of fraudulent activities and unauthorized modifications.

Moreover, blockchain can enable real-time monitoring and auditing of energy transactions. By integrating IoT (Internet of Things) devices and smart meters with blockchain technology, power grid operators can gather accurate and real-time data on energy production, consumption, and distribution. This data can be securely recorded on the blockchain, enabling better monitoring of energy flows, identification of anomalies or abnormalities, and timely response to potential security threats.

The adoption of blockchain for secure and efficient energy transactions in power grids represents a significant advancement in enhancing security and reducing vulnerabilities. By leveraging the decentralized and transparent nature of blockchain, power grid operators can streamline energy trading processes, eliminate intermediaries, improve transaction efficiency, and strengthen overall security. The increased transparency, auditability, and automation provided by blockchain contribute to a more resilient and trustworthy power grid ecosystem, ensuring the reliable and secure delivery of energy to consumers.

Section 5.3: Immutable and Transparent Grid Monitoring and Control

In addition to securing data storage and energy transactions, blockchain technology can play a crucial role in enhancing power grid security through immutable and transparent grid monitoring and control.

Traditionally, power grid monitoring and control systems rely on centralized databases and control centers, which can be vulnerable to cyber-attacks and system failures. By integrating blockchain into grid monitoring and control processes, power grid operators can establish a decentralized and transparent network that enhances the security and reliability of the grid.

Blockchain's immutable nature ensures that all grid monitoring data, including energy generation, consumption, and transmission information, is securely recorded and cannot be altered or tampered with. This provides an accurate and trustworthy source of data for monitoring grid operations, identifying anomalies, and detecting potential security breaches.

Moreover, blockchain enables real-time data sharing and transparency among relevant stakeholders, such as grid operators, energy producers, consumers, and regulatory authorities. Each participant can have access to the same set of data, ensuring transparency and enabling collaborative monitoring and control of the grid. This shared view of data fosters trust and accountability among stakeholders, as any changes or transactions are recorded on the blockchain and can be easily audited and verified.

The integration of blockchain with IoT devices and sensors further enhances grid monitoring and control capabilities. These devices can collect real-time data on grid performance, equipment status, and environmental factors, which is securely recorded on the blockchain. This data can then be analyzed and used to optimize grid operations, detect and respond to anomalies, and ensure the efficient and reliable delivery of electricity.

Additionally, blockchain-based smart contracts can automate grid control processes based on predefined rules and conditions. For example, smart contracts can automatically adjust energy distribution and reroute power in case of grid failures or security breaches. This automation reduces the reliance on manual interventions and improves the response time to potential threats, ensuring the continuity and stability of the power grid.

By leveraging blockchain technology for grid monitoring and control, power grid operators can enhance the security, reliability, and resilience of power infrastructures. The immutable and transparent nature of blockchain ensures the integrity and trustworthiness of grid data, while real-time data sharing and automation improve the efficiency and responsiveness of grid operations. This integrated approach strengthens power grid security and reduces vulnerabilities, ultimately ensuring the uninterrupted supply of electricity to consumers.

Proactive Threat Intelligence and Analytics

Power grid operators face an ever-evolving landscape of cyber threats, requiring proactive measures to detect and mitigate potential attacks. Blockchain technology can play a crucial role in enhancing threat intelligence and analytics capabilities, empowering power grid security teams to stay one step ahead of adversaries.

By leveraging blockchain's decentralized and immutable nature, power grid operators can establish a distributed threat intelligence network. This network allows different entities, such as utilities, vendors, regulatory bodies, and security agencies, to securely share and exchange threat intelligence data. Information about emerging threats, attack patterns, and vulnerabilities can be recorded on the blockchain, ensuring its integrity and preventing tampering. This collaborative approach enables power grid operators to access real-time threat intelligence and make informed decisions to enhance their security posture.

Blockchain's transparency and auditability also facilitate the collection and analysis of security-related data within the power grid ecosystem. Security events, alerts, and anomalies can be recorded on the blockchain, creating a comprehensive and immutable record of security incidents. This historical data can be analyzed using advanced analytics and machine learning techniques to identify patterns, detect potential threats, and predict future attack vectors. The insights gained from these analytics can be used to proactively strengthen the security infrastructure and implement preventive measures against known and emerging threats.

Furthermore, blockchain-enabled threat intelligence platforms can leverage smart contracts to automate security-related actions and responses. When a threat or anomaly is detected, smart contracts can trigger predefined actions, such as isolating compromised systems, redirecting network traffic, or initiating incident response procedures. This automation reduces response times and ensures consistent and efficient security incident management across the power grid infrastructure.

Collaboration and information sharing with other industries and sectors are also crucial in mitigating cyber threats. Blockchain can facilitate secure intersectoral information exchange, enabling power grid operators to benefit from threat intelligence shared by other sectors, such as finance, healthcare, and defense. By leveraging blockchain's interoperability and secure data-sharing capabilities, power grid operators can enhance their understanding of emerging threats and adopt best practices from other industries to strengthen their security defenses.

In summary, blockchain technology provides a powerful framework for proactive threat intelligence and analytics in power grid security. By establishing a decentralized threat intelligence network, leveraging transparent and auditable data, and automating security actions through smart contracts, power grid operators can enhance their ability to detect, analyze, and respond to cyber threats. This proactive approach strengthens the overall security posture of power grids and ensures the continuous delivery of reliable and secure electricity to communities and industries.

Section 5.5: Resilient and Decentralized Energy Management

One of the key challenges in power grid security is maintaining the resilience and availability of energy supply, especially during a cyberattack. Blockchain technology offers a promising solution by enabling resilient and decentralized energy management systems that can withstand disruptions and ensure continuous power delivery.

Traditionally, power grids rely on centralized control and management systems, making them susceptible to single points of failure. In the event of a cyberattack, these centralized systems can be targeted and compromised, leading to widespread power outages and disruptions. However, with blockchain, power grid operators can transition toward a decentralized energy management model.

By leveraging blockchain's distributed ledger and consensus mechanisms, power grid operations can be decentralized across a network of nodes. Each node in the network maintains a copy of the blockchain, ensuring redundancy and eliminating the reliance on a single central authority. This decentralized approach enhances the resilience of the power grid, as even if some nodes or components are compromised, the overall system remains operational and capable of delivering power.

Blockchain also enables the implementation of peer-to-peer energy trading and management. Through smart contracts, consumers and prosumers (consumers who also produce energy) can directly transact with each other without the need for intermediaries. This peer-to-peer energy trading system allows for a more efficient utilization of energy resources and promotes renewable energy integration into the grid. Additionally, the transparency and immutability of blockchain ensure the integrity and traceability of energy transactions, reducing the risk of fraud or manipulation.

Moreover, blockchain-based energy management systems can facilitate demand response mechanisms. During times of peak demand or supply constraints, smart contracts can automatically adjust energy consumption or incentivize consumers to reduce their usage. This dynamic management of energy demand and supply helps balance the grid, optimize resource allocation, and ensure the stability and reliability of the power system.

In the event of a cyberattack, the decentralized nature of blockchain-based energy management systems enhances the system's resilience and ability to recover. Since there is no single point of control, attackers would need to compromise multiple nodes simultaneously to disrupt the power grid. This significantly increases the complexity and effort required for a successful attack, making it more challenging for adversaries to cause widespread damage.

Furthermore, blockchain's immutable nature provides an auditable and tamper-proof record of energy transactions and system operations. This transparency enables power grid operators to detect anomalies or malicious activities, quickly identify the source of the attack, and take appropriate remedial actions. The ability to trace and attribute actions within the blockchain enhances accountability and facilitates post-attack analysis for continuous improvement of the system's security.

In conclusion, blockchain technology offers a resilient and decentralized approach to energy management in power grids. By leveraging blockchain's distributed ledger, peer-to-peer energy trading, and demand response mechanisms, power grid operators can enhance the resilience, efficiency, and reliability of energy supply. Furthermore, the transparency and immutability of blockchain ensure the integrity of energy transactions and enable effective detection and response to cyber-attacks. Embracing blockchain-based energy management systems can revolutionize the power grid infrastructure, paving the way for a more secure and sustainable energy future.

Continuous Monitoring and Incident Response

Continuous monitoring and proactive incident response are critical components of enhancing power grid security with blockchain technology. By implementing robust monitoring systems and efficient incident response procedures, power grid operators can quickly detect and respond to cyber threats, minimizing the potential damage and downtime caused by cyber-attacks.

Blockchain technology can play a significant role in continuous monitoring by providing a transparent and immutable record of power grid operations. Through the distributed ledger, all transactions, events, and system activities are recorded and stored securely. Power grid operators can leverage this data to establish a comprehensive monitoring system that tracks and analyzes network traffic, system performance, and security events in real time.

By integrating blockchain with advanced analytics and machine learning techniques, power grid operators can identify anomalous patterns and potential indicators of compromise. These analytics can detect suspicious activities, such as unauthorized access attempts, unusual data transfers, or changes to critical system settings. Early detection of these anomalies can prompt immediate investigation and response, preventing further exploitation and potential disruptions.

Additionally, blockchain technology enables the creation of incident response workflows and smart contracts that automate certain response actions.

In the event of a detected threat or cyberattack, predefined response protocols can be triggered automatically, minimizing the time between detection and remediation. These response protocols can include isolating affected components, disabling compromised accounts, or activating backup systems to ensure the continuity of power supply.

Furthermore, blockchain's transparent and auditable nature facilitates post-incident analysis and forensic investigations. The immutable record of transactions and system events enables the identification of the attack's origin, impact, and propagation path. This information is crucial for understanding the attack vectors, closing security gaps, and improving incident response procedures to prevent future cyber threats.

Continuous monitoring and incident response in a blockchain-based power grid security framework require collaboration and information sharing among stakeholders. Power grid operators, regulatory bodies, and cybersecurity experts can establish partnerships and share threat intelligence to collectively enhance the security posture of the power grid. Blockchain technology can facilitate secure and private information sharing through encrypted channels, ensuring the confidentiality of sensitive data.

Regular vulnerability assessments and penetration testing should be conducted to identify potential weaknesses in the power grid infrastructure. These assessments can help identify vulnerabilities that could be exploited by attackers and inform the implementation of appropriate security measures.

In conclusion, continuous monitoring and proactive incident response are essential strategies for enhancing power grid security. By leveraging blockchain technology, power grid operators can establish a robust monitoring system, automate incident response procedures, and facilitate post-incident analysis. The transparency and immutability of blockchain provide a reliable audit trail and enable effective collaboration among stakeholders. By adopting these strategies, the power grid can strengthen its defenses against cyber threats and ensure the reliable and secure delivery of electricity to consumers.

5
Safeguarding Wealth: Cybersecurity in the Financial Sector

Money Trails: Understanding How Financial Systems Work

Financial systems play a critical role in facilitating economic activities and the flow of money. Section 1 provides a comprehensive exploration of the intricacies of financial systems, shedding light on the fundamental mechanisms and processes that underpin their operations.

The section begins by examining the various components of financial systems, including central banks, commercial banks, financial markets, and regulatory bodies. It delves into the roles and responsibilities of these entities, highlighting how they contribute to the overall functioning of the financial sector.

Central banks are at the core of financial systems, responsible for managing monetary policy, regulating the supply of money, and ensuring the stability of the economy. Section 1 explores the functions of central banks, including interest rate setting, currency issuance, and oversight of financial institutions.

Commercial banks, on the other hand, provide a range of financial services to individuals, businesses, and governments. Section 1 delves into the operations of commercial banks, such as accepting deposits, granting loans, facilitating payments, and offering investment products.

Financial markets, including stock exchanges, bond markets, and commodity markets, enable the trading and investment of various financial instruments. Section 1 examines the role of these markets in facilitating capital allocation, price discovery, and risk management.

Regulatory bodies and compliance frameworks play a crucial role in ensuring the integrity and stability of financial systems. Section 1 explores the regulatory landscape, discussing the importance of prudential regulations, anti-money laundering (AML) measures, and consumer protection rules.

By understanding the intricacies of financial systems, Section 1 sets the stage for comprehending the cybersecurity challenges that exist within the financial sector. It provides a solid foundation for the subsequent sections, which delve into the threats, solutions, and strategies related to cybersecurity in the financial industry.

Threats to the Treasury: Unmasking Cyber-attacks on Financial Systems

Financial systems are a prime target for cyber-attacks due to the significant value of assets and sensitive data they hold. Section 2 delves into the various threats faced by financial systems, shedding light on the sophisticated techniques employed by cybercriminals to compromise these systems and exploit their vulnerabilities.

This section explores the diverse range of cyber threats targeting the financial sector. It examines the tactics used by hackers, including phishing, malware, ransomware, insider threats, and advanced persistent threats (APTs). Each attack vector is dissected to understand how adversaries exploit vulnerabilities in networks, systems, and human behavior to gain unauthorized access, steal sensitive information, or disrupt financial operations.

To expand upon the example, consider a case where a sophisticated phishing campaign targets banking customers. Cybercriminals craft convincing emails, impersonating reputable financial institutions, and deceive recipients into divulging their login credentials or personal information. With this stolen data, attackers gain unauthorized access to the victims' bank accounts, allowing them to carry out fraudulent transactions or initiate identity theft.

Moreover, Section 2 analyzes the motivations behind cyber-attacks on financial systems. It explores the financial incentives that drive cybercriminals, such as monetary gain through fraud, theft, or extortion. It also delves into state-sponsored attacks targeting financial institutions for political or economic espionage purposes, as well as hacktivist activities aimed at disrupting the financial system to convey ideological messages.

To illustrate further, imagine a scenario where a nation-state actor targets a stock exchange with the objective of manipulating financial markets. By gaining unauthorized access to the trading platform, the attacker can execute unauthorized trades or disrupt trading activities, causing significant financial losses and undermining investor confidence.

The impact of cyber-attacks on the financial sector is profound. Section 2 examines the consequences of successful attacks, including financial losses, reputational damage, regulatory penalties, and erosion of customer trust. It emphasizes the importance of swift incident response, effective threat intelligence, and collaboration among financial institutions, government agencies, and cybersecurity experts to mitigate the impact of cyber-attacks and protect the stability of the financial system.

As the financial sector continues to be a prime target for cybercriminals, it is crucial for financial institutions to remain vigilant and employ robust cybersecurity measures. Section 2 highlights the evolving nature of cyber threats in the financial sector, encouraging organizations to continuously update their defenses, educate employees on best practices, and foster a culture of cybersecurity awareness. By understanding the threats, financial institutions can take proactive steps to mitigate risks and protect their assets, customers, and reputation.

Banking on Blockchain: How Blockchain Can Secure Financial Transactions

Blockchain technology has emerged as a game-changer in the financial sector, revolutionizing the way financial transactions are conducted and secured. This section explores the potential of blockchain in enhancing the security, transparency, and efficiency of financial transactions, offering a promising solution to the cybersecurity challenges faced by the financial sector.

Blockchain, as a decentralized and immutable ledger, provides a tamper-proof and transparent record of financial transactions. It eliminates the need for intermediaries and central authorities, allowing for direct peer-to-peer transactions. The distributed consensus mechanism ensures that transactions are securely validated and recorded on the blockchain, reducing the risk of fraud, manipulation, and unauthorized access.

One of the key strengths of blockchain in securing financial transactions is the use of smart contracts. Smart contracts are self-executing agreements with predefined rules and conditions that automatically execute actions when specific criteria are met. This eliminates the need for manual intervention and reduces the potential for human error or malicious intent. Smart contracts ensure the proper execution and enforcement of financial agreements, such as the transfer of assets, payment settlements, or the execution of complex financial transactions.

Blockchain's immutability and transparency provide an additional layer of security to financial transactions. Once a transaction is recorded on the blockchain, it becomes virtually impossible to alter or delete, ensuring an accurate and tamper-resistant record. This feature enhances auditability, allowing participants to trace and verify the integrity and authenticity of transactions. It also enables regulators and auditors to conduct efficient and thorough audits, reducing the risk of fraudulent activities and enhancing compliance with regulatory requirements.

Moreover, blockchain technology can address challenges related to identity verification and fraud prevention. Traditional financial transactions often involve extensive verification processes and the exchange of sensitive personal information. Blockchain-based identity solutions, powered by cryptographic mechanisms, offer secure and decentralized identity management. By leveraging blockchain, financial institutions can streamline identity verification processes, reduce the risk of identity theft, and enhance customer privacy and data protection.

Additionally, blockchain's potential for cross-border transactions and international remittances is significant. Traditional cross-border transactions often involve multiple intermediaries, resulting in delays, high costs, and increased security risks. Blockchain-based solutions can enable near-instantaneous and cost-effective cross-border transfers, leveraging the transparency and efficiency of blockchain technology. This has the potential to revolutionize global financial transactions, making them faster, cheaper, and more accessible.

To illustrate the potential of blockchain in securing financial transactions, consider the example of trade finance. Traditionally, trade finance involves complex documentation and multiple intermediaries, resulting in delays and increased risk. By utilizing blockchain, all parties involved in the trade, including exporters, importers, banks, and regulatory authorities, can access a shared and secure platform. The transparent and immutable nature of blockchain ensures trust and transparency in the transaction process, reducing the risk of fraud, improving efficiency, and accelerating the settlement of trade transactions.

As with any emerging technology, challenges and considerations exist in implementing blockchain for financial transactions. Scalability, privacy, regulatory compliance, and interoperability are among the key factors that need to be addressed for widespread adoption. However, the potential benefits of blockchain in securing financial transactions far outweigh the challenges, making it a compelling solution for the financial sector.

In summary, blockchain technology has the potential to revolutionize the way financial transactions are conducted and secured. Its decentralized nature, smart contracts, immutability, and transparency offer significant advantages in enhancing the security, efficiency, and trustworthiness of financial transactions. By embracing blockchain technology, the financial sector can mitigate cybersecurity risks, reduce costs, streamline processes, and ultimately provide a more secure and seamless financial experience for individuals and businesses alike.

Banking on Blockchain: How Blockchain Can Secure Financial Transactions

Blockchain technology has emerged as a transformative solution for the financial sector, offering enhanced security, transparency, and efficiency in financial transactions. This section explores the potential of blockchain in revolutionizing the way financial transactions are conducted and secured, providing a robust defense against cyber threats in the banking industry.

1. **Immutable and Tamper-Proof Transactions:**
   Blockchain's core strength lies in its ability to create immutable and tamper-proof records of transactions. By utilizing cryptographic hashing and distributed consensus mechanisms, blockchain ensures that once a transaction is recorded on the blockchain, it cannot be altered or deleted without the consensus of the network. This immutability provides a strong layer of security, making it extremely challenging for cybercriminals to manipulate or falsify financial transactions.
   Furthermore, blockchain's transparency enables participants to have visibility into the entire transaction history. Every transaction recorded on the blockchain is visible to all network participants, providing a

comprehensive audit trail. This transparency fosters trust, accountability, and auditability, as financial institutions, regulators, and customers can independently verify the integrity and authenticity of transactions.

2. **Smart Contracts for Automated and Secure Execution:**
Smart contracts, powered by blockchain, offer automated and secure execution of financial agreements. These self-executing contracts automatically enforce predefined conditions and execute actions when the specified criteria are met. By removing the need for intermediaries, smart contracts streamline processes, reduce costs, and eliminate potential vulnerabilities associated with human error or malicious intent. Smart contracts can facilitate a wide range of financial transactions, such as the transfer of assets, settlement of payments, issuance of digital currencies, and compliance with regulatory requirements. The automated nature of smart contracts ensures that transactions are executed accurately, efficiently, and in a tamper-resistant manner, mitigating the risk of fraud and ensuring compliance with established rules and regulations.

3. **Enhanced Security in Identity Management:**
Identity theft and fraudulent activities pose significant risks in the financial sector. Blockchain technology offers enhanced security in identity management by providing a decentralized and secure framework for storing and managing identities. Personal information can be encrypted and stored on the blockchain, reducing the risk of unauthorized access or data breaches.

Through blockchain-based identity solutions, individuals can have control over their own digital identities, granting selective access to trusted entities through cryptographic mechanisms. This decentralized approach enhances privacy, reduces the reliance on centralized databases, and minimizes the risk of identity theft and fraud. By leveraging blockchain for identity management, financial institutions can strengthen customer trust, improve compliance with data protection regulations, and reduce the risk of unauthorized transactions.

4. **Streamlined Cross-Border Transactions:**
Traditional cross-border transactions are often complex, time-consuming, and costly, involving multiple intermediaries and lengthy settlement processes. Blockchain technology has the potential to streamline cross-border transactions, enabling near-instantaneous transfers with reduced costs and increased efficiency.

Blockchain-based solutions for cross-border transactions leverage the transparent and decentralized nature of blockchain to eliminate intermediaries and automate the settlement process. By providing a shared and secure platform for participants, blockchain ensures transparency, reduces the risk of errors or delays, and enhances the traceability of funds throughout the transaction lifecycle. This streamlined approach simplifies cross-border transactions, enhances liquidity, and promotes financial inclusion.

5. **Regulatory Compliance and Auditing:**
Regulatory compliance is of utmost importance in the financial sector. Blockchain technology offers benefits in terms of regulatory compliance and auditing processes. The transparent and immutable nature of blockchain simplifies auditing procedures by providing a verifiable and tamper-proof record of transactions. Regulators can independently verify compliance, detect anomalies, and identify potential risks more efficiently.

Additionally, blockchain's ability to automate compliance through smart contracts ensures that financial transactions adhere to established regulations and protocols. Compliance rules can be embedded within smart contracts, enabling real-time monitoring and enforcement of regulatory requirements.

This automated approach reduces the burden of manual compliance and enhances the accuracy and timeliness of compliance processes.

Furthermore, the use of blockchain in financial transactions enables greater transparency and traceability of funds, making it easier to detect and prevent money laundering, fraud, and other financial crimes. The immutability of blockchain records ensures that transaction histories cannot be altered, providing an auditable trail for regulatory authorities and law enforcement agencies.

6. **Collaborative Security and Fraud Detection:**
   Blockchain technology can facilitate collaborative security measures and enhance fraud detection in the financial sector. By leveraging blockchain's decentralized and distributed nature, financial institutions can share threat intelligence and collaborate in real-time to identify and respond to emerging cyber threats.

Blockchain can be utilized to create shared security platforms where financial institutions can exchange information about cybersecurity incidents, attack patterns, and vulnerabilities. This collaborative approach strengthens the collective defense against cyber-attacks, enabling rapid response and mitigation.

Moreover, the use of advanced technologies such as artificial intelligence (AI) and machine learning (ML) in conjunction with blockchain can enhance fraud detection capabilities. By analyzing large volumes of transaction data stored on the blockchain, AI and ML algorithms can identify patterns and anomalies indicative of fraudulent activities. This proactive approach allows financial institutions to detect and prevent fraudulent transactions in real time, safeguarding the integrity of financial systems.

In summary, blockchain technology holds significant potential for securing financial transactions and mitigating cyber threats in the banking industry. Its features of immutability, transparency, smart contracts, enhanced identity management, streamlined cross-border transactions, regulatory compliance, and collaborative security provide a strong foundation for building a more secure and efficient financial ecosystem. By embracing blockchain technology, financial institutions can enhance customer trust, reduce costs, streamline processes, and bolster the overall cybersecurity posture of the financial sector.

Section 4: Case Studies: Examining Past Financial Cyber-attacks

Financial institutions have become prime targets for cybercriminals due to the high-value assets and sensitive data they possess. This section delves into notable case studies of past financial cyber-attacks, providing insights into the tactics employed by attackers and the consequences faced by the targeted organizations. By examining these case studies, we can gain a better understanding of the evolving nature of financial cyber threats and the importance of robust cybersecurity measures.

1. Case Study 1: The Bangladesh Bank Heist (2016)

The Bangladesh Bank cyber heist is one of the most significant financial cyber-attacks in recent history. Attackers used sophisticated malware to gain access to the bank's SWIFT (Society for Worldwide Interbank Financial Telecommunication) credentials. They manipulated the SWIFT system to initiate fraudulent fund transfers, attempting to steal nearly $1 billion. While most of the transactions were blocked, the attackers still managed to successfully transfer around $81 million. This case highlights the importance of robust security measures, particularly in securing critical financial systems and employing stringent access controls.

2. Case Study 2: JP Morgan Chase Data Breach (2014)

In 2014, JPMorgan Chase, one of the largest financial institutions in the United States, suffered a significant data breach. Attackers gained access to the bank's network and compromised sensitive customer data, including names, addresses, and email addresses of approximately 76 million households and 7 million small businesses. The breach was attributed to a combination of sophisticated spear-phishing techniques and vulnerabilities in the bank's security infrastructure. This case emphasizes the critical need for comprehensive security measures, including robust authentication protocols and continuous monitoring to detect and respond to cyber threats.

3. Case Study 3: Equifax Data Breach (2017)

Equifax, one of the largest credit reporting agencies in the world, experienced a massive data breach in 2017. Attackers exploited a vulnerability in a web application, gaining access to personal information, including social security numbers, dates of birth, and addresses, of approximately 147 million individuals. The breach had severe implications for the affected individuals, as it exposed sensitive financial and personal data. This case highlights the importance of proactive vulnerability management, regular security assessments, and prompt patching of known vulnerabilities.

4. Case Study 4: SWIFT-related Cyber-attacks (2016-2018)

Several financial institutions worldwide fell victim to a series of cyber-attacks targeting the SWIFT messaging system between 2016 and 2018. Attackers exploited vulnerabilities in the banks' security controls and compromised the SWIFT network, allowing them to send fraudulent payment instructions. This led to significant financial losses for some institutions and exposed the vulnerabilities in the global financial messaging system. This case underscores the need for enhanced security measures and continuous monitoring of critical financial infrastructure.

5. Case Study 5: Cryptocurrency Exchange Hacks (e.g., Mt. Gox, Coincheck)

Numerous cryptocurrency exchanges have experienced high-profile hacks, resulting in the theft of millions of dollars' worth of digital assets. For example, the Mt. Gox exchange hack in 2014 led to the loss of approximately 850,000 bitcoins. Similarly, the Coincheck hack in 2018 resulted in the theft of over $500 million worth of NEM cryptocurrency. These attacks highlight the unique cybersecurity challenges faced by the cryptocurrency industry and the need for robust security measures, including secure wallet storage, multifactor authentication, and proactive threat intelligence.

These case studies represent just a fraction of the financial cyber-attacks that have occurred in recent years. They demonstrate the evolving sophistication of cybercriminals and the potential ramifications for targeted organizations and individuals. Examining these attacks provides valuable insights into the techniques employed by attackers, the vulnerabilities they exploit, and the consequences faced by the targeted entities. These case studies emphasize the importance of implementing robust cybersecurity measures and adopting proactive defense strategies to mitigate the risks associated with financial cyber-attacks.

It is essential for financial institutions to continuously assess and strengthen their security posture by implementing measures such as:

- Regular security assessments and vulnerability scanning to identify and remediate weaknesses in systems and applications.

- Multifactor authentication and strong access controls to prevent unauthorized access to sensitive financial systems and data.
- Employee training and awareness programs to educate staff about cybersecurity best practices and the importance of vigilant behavior.
- Network segmentation and isolation to limit the lateral movement of attackers within the infrastructure.
- Continuous monitoring and threat intelligence integration to detect and respond to cyber threats in real-time.
- Incident response plans and drills to ensure an organized and efficient response to security incidents.

By analyzing past financial cyber-attacks, financial institutions can gain valuable insights into the tactics employed by attackers and the impact of these attacks. This knowledge can inform the development of robust cybersecurity strategies and the implementation of effective security controls. It is crucial for organizations to collaborate with industry peers, share threat intelligence, and stay updated on emerging threats and best practices.

Furthermore, regulatory bodies play a vital role in the financial sector's cybersecurity. They should continue to develop and enforce regulations that require financial institutions to adhere to robust security standards and implement necessary controls to protect customer data and financial systems.

By leveraging the lessons learned from these case studies and adopting a proactive and collaborative approach to cybersecurity, financial institutions can better safeguard their assets, customer data, and reputation. They can enhance their resilience in the face of evolving cyber threats and maintain the trust of their customers in the increasingly digital financial landscape.

Future-Proofing Finances: Strategies to Shield Our Money

In an increasingly digitized financial landscape, it is crucial to implement strategies that not only protect our money but also future-proof our financial systems against emerging cyber threats. This section explores key strategies and measures that individuals, financial institutions, and regulatory bodies can adopt to safeguard money and ensure the long-term security and stability of the financial sector.

1. **Embracing Strong Authentication Mechanisms:**
   One of the fundamental strategies to shield our money is to embrace robust and multifactor authentication mechanisms. Traditional username and password combinations are no longer sufficient to protect financial accounts. By incorporating additional factors such as biometrics (fingerprint, face recognition), hardware tokens, or one-time passwords, individuals can enhance the security of their financial transactions. Multifactor authentication adds an extra layer of protection, making it significantly more difficult for cybercriminals to gain unauthorized access to financial accounts.

2. **Educating and Empowering Individuals:**
   Education plays a crucial role in safeguarding finances. Financial institutions and regulatory bodies should invest in comprehensive awareness campaigns to educate individuals about common cyber threats, phishing attacks, and safe online practices. By providing individuals with the necessary knowledge and tools to recognize and mitigate potential risks, they can actively participate in protecting their own financial well-being. Topics such as password hygiene, secure online transactions, and recognizing social engineering attempts should be emphasized to empower individuals to make informed decisions and take proactive measures to secure their money.

3. **Continuous Monitoring and Early Detection:**
   A proactive approach to financial security involves the implementation of continuous monitoring and early detection systems. Financial institutions should invest in advanced security solutions that utilize machine learning algorithms and behavioral analytics to detect anomalous activities and potential breaches in real-time. By continuously monitoring financial transactions, user behavior, and system logs, suspicious activities can be promptly identified and flagged for investigation. Early detection enables timely response and mitigation, reducing the potential impact of cyber-attacks on financial systems and preventing financial losses.

4. **Robust Data Encryption and Storage:**
   Data encryption is a critical component of protecting sensitive financial information. Financial institutions should employ strong encryption techniques to secure data both at rest and in transit. Encryption ensures that even if data is compromised, it remains unreadable and unusable to unauthorized individuals. Secure storage practices, such as leveraging secure cloud solutions or implementing on-premises data centers with strict access controls, are also essential to prevent data breaches and unauthorized access. Additionally, implementing data loss prevention measures can help mitigate the risk of data leakage and unauthorized data exfiltration.

5. **Collaborative Threat Intelligence Sharing:**
   Collaboration and information sharing among financial institutions, industry peers, and regulatory bodies are vital to combat evolving cyber threats effectively. Establishing channels for sharing threat intelligence, indicators of compromise, and insights about emerging threats can significantly enhance the collective ability to detect, prevent, and respond to financial cyber-attacks. Collaborative efforts enable the financial sector to leverage the experiences and knowledge of others, enhancing the overall security posture and resilience against cyber threats.

6. **Regular Security Assessments and Penetration Testing:**
   Financial institutions should conduct regular security assessments and penetration testing to identify vulnerabilities and address potential weaknesses in their systems and applications. Proactive testing and auditing help uncover security gaps and provide an opportunity to remediate them before they can be exploited by attackers. Regular assessments also ensure compliance with security standards and best practices. Penetration testing, performed by skilled professionals, allows organizations to simulate real-world attacks and identify potential entry points and vulnerabilities in their infrastructure.

7. **Regulatory Compliance and Industry Standards:**

   Regulatory bodies play a critical role in establishing and enforcing cybersecurity standards within the financial sector. Compliance with industry standards such as PCI-DSS (Payment Card Industry Data Security Standard) and GDPR (General Data Protection Regulation) ensures that financial institutions adhere to best practices in securing customer data and financial transactions.

   Compliance frameworks drive the adoption of security controls, risk management practices, and incident response protocols, which are crucial for safeguarding financial systems. Financial institutions should actively collaborate with regulatory bodies, participate in industry forums, and stay updated on emerging regulations to ensure they meet the required security standards.

8. **Investing in Emerging Technologies:**

   To future-proof finances, financial institutions should embrace emerging technologies that have the potential to enhance security and resilience. Blockchain technology, for example, can revolutionize financial transactions by providing decentralized and tamper-proof ledgers. By leveraging blockchain, financial institutions can enhance the security, transparency, and traceability of transactions while reducing the risk of fraud and unauthorized alterations. Additionally, artificial intelligence (AI) and machine learning (ML) technologies can be employed to analyze vast amounts of data, identify patterns, and detect anomalies that may indicate potential cyber threats or fraudulent activities.

9. **Cybersecurity Training and Skill Development:**

   Building a strong cybersecurity culture within financial institutions requires ongoing training and skill development programs. Organizations should invest in providing cybersecurity training to their employees, ensuring they are equipped with the knowledge and skills to identify and respond to potential threats. This includes training on social engineering awareness, incident response protocols, secure coding practices, and data protection guidelines. Continuous education and skill development enable employees to become proactive defenders of financial systems, contributing to the overall security posture of the organization.

10. **Enhancing Collaboration with Law Enforcement and Security Partners:**
Financial institutions should establish strong partnerships with law enforcement agencies and other security partners to combat cyber threats effectively. Collaborating with law enforcement can facilitate the sharing of information related to cybercrime trends, emerging threats, and investigative techniques. Financial institutions can also benefit from partnerships with cybersecurity vendors, threat intelligence providers, and incident response teams to enhance their incident response capabilities and access up-to-date information on the latest threats and vulnerabilities.

By implementing these strategies and measures, individuals, financial institutions, and regulatory bodies can enhance the security of financial systems and future-proof their finances against emerging cyber threats. It requires a collaborative effort, continuous investment in cybersecurity practices, and staying ahead of evolving threats to ensure the resilience and integrity of the financial sector. By safeguarding our money and financial systems, we can foster trust, protect assets, and enable the growth and stability of the global economy.

6
Democracy at Risk: Election System Hacking

The U.S. Election System: An Overview

The U.S. election system stands as a cornerstone of democracy, ensuring that the voices of the people are heard and political leaders are selected through a fair and transparent process. In this section, we delve into the intricacies of the U.S. election system, providing a comprehensive overview that explores its key components, processes, and inherent vulnerabilities. By understanding the complex nature of the system, we can better comprehend the challenges it faces in the realm of cybersecurity.

To begin, we examine the structure of the U.S. election system, which operates as a decentralized framework with a blend of federal and state-level governance. We explore the roles and responsibilities of the various stakeholders involved, including election officials, political parties, candidates, and the electorate. Understanding the distribution of power and decision-making processes among these entities is crucial in comprehending the vulnerabilities that can arise within the system.

Moving forward, we explore the stages of the election process, which encompasses a series of interconnected activities. From voter registration to candidate nominations, campaign financing, voter education, and the casting and counting of ballots, each step holds significance in ensuring a fair and accurate representation of the public's will. We delve into the technologies, infrastructure, and data management systems employed throughout these stages, including voter registration databases, electronic voting machines, and secure communication networks. Moreover, we shine a light on the evolving landscape of election security within the U.S. election system. We delve into the adoption of cybersecurity measures, such as risk assessment, threat monitoring, and incident response protocols, that seek to safeguard the integrity of the election process. Additionally, we explore the role of legislative frameworks and regulations aimed at protecting voter privacy, preventing voter suppression, and ensuring transparency in campaign financing.

Furthermore, we examine the challenges faced in securing the U.S. election system from cyber threats. The increasing sophistication of hacking techniques, potential vulnerabilities in voting systems, and the protection of voter data are among the key concerns. We explore the importance of robust authentication mechanisms, secure communication channels, and encryption protocols in safeguarding the confidentiality, integrity, and availability of election-related information.

In addition, we analyze the impact of external factors on the integrity of elections, such as disinformation campaigns, social media manipulation, and foreign interference. We delve into the challenges posed by the rapid dissemination of misleading information, the influence of online platforms, and the need for media literacy among the electorate. Understanding these dynamics is crucial in developing comprehensive strategies to protect the democratic process from undue influence and manipulation.

Lastly, we delve into the historical context of election system vulnerabilities, examining notable incidents of cyber-attacks and data breaches that have targeted the U.S. election system. By analyzing these past instances, we gain insights into the potential consequences and risks associated with election system vulnerabilities, highlighting the urgency for robust cybersecurity measures and continuous improvement of election infrastructure.

Overall, Section 1 provides an in-depth overview of the U.S. election system, uncovering its structure, processes, and vulnerabilities. By understanding the complexities and challenges faced within the system, we can delve deeper into the subsequent sections that explore cybersecurity threats, solutions, and strategies aimed at safeguarding the democratic process.

The 2020 Election: A Case Study: Here, you can dive into the specifics of the 2020 U.S. elections, any reported incidents of hacking, suspected vulnerabilities that were exploited, and the impacts.

The 2020 U.S. election stands as a compelling case study that allows us to delve into the specifics of a pivotal election, examining any reported incidents of hacking, suspected vulnerabilities that were exploited, and the consequential impacts on the democratic process. By analyzing this case study, we gain valuable insights into the evolving landscape of election security and the urgent need for robust cybersecurity measures to safeguard the integrity of elections.

To begin, we provide an overview of the 2020 U.S. election, a highly contested and closely watched event that had significant implications for the nation's political landscape. We explore the key issues and dynamics that shaped the election, including policy debates, voter turnout, and the influence of social media.

Next, we examine the reported incidents of hacking and cyber threats that emerged during the 2020 election cycle. One notable incident involved a targeted disinformation campaign aimed at sowing doubt about the electoral process and the validity of the election results. Additionally, there were reports of attempts to breach election infrastructure, such as voter registration databases, with the intention of manipulating voter information or disrupting the electoral process. These incidents shed light on the vulnerability of the election system to external interference and emphasize the need for robust cybersecurity measures.

Furthermore, we analyze the suspected vulnerabilities that were exploited during the 2020 election. For example, the reliance on outdated voting machines and inadequate cybersecurity protocols in certain jurisdictions created potential entry points for malicious actors. Additionally, the challenge of ensuring the accuracy and integrity of mail-in ballots during a highly contentious election posed unique vulnerabilities. These vulnerabilities highlight the importance of investing in secure and modernized election infrastructure to safeguard the electoral process.

We also explore the impacts of the 2020 election and the challenges that arose in its aftermath. One significant development was the contested election results and the legal battles that ensued. The losing candidate, Donald Trump, challenged the election results, claiming widespread voter fraud and irregularities. This led to heightened tensions and a deepening of political divisions, undermining public trust in the electoral process. The repercussions extended beyond the 2020 election and influenced subsequent political events, such as the midterm elections.

Moreover, we examine the implications of the 2020 case study on election security and the responses taken to address the identified vulnerabilities. The challenges faced during this election served as a catalyst for reforms in election infrastructure, cybersecurity protocols, and transparency measures. Efforts were made to enhance public confidence in the electoral process, strengthen voter education, and improve collaboration between election officials, cybersecurity experts, and law enforcement agencies. These responses aimed to fortify the democratic process against cyber threats and ensure the integrity of future elections.

By thoroughly analyzing the 2020 U.S. election as a case study, we gain valuable insights into the specific challenges and implications of cyber threats on the democratic process. This case study serves as a powerful reminder of the urgent need for comprehensive cybersecurity measures, continuous monitoring, and proactive responses to safeguard the integrity and trustworthiness of elections in the face of evolving threats.

Blockchain for Elections: A New Hope: This section can focus on how blockchain technology could be (or was) applied to secure the U.S. elections, ensuring transparency, and reducing opportunities for manipulation.

Blockchain technology has emerged as a promising solution to enhance the security and transparency of elections. In this section, we explore how blockchain has the potential to be applied (or has been applied) to secure U.S. elections, ensuring transparency and reducing opportunities for manipulation. By leveraging the unique features of blockchain, we can reimagine the electoral process and instill greater trust in democratic systems.

To begin, we delve into the fundamental principles of blockchain technology that make it an ideal candidate for securing elections. Blockchain's decentralized nature eliminates the reliance on a single central authority, mitigating the risk of a single point of failure and reducing the vulnerability to external interference. The immutability of blockchain ensures that once a transaction or record is added to the blockchain, it cannot be altered or tampered with, ensuring the integrity of the data.

One notable example of blockchain application in elections is the pilot project conducted in West Virginia during the 2018 midterm elections. The state implemented a blockchain-based mobile voting platform that allowed military personnel stationed overseas to cast their votes securely and conveniently. The platform utilized cryptographic techniques to ensure the privacy and integrity of the votes, providing an auditable trail that could be verified by stakeholders.

Furthermore, blockchain technology can enable transparent and verifiable elections by allowing all participants to have access to a shared, tamper-proof ledger of all transactions and voting records. Each vote cast on the blockchain is encrypted and recorded as a unique transaction, making it practically impossible for unauthorized entities to alter or manipulate the results. This transparency fosters trust among voters, candidates, and election officials, as anyone can independently verify the accuracy and fairness of the election outcome.

Additionally, blockchain technology can provide greater accessibility to the electoral process, particularly for disenfranchised or marginalized populations. By enabling remote voting through secure digital platforms, blockchain can eliminate geographical barriers and enhance participation. This could be particularly beneficial for individuals who face challenges in physically accessing polling stations or those residing in remote areas.

However, it is essential to acknowledge the challenges and limitations of implementing blockchain in elections. Scalability, privacy concerns, and the need to ensure secure digital identities are among the key considerations. Robust cybersecurity measures must be in place to protect the blockchain infrastructure from cyber-attacks and to prevent unauthorized access to sensitive voter information.

As blockchain technology continues to evolve and mature, further research, development, and real-world testing are necessary to address these challenges. Collaboration between election officials, cybersecurity experts, blockchain developers, and policymakers is crucial to design and implement effective blockchain solutions tailored to the unique requirements of election systems.

In conclusion, blockchain technology offers a new hope for securing elections by providing transparency, immutability, and enhanced accessibility. The West Virginia pilot project serves as a promising example of how blockchain can be applied to enable secure and auditable voting. While challenges remain, continued exploration of blockchain's potential in the electoral process holds the promise of transforming elections into more transparent, secure, and inclusive democratic exercises.

From Theory to Practice: Implementing Blockchain in Elections

Delve into the practical aspects of implementing blockchain technology in the election system, with a focus on the U.S. 2020 elections.

The potential of implementing blockchain technology in the electoral process is promising, but it requires careful consideration and planning to transition from theory to practice. In this section, we delve into the practical aspects of implementing blockchain technology in the election system, with a specific focus on the U.S. 2020 elections. By exploring the key considerations and challenges involved, we can gain a deeper understanding of the steps required to transform the theoretical benefits of blockchain into a practical reality.

To begin, the implementation of blockchain in elections requires the development of a secure and robust blockchain infrastructure. This infrastructure serves as the foundation for storing and managing election-related data securely and immutably. It involves setting up a network of distributed nodes that will collectively validate and record transactions, ensuring transparency and reducing the risk of manipulation. The selection of an appropriate blockchain platform or framework, such as Ethereum or Hyperledger, must be carefully evaluated based on factors like scalability, security, and interoperability.

Once the blockchain infrastructure is in place, the next step is to establish clear protocols and standards for data management and transaction validation. This includes defining the rules and processes for registering voters, casting and counting votes, and auditing the election results. Smart contracts, which are self-executing programs stored on the blockchain, can be developed to automate and enforce these rules, ensuring the integrity of the election process. Smart contracts enable tamper-proof execution of predefined actions, reducing human error and minimizing the risk of fraud.

Integrating the existing election systems with the blockchain infrastructure is another crucial aspect of implementation. This involves securely connecting voter registration databases, voting machines, and other election-related systems to the blockchain network. The integration process must ensure compatibility and interoperability, allowing for the seamless flow of data between the existing systems and the blockchain. Collaboration between election officials, technology experts, and blockchain developers is essential to address technical challenges and ensure a smooth integration process.

Addressing the challenges associated with implementing blockchain in elections is crucial for success. Scalability is a significant consideration, as the blockchain network must be capable of handling a large volume of transactions during peak voting periods. Privacy is another critical aspect, as sensitive voter information must be protected while still ensuring transparency and auditability.

Compliance with legal and regulatory frameworks, such as data protection and election laws, must also be carefully considered to ensure the implementation aligns with existing regulations.

Robust cybersecurity measures are paramount in safeguarding the blockchain infrastructure from cyber threats. Encryption techniques, secure key management, and continuous monitoring of the network help prevent unauthorized access and tampering. Regular vulnerability assessments and audits should be conducted to identify and address any potential weaknesses in the system. Public trust and acceptance of blockchain-based election systems can be fostered through transparency initiatives, providing clear information about how the blockchain technology is used, addressing concerns about data security and privacy, and engaging the public in the decision-making process.

In addition to securing voter registration and voting processes, blockchain technology can also play a vital role in enhancing the auditing and result tabulation processes. The transparency and immutability of the blockchain allow auditors and election observers to independently verify the integrity of the election results. Each vote recorded on the blockchain is traceable and auditable, making it difficult for any tampering or manipulation to go undetected. This enhances the accuracy and trustworthiness of the final election outcome, instilling confidence in the electoral process.

Pilots and small-scale deployments can serve as valuable testing grounds to refine the implementation process before scaling up to larger elections. Lessons learned from successful pilot projects, such as the West Virginia mobile voting pilot during the 2018 midterms, can provide insights into the challenges and opportunities of implementing blockchain in elections. Collaboration between election officials, technology experts, and relevant stakeholders is crucial throughout the implementation process to ensure that the unique requirements and complexities of the election system are effectively addressed.

In conclusion, the implementation of blockchain technology in the U.S. 2024 elections holds immense potential to transform the electoral process, ensuring security, transparency, and trust. By carefully considering and addressing the practical aspects of implementation, including infrastructure development, smart contract integration, and data privacy, we can pave the way for more resilient and tamper-proof elections. While challenges exist, continuous research, collaboration, and learning from successful pilot projects will help refine the implementation process, leading to a future where blockchain-enabled elections are a reality. The U.S. 2024 elections serve as a crucial opportunity to explore and showcase the potential of blockchain technology in safeguarding the democratic process, fostering trust among voters, and ensuring the integrity of election outcomes.

The Future of Elections: Envisioning Blockchain-Secured Democracy

In this final section, we paint a vision of a future where elections are secure, transparent, and verifiable, thanks to the transformative power of blockchain technology. Drawing lessons from the U.S. 2020 election and the implementation of blockchain in the electoral process, we explore the potential impact and benefits that blockchain can bring to democratic systems.

Imagine a future where voters have complete confidence in the integrity of the electoral process. Blockchain technology has the potential to provide a tamper-proof, transparent, and auditable platform for casting and counting votes. Every vote recorded on the blockchain is encrypted, time-stamped, and stored in a distributed ledger that is accessible to all stakeholders. This ensures that no single entity can manipulate or alter the results, fostering trust among voters and candidates.

The transparency offered by blockchain also allows for greater scrutiny and accountability. Election observers, auditors, and even the general public can independently verify the integrity of the voting process. The immutability of the blockchain ensures that once a vote is recorded, it cannot be tampered with or erased. This provides a clear and verifiable trail of every vote cast, reducing the potential for fraud and ensuring the accuracy of the final election outcome.

Furthermore, blockchain technology can enable secure and anonymous voting, safeguarding voter privacy while ensuring the integrity of the electoral process. By leveraging advanced cryptographic techniques, voters can cast their ballots without fear of their identities being compromised. The use of unique digital signatures and secure key management ensures that only eligible voters can participate, preventing double voting or unauthorized access to the system.

In this envisioned future, blockchain technology also plays a crucial role in enhancing voter registration and identity verification. By securely storing and verifying voter information on the blockchain, the risk of voter impersonation and fraudulent registrations is significantly reduced. Blockchain-based digital identities allow for seamless and secure verification, enabling more inclusive participation in the electoral process.

The lessons learned from the U.S. 2020 election and the successful implementation of blockchain in the electoral process serve as a foundation for further advancements in securing democracy. As technology continues to evolve and blockchain matures, we can expect continued research and innovation to address the scalability, privacy, and regulatory challenges associated with blockchain-based elections.

Collaboration between governments, election officials, technology experts, and the public is essential to foster trust, transparency, and acceptance of blockchain-enabled elections. Public education and awareness campaigns can help bridge the gap between the perceived complexity of blockchain and its potential to revolutionize the democratic process. Open dialogue and stakeholder engagement are necessary to address concerns, build consensus, and ensure the responsible and ethical implementation of blockchain technology in elections.

As we move forward, the vision of blockchain-secured democracy becomes more tangible. While challenges remain, the potential benefits of blockchain technology in ensuring secure, transparent, and verifiable elections are immense. By leveraging the lessons learned and continuously refining the implementation process, we can pave the way for a future where elections are safeguarded by blockchain, restoring trust and confidence in democratic systems worldwide.

7

The Dark Side of Connectivity: Exploitation of IoT Systems

The IoT Revolution: Understanding the Impact of Connectivity

In this section, we explore the profound impact of the Internet of Things (IoT) revolution and the implications it has for cybersecurity. The IoT has ushered in an era of unprecedented connectivity, where everyday objects are equipped with sensors, software, and network connectivity, enabling them to collect and exchange data. This connectivity has transformed industries and our daily lives, offering immense benefits but also posing significant security challenges.

We begin by examining the scope and scale of the IoT revolution, highlighting its vast potential and the exponential growth of interconnected devices. From smart homes and wearable devices to industrial automation and smart cities, the IoT has permeated various sectors, revolutionizing how we live and work.

Next, we delve into the implications of this widespread connectivity, discussing the benefits and opportunities it brings. The IoT has improved efficiency, productivity, and convenience in countless ways. It has enabled real-time monitoring, predictive maintenance, and data-driven decision-making, leading to increased operational efficiency and cost savings. We explore real-world examples across industries, showcasing the transformative power of IoT-enabled solutions.

However, as we embrace the IoT's benefits, we must also confront its dark side. The proliferation of interconnected devices and the sheer volume of data they generate create a vast attack surface for cybercriminals. We discuss the inherent security challenges and vulnerabilities associated with the IoT, including:

1. **Inadequate Security Measures:** Many IoT devices are designed with limited security features, making them easy targets for hackers. Weak or default passwords, unencrypted communications, and lack of firmware updates create vulnerabilities that can be exploited.
2. **Lack of Standardization:** The IoT landscape is fragmented, with various manufacturers using different protocols and standards. This lack of standardization makes it difficult to establish consistent security measures across devices, leaving room for vulnerabilities.
3. **Complexity and Scale:** The interconnected nature of IoT systems introduces complex and dynamic security challenges. Managing a large number of devices, ensuring secure communication, and protecting data privacy become daunting tasks as the IoT ecosystem expands.
4. **Privacy Concerns:** The IoT collects vast amounts of personal data, raising concerns about privacy and data protection. Unauthorized access to sensitive information can lead to identity theft, surveillance, and other privacy infringements.

By understanding the impact of connectivity and the security challenges posed by the IoT, we can begin to address the risks associated with this revolution. As we move forward, it is essential to prioritize security, privacy, and robust cybersecurity measures to safeguard against potential threats and ensure a safe and trustworthy IoT ecosystem.

Insecurity of Things: Unveiling IoT Exploitation Tactics

In this section, we delve into the world of IoT exploitation and the tactics employed by cybercriminals to compromise and exploit vulnerable IoT systems. As the number of interconnected devices continues to rise, so does the risk of malicious actors exploiting their inherent weaknesses. By understanding these tactics, we can better defend against IoT-related cyber threats.

We begin by exploring common IoT exploitation tactics used by cybercriminals, including:

1. **Default or Weak Credentials:** Many IoT devices come with default usernames and passwords, and users often fail to change them. Cybercriminals take advantage of this oversight to gain unauthorized access and control over the devices.
2. **Firmware and Software Vulnerabilities:** IoT devices may have outdated firmware or software with known vulnerabilities. Cybercriminals exploit these weaknesses to execute remote code execution attacks, gaining control over the devices.
3. **Man-in-the-Middle Attacks:** In this type of attack, cybercriminals intercept and alter the communication between IoT devices and their intended destinations. By compromising the data flow, they can manipulate or steal sensitive information.
4. **Physical Tampering:** Physical access to IoT devices opens up opportunities for malicious actors to manipulate or tamper with the devices. This can involve inserting malicious hardware or modifying device components to compromise their functionality.
5. **Distributed Denial of Service (DDoS) Attacks:** IoT devices can be recruited into botnets and used to launch powerful DDoS attacks. By flooding targeted systems with overwhelming traffic, cybercriminals disrupt services, causing significant downtime and financial losses.
6. **Data Interception and Theft:** IoT devices generate and transmit vast amounts of data, including personal and sensitive information. Cybercriminals intercept and steal this data to exploit it for various purposes, such as identity theft, blackmail, or financial fraud.
7. **Supply Chain Attacks:** Cybercriminals may compromise the supply chain of IoT devices, injecting malicious components or manipulating the manufacturing process. This allows them to gain control over the devices from the moment they are deployed, making it difficult to detect and mitigate the compromise.

It is crucial to recognize and understand these IoT exploitation tactics to implement effective cybersecurity measures. Organizations and individuals must prioritize the security of IoT devices by regularly updating firmware, using strong and unique passwords, and implementing network segmentation to limit the impact of potential compromises.

Furthermore, manufacturers need to take a proactive approach to security, incorporating security measures into the design and development of IoT devices. This includes rigorous vulnerability testing, secure firmware updates, and adherence to industry best practices.

By shedding light on the insecurity of IoT and the tactics employed by cybercriminals, we can raise awareness and foster a proactive mindset toward securing IoT systems. With proper cybersecurity measures in place, we can mitigate the risks and create a safer and more resilient IoT ecosystem.

Case Studies: When IoT Devices Become Cyber Weapons

In this section, we delve deeper into real-world case studies that provide concrete evidence of the risks and consequences associated with IoT devices turning into cyber weapons. These examples highlight the severity of IoT-related cyber threats and underscore the urgent need for robust security measures and proactive defense strategies.

1. **Mirai Botnet Attack (2016):** The Mirai botnet attack serves as a stark reminder of the vulnerabilities and potential impact of compromised IoT devices. This attack exploited default or weak credentials on IoT devices such as routers, IP cameras, and DVRs, assembling a massive botnet army of compromised devices. The attackers then directed this botnet to launch devastating distributed denial of service (DDoS) attacks against prominent websites and online services. The attack disrupted critical internet infrastructure and highlighted the substantial power that can be harnessed from a network of interconnected IoT devices. The Mirai botnet attack affected major organizations, including Dyn, a DNS service provider, leading to widespread internet outages for users across the globe.

2. **Triton Malware Attack (2017):** The Triton malware attack targeted an industrial control system (ICS) used in a critical infrastructure facility, specifically focusing on the safety instrumentation system. The attackers exploited vulnerabilities in the IoT-based safety devices to gain unauthorized access and manipulate the systems. The goal of the attack was to disrupt the facility's operations and potentially cause physical

harm. This incident highlighted the significant risks associated with compromised IoT devices in critical infrastructure, emphasizing the need for robust security measures to safeguard against potential intrusions that can compromise public safety and national security.

3. **Stuxnet Worm (2010):** The Stuxnet worm was a highly sophisticated piece of malware that specifically targeted industrial control systems, including those used in nuclear facilities. While not exclusively an IoT attack, Stuxnet exploited vulnerabilities in IoT-based systems to disrupt the operation of centrifuges. This cyber weapon demonstrated the potential for malicious actors to exploit IoT devices within critical infrastructure and highlighted the potential for cyber-attacks to have physical consequences. The Stuxnet worm revealed the need for enhanced security measures in IoT systems, particularly those deployed in critical sectors such as energy, transportation, and healthcare.

4. **Jeep Cherokee Hack (2015):** In a controlled experiment, researchers demonstrated the vulnerability of connected vehicles by remotely hacking into a Jeep Cherokee's entertainment system. Through this exploit, they gained control over critical functions such as braking and steering. This eye-opening demonstration highlighted the potential risks associated with inadequate security measures in IoT-enabled vehicles. It showcased how a compromised IoT device in a vehicle could pose significant threats to driver safety and potentially result in accidents or even loss of life. The Jeep Cherokee hack served as a wake-up call for the automotive industry to prioritize cybersecurity in the design and implementation of IoT systems within vehicles.

These case studies provide compelling evidence of the risks posed by compromised IoT devices and the potential consequences of IoT-related cyber-attacks. They underscore the urgent need for robust security measures, standardized protocols, and proactive defense strategies to mitigate the vulnerabilities associated with interconnected devices. The lessons learned from these incidents must inform the development of comprehensive security frameworks, industry-wide collaborations, and regulatory efforts to protect against IoT-based cyber threats. By analyzing these case studies and their implications, we can better understand the challenges and make informed decisions to safeguard our increasingly connected world.

IoT Security Enhanced: Role of Blockchain in Securing IoT Devices

In this section, we explore the role of blockchain technology in enhancing the security of IoT devices. As the Internet of Things (IoT) continues to grow, ensuring the security and integrity of these interconnected devices becomes increasingly critical. Blockchain, with its decentralized and tamper-proof nature, offers promising solutions to address the security challenges faced by IoT systems.

1. Data integrity and immutability are critical aspects of securing IoT devices, and blockchain technology offers robust solutions in this regard. By leveraging blockchain, the integrity and authenticity of data generated by IoT devices can be ensured throughout its lifecycle.

The decentralized and distributed nature of blockchain makes it an ideal platform for storing IoT-generated data. Each transaction or data entry is cryptographically linked to the previous one, forming a chain of blocks, commonly referred to as the blockchain. This chain serves as a transparent and tamper-proof ledger that records every interaction and data exchange involving IoT devices.

Through the use of cryptographic hashing algorithms, the data is transformed into a fixed-size string of characters known as a hash. These hashes act as digital fingerprints of the original data, uniquely identifying its contents. Any alteration to the data will result in a different hash value, making it easily detectable. Thus, even a minor change in the data will break the cryptographic link with the previous block, alerting network participants to the tampering attempt.

The immutability of the blockchain ensures that once data is recorded, it cannot be altered or deleted without consensus from the network. This feature provides a strong safeguard against unauthorized modifications or data manipulation, making it highly resistant to cyber-attacks.

Additionally, blockchain's transparency contributes to data integrity. Every transaction recorded on the blockchain is visible to all network participants, creating a level of transparency that enables data validation and verification.

This transparency helps build trust among stakeholders and provides an audit trail for data integrity.

Expanding on the benefits of data integrity and immutability in securing IoT devices, consider the example of a smart home system. Smart home devices, such as thermostats, security cameras, and door locks, generate data about temperature settings, occupancy, and security events. By utilizing blockchain, this data can be securely recorded and stored, ensuring its integrity and eliminating the risk of unauthorized access or manipulation.

For instance, if a security camera detects a suspicious activity, the recorded video footage and associated metadata can be securely stored on the blockchain. The cryptographic hashing of each data block ensures that the footage remains intact and unaltered, providing a reliable record that can be used for investigations or legal purposes. This not only strengthens the security of the smart home system but also enhances trust between homeowners, service providers, and law enforcement agencies.

Moreover, in sectors such as healthcare and supply chain management, where data integrity and provenance are crucial, blockchain can play a vital role. By leveraging blockchain technology, IoT devices in these domains can securely record and share critical information, such as patient health records or product origin and authenticity. The immutable nature of the blockchain ensures the integrity and trustworthiness of this data, mitigating the risks associated with data tampering, unauthorized access, or counterfeit products. In summary, the ability of blockchain to provide data integrity and immutability is a significant advantage in securing IoT devices. By leveraging cryptographic hashing, transparent transactions, and the immutability of the blockchain, the integrity and authenticity of data generated by IoT devices can be effectively preserved. This not only enhances the security of IoT systems but also instills trust among stakeholders and enables the full potential of IoT applications in various domains.

2. Secure device identity and authentication are paramount in ensuring the integrity and security of IoT systems. Blockchain technology offers a robust solution to address the challenges associated with device identity and authentication in the IoT landscape.

In a blockchain-based IoT system, each device is assigned a unique digital identity that is securely stored on the blockchain. This digital identity consists of cryptographic keys, certificates, or other identifiers that uniquely represent the device. The device's identity is verified and authenticated through cryptographic mechanisms, ensuring that only authorized devices can participate in the network.

By leveraging blockchain for device identity and authentication, several benefits are realized. Firstly, the decentralized nature of blockchain eliminates the need for a centralized authority or certificate authority to validate device identities. Instead, the blockchain acts as a distributed ledger that records and verifies the identity of each device in a transparent and tamper-proof manner. This reduces the reliance on a single point of failure and enhances the overall security of the IoT ecosystem.

Furthermore, the immutability of the blockchain ensures that device identities cannot be altered or forged without consensus from the network participants. Once a device identity is recorded on the blockchain, it becomes an irrefutable record of the device's authenticity. This eliminates the risk of identity spoofing or unauthorized access, as any attempts to tamper with the device identity would be immediately detected by the network.

Expanding on the benefits of secure device identity and authentication, consider the example of a smart home system. Each IoT device, such as a smart thermostat or a smart lock, has its own unique digital identity recorded on the blockchain. When a user interacts with the smart home system, the device's identity is verified through cryptographic means, such as digital signatures or public-private key pairs. This ensures that only authorized devices can control or access the smart home system, preventing unauthorized individuals from tampering with the system or gaining unauthorized access to the user's home.

Moreover, secure device identity and authentication can enhance the security of IoT systems in industrial settings. In industrial IoT applications, devices such as sensors, actuators, and machinery play critical roles in monitoring and controlling various processes. By leveraging blockchain for device identity and authentication, the integrity and authenticity of these devices can be ensured. This reduces the risk of unauthorized devices entering the network and provides a secure framework for trusted interactions between devices, leading to safer and more reliable industrial operations.

Implementing secure device identity and authentication on the blockchain requires careful consideration of cryptographic protocols, key management practices, and secure communication channels. Standardization efforts and industry collaborations are necessary to establish best practices and interoperable solutions that enable seamless integration of blockchain-based device identity and authentication in IoT systems.

In conclusion, blockchain technology offers a powerful solution for establishing secure device identity and authentication in IoT systems. By leveraging the decentralized and tamper-proof nature of the blockchain, device identities can be securely recorded, verified, and authenticated. This enhances the overall security of IoT systems, mitigates the risks of unauthorized access or identity spoofing, and enables the trusted and reliable operation of interconnected devices in various domains.

3. Distributed Trust and Consensus: Blockchain's decentralized nature enables the establishment of distributed trust and consensus within IoT networks. Traditional centralized systems rely on a single authority to manage and validate transactions or interactions. In contrast, blockchain allows for the creation of a distributed network of nodes that collectively validate and agree upon the integrity of data and transactions. This distributed trust model enhances the security of IoT systems by eliminating the reliance on a single point of failure or a central authority that could be compromised.

4. Enhanced Security for Firmware and Software Updates: IoT devices often require regular firmware and software updates to patch vulnerabilities and address security issues. Blockchain technology can provide a secure and transparent mechanism for managing these updates. By leveraging blockchain's immutable ledger, device manufacturers can securely distribute updates to IoT devices, ensuring the authenticity and integrity of the updates. This mitigates the risk of compromised or malicious updates being installed on the devices, enhancing the overall security of the IoT ecosystem.

5. Improved supply chain security is a critical aspect of ensuring the integrity and trustworthiness of IoT devices. Blockchain technology offers a powerful solution to enhance the security and transparency of the supply

chain for IoT devices, mitigating risks such as tampering, counterfeit devices, and unauthorized modifications.

By leveraging blockchain, every step of the device's lifecycle can be securely recorded and tracked, providing a verifiable and auditable record of its journey through the supply chain. This includes manufacturing, assembly, testing, distribution, and installation. Each transaction and interaction involving the device is recorded on the blockchain, creating an immutable trail of information.

The use of blockchain in the supply chain brings several benefits. Firstly, it enables transparency and visibility throughout the entire supply chain. All stakeholders, including manufacturers, distributors, retailers, and customers, can access the blockchain and trace the device's origin, verifying its authenticity and ensuring it has not been compromised or tampered with. This transparency helps in identifying and mitigating risks associated with counterfeit devices or unauthorized modifications that may compromise the security and functionality of the IoT system.

Furthermore, blockchain can facilitate the integration of additional data points and information related to the device's journey. This can include details such as quality control checks, certifications, firmware updates, and maintenance records. By incorporating such data on the blockchain, stakeholders can have a comprehensive view of the device's history, enabling better decision-making and risk assessment.

Expanding on the benefits of improved supply chain security, consider the example of a smart home device. The blockchain can securely record and store information about the device's manufacturing process, including the suppliers of components, assembly details, and quality control checks. It can then track the device's distribution, ensuring that it is delivered to authorized retailers or directly to end-users without being tampered with or substituted with counterfeit products. Finally, the blockchain can capture installation and activation data, providing a clear audit trail and ensuring that only genuine and trusted devices are integrated into the IoT ecosystem.

Implementing blockchain-based supply chain security requires collaboration and integration among various stakeholders. This includes manufacturers, suppliers, logistics providers, and regulatory bodies. Standardization efforts, such as the development of interoperable protocols and industry-wide guidelines, are essential to ensure seamless integration and data exchange on the blockchain.

In conclusion, blockchain technology offers significant potential to improve supply chain security for IoT devices. By securely recording and tracking the device's journey on the blockchain, stakeholders can have greater transparency, traceability, and assurance of the device's authenticity and integrity. This helps prevent risks associated with counterfeit devices, tampering, and unauthorized modifications, ensuring that only genuine and trusted devices enter the IoT ecosystem. The application of blockchain in the supply chain holds promise for building a more secure and trustworthy IoT ecosystem.

6. Privacy and Data Ownership: With the proliferation of IoT devices, concerns about privacy and data ownership have become significant. Blockchain technology can provide solutions by enabling users to have control over their data and determine who has access to it. Through blockchain-based smart contracts, users can define the terms of data usage and grant permissions to entities requesting access. This empowers individuals to maintain ownership and control over their personal data, fostering trust and privacy in the IoT environment.

By leveraging the unique characteristics of blockchain, including data immutability, secure authentication, distributed trust, and enhanced supply chain security, IoT devices can be better protected against cyber threats. Blockchain technology offers a promising framework to establish a secure and trustworthy IoT ecosystem, where devices can interact with each other and exchange data with confidence. While there are still challenges to overcome, such as scalability and interoperability, the integration of blockchain in securing IoT devices holds great potential for addressing the security vulnerabilities associated with connectivity. The role of blockchain in securing IoT devices is not only limited to the aforementioned aspects but extends to various other areas as well. The integration of blockchain technology in IoT security is an ongoing area of research and development, with new solutions and approaches continually emerging.

It is important to note that while blockchain can enhance the security of IoT devices, it is not a panacea. Implementing blockchain technology requires careful consideration of the specific use cases, technical requirements, and potential trade-offs. Additionally, collaboration between industry stakeholders, policymakers, and researchers is crucial to establish standardized protocols, security frameworks, and regulatory guidelines to ensure the safe and effective deployment of blockchain-enabled IoT systems.

As the IoT ecosystem continues to expand and interconnect various aspects of our lives, safeguarding the integrity, privacy, and security of these devices becomes increasingly vital. The role of blockchain in securing IoT devices offers promising solutions that can help mitigate the risks and vulnerabilities associated with this interconnected landscape. By leveraging the unique features of blockchain, such as decentralization, immutability, and distributed trust, we can lay the foundation for a more secure and resilient IoT future.

Envisioning a Secure IoT: Blockchain-Integrated IoT Systems

The integration of blockchain technology in IoT systems holds great promise for creating a secure and trustworthy IoT ecosystem. By leveraging the unique properties of blockchain, such as decentralization, immutability, and transparency, we can envision a future where IoT devices are protected against cyber threats and data breaches. Section 5 explores this vision and highlights the potential benefits of blockchain-integrated IoT systems.

In a blockchain-integrated IoT system, the blockchain acts as a foundational layer that enhances the security, privacy, and reliability of IoT devices and their interactions. Let's delve into some key aspects of how blockchain can contribute to a secure IoT:

1. Enhanced security and privacy are critical considerations in the context of IoT devices, which often collect and transmit sensitive data. Blockchain technology offers robust security mechanisms that can strengthen the protection of IoT devices and the data they generate.

One of the key features of blockchain technology is its ability to encrypt and securely store data on the distributed ledger. When sensitive data is transmitted by IoT devices, it can be encrypted using cryptographic algorithms before being recorded on the blockchain. This encryption ensures that even if the data is intercepted during transmission, it remains unintelligible to unauthorized individuals. The encrypted data is then securely stored on the distributed ledger, which is distributed across multiple nodes in the network. This decentralized storage mitigates the risk of data compromise, as there is no single point of failure or vulnerability that can be targeted by malicious actors.

Furthermore, the use of cryptographic techniques in blockchain ensures the integrity and authenticity of data. Each transaction or data entry on the blockchain is accompanied by a cryptographic hash, which is a unique identifier generated using cryptographic algorithms. This hash acts as a digital fingerprint of the data, allowing anyone to verify its integrity and authenticity. Even a slight modification to the data would result in a completely different hash, alerting the network to the tampering attempt. This makes it extremely difficult for malicious actors to manipulate or tamper with the data stored on the blockchain.

The decentralized consensus algorithms employed by blockchain also contribute to enhanced security and privacy. In traditional centralized systems, a single point of control or authority can be targeted by attackers, making them vulnerable to breaches. However, in a blockchain network, consensus is achieved through the agreement of multiple nodes in the network. This decentralized consensus mechanism ensures that no single entity has complete control over the system, making it highly resistant to attacks and manipulation. As a result, the data transmitted and stored by IoT devices on the blockchain remains secure and trustworthy.

Expanding on the concept of enhanced security and privacy, consider the example of a smart home system. The IoT devices within the smart home, such as surveillance cameras, door locks, and motion sensors, generate sensitive data about the occupants' activities and behaviors. By utilizing blockchain technology, the data collected by these devices can be encrypted, securely stored, and verified through cryptographic hashes on the blockchain. This ensures that the privacy of the homeowners is maintained, as the data remains encrypted and inaccessible to unauthorized individuals. Additionally, the use of decentralized consensus in the blockchain network provides an added layer of security, making it difficult for hackers to compromise the system and gain unauthorized access to the smart home devices.

In conclusion, the enhanced security and privacy offered by blockchain technology can significantly strengthen the protection of IoT devices and the data they generate. Through encryption, decentralized storage, cryptographic hashes, and decentralized consensus, blockchain provides a robust framework for securing sensitive data and ensuring its integrity. By leveraging blockchain in IoT systems, organizations and individuals can enhance the security and privacy of their IoT devices, mitigating the risks of unauthorized access, data breaches, and manipulation.

2. Improved device management and control is a crucial aspect of securing IoT systems, and blockchain technology offers innovative solutions in this regard. By leveraging blockchain-based smart contracts, device owners can establish predefined rules and conditions for device operation and access, bringing about significant improvements in device management and control.

Smart contracts are self-executing agreements with the terms of the agreement directly written into the code. In the context of IoT devices, smart contracts can be used to define the rules and conditions for device operation, access, and interactions. These rules can include parameters such as authorized users, permissible actions, and data-sharing permissions. Once the terms are defined in the smart contract, they are automatically executed without the need for intermediaries or manual intervention. This automated process enhances efficiency, reduces human error, and ensures that devices operate according to predetermined rules.

By implementing smart contracts on a blockchain, device owners can establish a transparent and auditable system for device management and control. The transparent nature of blockchain enables device owners to track and monitor the behavior and activities of their IoT devices in real-time. They can view the interactions, transactions, and events recorded on the blockchain, providing them with a comprehensive overview of how their devices are being used. This transparency fosters accountability and allows device owners to identify any suspicious activities or anomalies that may indicate unauthorized access or manipulation.

Additionally, the immutability of blockchain ensures that once the rules and conditions are set in the smart contract, they cannot be altered or tampered with without consensus from the network participants. This provides device owners with assurance that the established rules for device management and control remain intact and enforceable. Any attempts to deviate from the predefined rules would require consensus from the network, making it highly improbable for unauthorized individuals to gain control or manipulate the devices.

Expanding on the concept of improved device management and control, consider the example of a smart manufacturing facility. In this scenario, IoT devices such as sensors, actuators, and production equipment are interconnected to optimize operations. By utilizing blockchain-based smart contracts, the facility owner can establish rules and conditions for device interactions and data sharing. For example, smart contracts can define the conditions under which equipment can be accessed, the permissible actions that can be taken, and the data that can be shared among devices. The transparent and auditable nature of blockchain allows the facility owner to monitor and track the activities of the devices, ensuring that they operate within the predefined rules and detecting any unauthorized actions or deviations.

In conclusion, blockchain technology can revolutionize device management and control in IoT systems by leveraging smart contracts and the transparency of the blockchain. The implementation of predefined rules and conditions through smart contracts ensures that only authorized entities can interact with IoT devices, reducing the risk of unauthorized control or manipulation. Moreover, the transparency and immutability of blockchain enhance overall device accountability and allow device owners to monitor device behavior in real-time. By adopting blockchain-based solutions for device management and control, organizations can significantly enhance the security and integrity of their IoT systems.

3. Data integrity and trustworthiness are paramount in IoT systems, especially in domains where accurate and reliable data is critical, such as healthcare, supply chain, and logistics. Blockchain technology offers a robust solution to ensure the integrity and trustworthiness of the data generated by IoT devices.

One of the key features of blockchain that enhances data integrity is its immutability. Once data is recorded on the blockchain, it cannot be altered or tampered with without consensus from the network participants. Each transaction or data entry is cryptographically linked to the previous one, creating a chain of blocks that forms a permanent and unalterable record. This immutability ensures that the data remains tamper-proof, providing a high level of assurance regarding its integrity.

Furthermore, the consensus mechanisms employed by blockchain networks add an extra layer of trustworthiness to the data. In traditional centralized systems, data integrity relies on trusting a central authority. However, in a blockchain network, consensus is achieved through the agreement of multiple nodes in the network. This decentralized consensus mechanism ensures that data is validated and verified by a network of participants, making it more resistant to malicious tampering or falsification.

Each participant in the network has access to a copy of the blockchain, enabling them to independently verify the integrity of the data.

In the context of healthcare, the integration of blockchain in IoT systems can significantly improve data integrity and trustworthiness. For instance, in a patient monitoring scenario, IoT devices collect vital signs and health data, which are then recorded on the blockchain. The immutability of the blockchain ensures that the recorded data remains tamper-proof and cannot be modified without consensus. Healthcare providers can trust the authenticity and accuracy of the data, enabling them to make informed decisions about patient care.

Expanding on the concept of data integrity and trustworthiness, consider the example of a supply chain system utilizing IoT devices to track the movement of goods. By integrating blockchain technology, each transaction and data entry, such as shipment details and product information, can be recorded on the blockchain. The immutability of the blockchain ensures that the recorded data remains unchanged, providing an auditable trail of the product's journey through the supply chain. This enhances trust among stakeholders, as they can verify the authenticity and integrity of the recorded data, reducing the risk of counterfeit products or fraudulent activities.

In conclusion, the integration of blockchain in IoT systems enhances data integrity and trustworthiness by leveraging its immutability and decentralized consensus mechanisms. By recording data on the blockchain, organizations can ensure that the data remains tamper-proof and trustworthy. This is particularly crucial in critical domains such as healthcare and supply chain, where accurate and reliable data is essential. By adopting blockchain-integrated IoT systems, organizations can enhance the integrity of their data, foster trust among stakeholders, and make more informed decisions based on reliable information.

4. Interoperability and Seamless Integration: Blockchain technology can facilitate interoperability and seamless integration among diverse IoT devices and platforms. By adopting standardized protocols and interfaces, IoT devices can communicate and interact with each other in a secure and transparent manner. This interoperability enables the creation of complex IoT ecosystems, where devices from different manufacturers and platforms can seamlessly collaborate and share data, leading to more innovative and integrated IoT solutions.

Expanding on the vision of a secure IoT, consider the example of a smart city. In a blockchain-integrated smart city, various IoT devices, such as sensors, traffic lights, and surveillance cameras, can securely communicate and share data through the blockchain. This enables efficient management of city infrastructure, enhances public safety, and optimizes resource allocation. The immutable nature of blockchain ensures that data related to traffic patterns, air quality, and energy consumption remains tamper-proof and trustworthy, enabling data-driven decision-making for city administrators.

To realize this vision, collaboration among various stakeholders is essential. Manufacturers, technology providers, regulators, and standardization bodies need to work together to develop industry-wide standards, protocols, and best practices for integrating blockchain into IoT systems. Additionally, continuous research and innovation are necessary to address scalability, energy efficiency, and privacy challenges associated with blockchain-integrated IoT solutions.

In conclusion, the integration of blockchain technology in IoT systems offers significant potential to create a secure and trustworthy IoT ecosystem. By leveraging blockchain's inherent security features, IoT devices can be protected against cyber threats, data breaches, and unauthorized access. The vision of a secure IoT powered by blockchain holds promise for driving innovation, enhancing privacy, and fostering trust in the increasingly interconnected world of IoT.

8

The Economic Domino Effect: The Rise in Oil Prices

Tracing the Impact: How Cyber-attacks Affect Oil Prices

In today's interconnected world, cyber-attacks pose a significant threat to the stability of global oil markets, causing disruptions that can have a domino effect on oil prices. Section 1 of Chapter 8 explores the intricate relationship between cyber-attacks and the fluctuations in oil prices, shedding light on the far-reaching consequences of these attacks.

The section begins by examining notable incidents where cyber-attacks targeted oil infrastructure, leading to disruptions in various stages of the oil supply chain. These incidents include attacks on oil refineries, pipelines, storage facilities, and even maritime shipping systems. By analyzing these case studies, we can gain insights into the specific techniques and vulnerabilities exploited by hackers to disrupt the flow of oil.

One such example is the cyberattack on Saudi Aramco in 2012, where a sophisticated malware attack disrupted the company's computer systems, affecting oil production and temporarily reducing global oil supplies. This incident highlighted the vulnerability of critical oil infrastructure to cyber-attacks and demonstrated how such attacks can impact oil prices.

Another case study is the Shamoon malware attack on the Saudi Aramco network in 2012, which caused a temporary shutdown of the company's computer systems. This attack affected not only the operational efficiency of the company but also had broader implications for oil markets, contributing to a temporary rise in oil prices due to supply concerns.

Furthermore, Section 1 explores the ripple effects of these cyber-attacks on oil prices. Disruptions in oil supply can create supply-demand imbalances, leading to price hikes and market volatility. For example, the Colonial Pipeline cyberattack in 2021, which temporarily halted fuel transportation along the U.S. East Coast, caused panic buying and fuel shortages, resulting in a surge in gasoline prices in the affected regions.

By understanding the cause-and-effect relationship between cyber-attacks and oil prices, stakeholders can better prepare for and mitigate the economic consequences. This includes developing robust cybersecurity measures to protect critical oil infrastructure, enhancing information sharing and collaboration among industry players, and establishing contingency plans to address potential disruptions.

In summary, Section 1 of Chapter 8 provides an in-depth exploration of how cyber-attacks affect oil prices. Through case studies and analysis, it highlights the vulnerabilities of oil infrastructure and the potential economic consequences of cyber-attacks. By understanding these dynamics, stakeholders can work toward enhancing the resilience and security of critical oil systems to mitigate the impact on oil prices and maintain the stability of global energy markets.

A Crisis in the Pipeline: Unfolding the Colonial Pipeline Incident

The Colonial Pipeline incident stands as a stark reminder of the vulnerability of critical energy infrastructure to cyber-attacks. In this section, we delve into the timeline, tactics, and consequences of the Colonial Pipeline cyberattack, examining the far-reaching implications it had on energy security, national resilience, and economic stability.

The Colonial Pipeline, spanning over 5,500 miles, is a vital artery of the U.S. energy supply chain, transporting millions of barrels of gasoline, diesel, and jet fuel daily from refineries on the Gulf Coast to markets across the East Coast. In May 2021, the pipeline fell victim to a ransomware attack, forcing its operators to shut down operations for several days.

The attack utilized a sophisticated ransomware variant known as DarkSide, which targeted Colonial Pipeline's computer systems and encrypted critical data, effectively crippling their ability to operate. As a result, fuel deliveries along the pipeline came to a halt, leading to widespread panic-buying, fuel shortages, and price surges across the affected regions.

The consequences of the Colonial Pipeline incident were significant and far-reaching. It exposed the vulnerability of critical energy infrastructure to cyber-attacks, highlighting the potential disruptions and economic ramifications they can cause. The incident underscored the interdependencies between energy systems, transportation, and the broader economy, emphasizing the need for robust cybersecurity measures to safeguard against such threats.

Beyond the immediate impacts on fuel supply and prices, the Colonial Pipeline incident raised concerns about national resilience and the broader implications for critical infrastructure protection. It prompted discussions about the preparedness of energy systems to withstand and recover from cyber-attacks, as well as the importance of public-private collaboration in addressing cyber threats.

The incident also underscored the urgent need for enhanced cybersecurity practices within the energy sector. It served as a wake-up call for energy companies to reassess their security posture, implement robust safeguards, and enhance incident response capabilities. Furthermore, it spurred conversations around the importance of information sharing and collaboration between industry stakeholders, government agencies, and cybersecurity experts to collectively combat cyber threats.

The Colonial Pipeline incident serves as a critical case study, shedding light on the vulnerabilities and risks faced by energy infrastructure in an increasingly interconnected world. It highlights the imperative for proactive cybersecurity measures, including threat intelligence, employee training, network segmentation, and continuous monitoring, to detect and mitigate potential cyber-attacks.

As we move forward, the lessons learned from the Colonial Pipeline incident provide valuable insights into the need for ongoing investments in cybersecurity, resilience planning, and the adoption of emerging technologies like blockchain to bolster the security and integrity of critical energy infrastructure. By learning from this incident and taking proactive measures, we can strive to ensure the resilience and stability of our energy systems in the face of evolving cyber threats.

Economic Impact: Assessing the Broader Consequences of Cyber-attacks

The repercussions of cyber-attacks on oil infrastructure extend far beyond the immediate disruptions to oil prices. Section 3 delves into the broader economic impact of these attacks, analyzing the cascading effects that reverberate throughout the global economy, affecting various sectors, including transportation, manufacturing, and consumer goods.

When oil infrastructure is targeted by cyber-attacks, the consequences are not limited to the energy sector alone. Disruptions in oil supply and price volatility can have a domino effect on other industries that rely on a stable and affordable energy supply. Transportation systems, such as airlines and shipping companies, experience increased operational costs due to rising fuel prices, which can ultimately lead to higher ticket prices or shipping fees for consumers. Manufacturers, especially those reliant on petroleum-based products, face challenges in sourcing raw materials and may struggle to maintain production levels, impacting their ability to meet customer demand. The increased costs and uncertainties associated with cyber-attacks can also dampen investor confidence and disrupt financial markets.

Furthermore, cyber-attacks on oil infrastructure can have significant implications for national and global economies. Governments may need to allocate resources to address the immediate aftermath of the attacks, including emergency response efforts, investigations, and potential regulatory changes. The costs of recovery and rebuilding damaged systems can be substantial, further straining public finances. Businesses affected by cyber-attacks may experience prolonged periods of disruption and reduced profitability, which can have a broader impact on employment levels and economic growth.

The challenges of recovering from cyber-attacks and implementing resilience measures are multifaceted. Governments and businesses must invest in enhancing cybersecurity capabilities, fortifying critical infrastructure, and establishing robust incident response plans. Collaboration and information sharing between public and private entities are essential to develop comprehensive strategies that address evolving cyber threats. International cooperation is also crucial, as cyber-attacks on oil infrastructure can have transnational implications, necessitating coordinated efforts to mitigate risks and strengthen resilience.

By comprehensively assessing the broader economic consequences of cyber-attacks on oil infrastructure, stakeholders can better understand the interconnectedness of various sectors and the ripple effects that ensue. This understanding can inform the development of proactive measures to bolster cyber resilience, promote economic stability, and protect against future attacks.

A Blockchain Safety Net: How Blockchain Can Secure Economic Infrastructure

In the face of persistent cyber threats to economic infrastructure, Section 4 explores the potential of blockchain technology as a safeguard for securing critical systems. Blockchain offers a decentralized, transparent, and tamper-proof infrastructure that can enhance the security and resilience of economic systems.

One area where blockchain can make a significant impact is in securing supply chains. By utilizing blockchain's distributed ledger technology, stakeholders can track and verify the movement of goods and raw materials across the supply chain, reducing the risk of counterfeit products, unauthorized modifications, or fraudulent activities. Blockchain enables the recording of every transaction or interaction, providing an immutable and transparent audit trail that enhances trust among participants and improves the overall integrity of the supply chain.

Another key application of blockchain in securing economic infrastructure is through facilitating secure transactions. Traditional financial systems are often vulnerable to cyber-attacks and fraud, leading to financial losses and compromised economic stability. By leveraging blockchain technology, financial transactions can be conducted in a secure and transparent manner, utilizing smart contracts to automate and enforce predefined rules and conditions. This reduces the reliance on intermediaries and minimizes the risk of unauthorized access, manipulation, or fraud.

Furthermore, blockchain can enhance data integrity in the energy and oil sectors. By utilizing blockchain's immutable and consensus-based nature, energy-related data such as production, consumption, and distribution can be securely recorded and verified. This ensures the integrity and accuracy of the data, reducing the potential for manipulation or falsification. With transparent and trustworthy data, stakeholders can make more informed decisions and respond effectively to disruptions or emerging challenges in the economic infrastructure.

Real-world examples and initiatives showcase the practical implementation of blockchain in securing economic infrastructure. For instance, blockchain-based platforms have been developed to enhance transparency and efficiency in global trade, enabling secure and streamlined cross-border transactions. Additionally, energy companies are exploring blockchain solutions for peer-to-peer energy trading, enabling consumers to directly exchange energy resources and reducing dependence on centralized energy systems.

By integrating blockchain into economic infrastructure, stakeholders can benefit from enhanced security, increased transparency, and improved resilience. However, challenges such as scalability, interoperability, and regulatory considerations need to be addressed to fully harness the potential of blockchain in securing economic systems.

In summary, Section 4 highlights the role of blockchain as a safety net for economic infrastructure. By leveraging its decentralized and transparent characteristics, blockchain can help secure supply chains, facilitate secure transactions, and ensure data integrity, thereby strengthening the overall resilience of economic systems in the face of evolving cyber threats.

Energizing the Future: Blockchain in the Energy Sector

Section 5 sheds light on the transformative potential of blockchain technology in the energy sector. It explores how blockchain can revolutionize energy markets, supply chains, and sustainability efforts, paving the way for a more efficient, transparent, and decentralized energy landscape.

One of the key areas where blockchain can make a significant impact is in enabling peer-to-peer energy trading. By leveraging blockchain's smart contract functionality and decentralized nature, individuals and businesses can directly trade energy resources with each other. This peer-to-peer energy trading model eliminates the need for intermediaries and enables greater control and flexibility for energy consumers. It also promotes the use of renewable energy sources by allowing energy producers to sell excess energy back to the grid or directly to consumers, creating a more sustainable and decentralized energy ecosystem.

In addition to peer-to-peer energy trading, blockchain can facilitate the tracking and certification of renewable energy sources. Renewable energy certificates (RECs) can be recorded on the blockchain, providing a transparent and auditable record of the origin and attributes of renewable energy generation. This enhances trust and enables consumers and businesses to make informed choices by supporting renewable energy sources and reducing their carbon footprint.

Blockchain technology also holds the potential to enhance energy efficiency by enabling real-time monitoring and optimization of energy consumption. Smart meters and IoT devices can be integrated with blockchain, allowing for secure and transparent collection and analysis of energy data. This data can then be used to identify inefficiencies, implement energy-saving measures, and incentivize consumers to adopt more sustainable energy consumption patterns.

Several successful blockchain projects and initiatives in the energy sector serve as real-world examples of the technology's potential. For instance, blockchain-based platforms have been developed to streamline energy trading and settlement processes, enabling faster and more secure transactions. Some countries have also implemented blockchain solutions to track and verify the authenticity of green energy certificates, ensuring the credibility of renewable energy claims.

By harnessing the power of blockchain in the energy sector, stakeholders can benefit from increased transparency, efficiency, and sustainability. However, challenges such as scalability, regulatory frameworks, and interoperability need to be addressed to unlock the full potential of blockchain technology in transforming the energy landscape.

In summary, Section 5 highlights the role of blockchain in energizing the future of the energy sector. By enabling peer-to-peer energy trading, enhancing renewable energy certificate tracking, and optimizing energy consumption, blockchain has the potential to revolutionize energy markets and contribute to a more sustainable and resilient energy future.

9
National and Global Responses to Cyber Pandemics

Defending Nations: Unveiling National Cybersecurity Strategies

In Section 1 of Chapter 9, we explore the comprehensive strategies that nations adopt to defend against cyber threats and protect their critical infrastructures. These national cybersecurity strategies are vital in safeguarding national interests and ensuring the resilience of digital ecosystems. This section delves into the key components of these strategies and highlights their significance.

Risk assessment is a fundamental aspect that is examined in this section. Nations recognize the need to proactively identify and assess potential cybersecurity risks in order to develop effective strategies. By evaluating vulnerabilities, threats, and potential impacts, governments can prioritize and allocate resources accordingly.

Threat intelligence is another critical component of national cybersecurity strategies. Governments invest in intelligence gathering and analysis to stay ahead of emerging threats and identify potential adversaries. This information enables a more targeted and effective response by understanding the tactics, techniques, and procedures employed by cybercriminals and state-sponsored actors.

Incident response capabilities play a pivotal role in national cybersecurity strategies. Governments establish dedicated teams and frameworks to ensure a swift and coordinated response to cyber incidents. This includes incident detection, containment, investigation, and recovery, all aimed at minimizing the impact and disruption caused by cyber-attacks.

Capacity building is an integral part of national cybersecurity strategies as well. Governments invest in training programs, educational initiatives, and skill development to cultivate a strong and capable cybersecurity workforce. By bridging the skill gap, nations ensure that they have the expertise required to effectively combat cyber threats.

Moreover, national cybersecurity strategies emphasize the importance of public-private partnerships. Governments collaborate with industry stakeholders, academia, and research institutions to leverage their expertise, share information, and foster innovation. These partnerships enhance the collective defense posture and enable the rapid exchange of threat intelligence, best practices, and technological advancements.

In addition to these components, Section 1 further highlights the importance of proactive cybersecurity measures in national strategies. Governments focus on developing and implementing policies and regulations that enforce cybersecurity standards across critical sectors. This includes promoting the adoption of best practices, establishing incident reporting mechanisms, and ensuring compliance with industry-specific cybersecurity requirements.

Risk mitigation and resilience planning are also integral to national cybersecurity strategies. Governments identify critical assets and infrastructure that are vulnerable to cyber threats and implement appropriate measures to mitigate those risks. Regular security assessments, robust access controls, and backups and disaster recovery plans are implemented to minimize the impact of cyber incidents.

Furthermore, Section 1 emphasizes the role of international collaboration and information sharing in national cybersecurity strategies. Recognizing that cyber threats are borderless, governments actively engage in partnerships with other nations, international organizations, and cybersecurity alliances. Through this collaboration, they exchange threat intelligence, coordinate response efforts, and collectively address emerging challenges, strengthening the overall cybersecurity posture of nations.

The role of regulatory frameworks in ensuring compliance and accountability is also highlighted in this section. National cybersecurity strategies involve the development and enforcement of laws and regulations that promote secure practices, protect critical infrastructure, and deter cybercriminals. These legal frameworks establish a strong deterrent against cyber threats and provide a basis for international cooperation on cybercrime investigations and prosecutions.

Moreover, Section 1 discusses the significance of public awareness and education in national cybersecurity strategies. Governments invest in public campaigns and initiatives to educate individuals and organizations about cyber threats, safe online practices, and the importance of cybersecurity hygiene. By promoting a culture of cybersecurity awareness, nations empower their citizens to actively participate in safeguarding digital systems and contribute to the overall resilience of the nation's cybersecurity ecosystem.

Overall, Section 1 provides a comprehensive overview of national cybersecurity strategies, emphasizing their multifaceted approach in defending nations against cyber threats. By addressing risk assessment, threat intelligence, incident response, capacity building, public-private partnerships, and international cooperation, these strategies aim to enhance cybersecurity readiness, resilience, and coordination at the national level. Through a holistic and proactive approach, nations can effectively protect their critical infrastructures, secure sensitive information, and ensure the stability and security of their digital environments. By implementing robust national cybersecurity strategies, governments can mitigate cyber risks, respond effectively to incidents, and foster collaboration to address the evolving cyber threat landscape.

Unity Against Cyber Threats: Review of Global Cybersecurity Initiatives

In this section, we delve into the collaborative efforts undertaken by the international community to address cyber threats and promote global cybersecurity. This section provides a detailed and comprehensive review of various global cybersecurity initiatives, alliances, and partnerships that have been established to foster unity and cooperation among nations.

One of the key focuses of this section is to examine the collective response to cyber threats through international organizations, such as the United Nations' Cybersecurity Program, the International Telecommunication Union (ITU), and regional cooperation frameworks like the European Union Agency for Cybersecurity (ENISA). These initiatives serve as platforms for countries to come together, share knowledge, and develop common strategies to tackle cyber threats effectively.

The section highlights the shared goals and objectives of these global cybersecurity initiatives, which include the promotion of cybersecurity norms, the exchange of threat intelligence, capacity building, and collaborative research and development. It explores how these initiatives facilitate dialogue and cooperation among nations, aiming to create a cohesive and coordinated approach to cybersecurity at the global level.

An important aspect discussed in this section is the challenges and opportunities associated with global cybersecurity cooperation. The complexity of coordinating efforts among diverse nations with varying cybersecurity capabilities, legal frameworks, and geopolitical considerations is acknowledged. It emphasizes the need for trust-building, information sharing, and harmonization of approaches to foster effective collaboration.

Furthermore, this section emphasizes the significance of information sharing as a crucial component of global cybersecurity initiatives. It explores how timely and trusted exchange of threat intelligence, best practices, and lessons learned can enhance the collective situational awareness and response capabilities of nations. By sharing information, countries can proactively identify emerging threats, anticipate cyber-attacks, and collectively strengthen their defenses against evolving cyber threats.

Capacity building is another essential aspect examined in this section. It explores how global cybersecurity initiatives support the development of cybersecurity capabilities in less-resourced countries. This includes providing training programs, technical assistance, and knowledge sharing to enhance the cybersecurity posture of nations worldwide. By empowering countries with the necessary skills and expertise, global cybersecurity initiatives contribute to building a more secure and resilient global digital ecosystem.

Through a comparative analysis of global cybersecurity initiatives, this section identifies areas of convergence and divergence among nations in their approach to addressing cyber threats. It recognizes the diversity of perspectives, priorities, and resources among countries and highlights the importance of building trust, promoting responsible behavior, and developing international norms. These efforts aim to ensure the collective security of the digital realm and foster a global cybersecurity ecosystem that can effectively counter cyber threats.

In conclusion, this section provides a comprehensive review of global cybersecurity initiatives and underscores the significance of unity, collaboration, and information sharing in addressing cyber threats at the global level. By fostering international cooperation, capacity building, and the development of norms, the international community can collectively strengthen cybersecurity defenses, mitigate risks, and safeguard the global digital ecosystem from cyber threats.

Bridging Policy Gaps: Blockchain in National and Global Cybersecurity Policies

In this section of Chapter 9, we delve into the potential of blockchain technology in bridging policy gaps and enhancing cybersecurity at both the national and global levels. This section provides a comprehensive exploration of how blockchain can be leveraged to improve data integrity, enhance identity management, and strengthen the resilience of critical infrastructure.

One of the key focuses of this section is to discuss the integration of blockchain into national cybersecurity policies. It examines how blockchain technology can be utilized to secure digital identities, ensuring the authenticity and privacy of personal information. By employing blockchain-based identity management systems, nations can enhance their cybersecurity defenses, reduce the risk of identity theft, and provide individuals with greater control over their personal data.

Moreover, this section explores how blockchain can contribute to secure data sharing and enable trustworthy transactions. Blockchain's decentralized and immutable nature ensures the integrity and transparency of data exchanges, mitigating the risks associated with unauthorized access, data manipulation, or tampering. By integrating blockchain into national cybersecurity policies, governments can establish secure data ecosystems, foster digital trust, and facilitate secure and efficient transactions within their jurisdictions.

Another important aspect discussed in this section is the role of blockchain in addressing policy challenges related to privacy, data protection, and trust in the digital ecosystem. Blockchain technology can provide solutions to enhance privacy protection by enabling data anonymization and secure sharing protocols. It also offers mechanisms for data provenance, allowing individuals and organizations to verify the authenticity and origin of data, thereby fostering trust and accountability in the digital landscape.

Furthermore, the section explores the potential for blockchain to facilitate international cooperation and information sharing in the context of cybersecurity. It highlights initiatives and frameworks that promote the adoption of blockchain in cross-border data exchanges, secure supply chains, and collaborative threat intelligence platforms. Blockchain-based solutions can establish trust among participating entities, facilitate secure and transparent data sharing, and enable real-time information exchange to enhance the collective defense against cyber threats.

In addition, this section examines the challenges and considerations associated with the adoption of blockchain in national and global cybersecurity policies. It acknowledges the need for regulatory frameworks, interoperability standards, and international cooperation to harness the full potential of blockchain technology while addressing concerns related to governance, scalability, and energy consumption.

By leveraging blockchain in national and global cybersecurity policies, nations can bridge policy gaps, enhance data integrity, and strengthen the overall resilience of critical infrastructure. Blockchain's inherent features, such as decentralization, immutability, and transparency, offer innovative solutions to address existing challenges and ensure a more secure and trustworthy digital environment.

In conclusion, this section provides a comprehensive exploration of how blockchain technology can bridge policy gaps and enhance cybersecurity at both the national and global levels. By integrating blockchain into cybersecurity policies, nations can leverage its capabilities to improve data integrity, enhance identity management, and foster international cooperation in combating cyber threats. With careful consideration of regulatory frameworks and collaborative efforts, blockchain can play a transformative role in shaping the future of cybersecurity policy and practice.

Comparative Analysis: Examining Different National Responses to Cyber Threats

In this section of Chapter 9, we conduct a comprehensive comparative analysis of different national responses to cyber threats. This section aims to examine the diverse approaches adopted by countries worldwide, their respective strengths and weaknesses, and the factors that shape their national cybersecurity strategies.

To provide a comprehensive understanding, this section delves into case studies of various countries, showcasing their unique strategies, policies, and initiatives in combating cyber threats. By examining these real-world examples, we gain valuable insights into the effectiveness of different approaches and the outcomes they produce. The case studies also shed light on the factors that influence national cybersecurity strategies, such as geopolitical considerations, technological capabilities, and cultural contexts.

The comparative analysis highlights the strengths and weaknesses of different national responses to cyber threats. It explores the success stories and best practices that can serve as benchmarks for other countries to learn from. By identifying common challenges faced by nations, such as limited resources, evolving threat landscapes, and the need for talent and skill development, we can gain a deeper understanding of the complex cybersecurity landscape.

Moreover, this section emphasizes the importance of knowledge sharing and international collaboration. By examining the diverse national responses to cyber threats, policymakers, cybersecurity professionals, and stakeholders can identify areas for improvement in their own strategies and policies. Lessons learned from different countries can inform the development of more effective and comprehensive cybersecurity approaches.

Through this comparative analysis, countries can identify opportunities for collaboration, build upon successful initiatives, and foster international partnerships to address shared cybersecurity challenges. The insights gained from the examination of different national responses can contribute to the development of global cybersecurity frameworks and promote the collective defense against cyber threats.

By examining the diversity of national responses to cyber threats, this section highlights the importance of context-specific approaches in cybersecurity. It recognizes that there is no one-size-fits-all solution and encourages countries to adapt strategies to their own unique circumstances, taking into account their geopolitical, technological, and cultural contexts.

In conclusion, Section 4 provides a comprehensive comparative analysis of different national responses to cyber threats. By examining case studies, identifying strengths and weaknesses, and highlighting common challenges, this section empowers policymakers, cybersecurity professionals, and stakeholders to assess their own national strategies, learn from successful approaches, and foster international collaboration. By promoting knowledge sharing and embracing context-specific solutions, countries can strengthen their cybersecurity defenses and collectively address the evolving landscape of cyber threats.

Moving Forward: Future of National and Global Cybersecurity

This section of Chapter 9 concludes by looking toward the future of national and global cybersecurity. It explores emerging trends, technologies, and challenges that will shape the cybersecurity landscape in the coming years, providing insights and recommendations for policymakers, cybersecurity professionals, and stakeholders.

This section examines the potential impact of emerging technologies on cyber threats and defense strategies. It delves into the implications of artificial intelligence, quantum computing, and the Internet of Things (IoT) on the evolving threat landscape. It emphasizes the need for proactive measures to address the risks associated with these technologies and develop effective security solutions.

Furthermore, Section 5 highlights the importance of continuous adaptation and innovation in response to evolving threats. It emphasizes the need for cybersecurity strategies to be dynamic and flexible, capable of adjusting to emerging risks and vulnerabilities. It also underscores the importance of interdisciplinary approaches that bring together expertise from various fields, including technology, policy, law, and psychology, to develop comprehensive and effective cybersecurity measures.

The section discusses the critical role of public-private partnerships in strengthening national and global cybersecurity. It recognizes the need for collaboration between governments, industry stakeholders, academia, and civil society to collectively address cyber threats. It emphasizes the importance of information sharing, joint research and development, and coordinated response efforts to enhance the resilience of cyberspace.

Moreover, Section 5 addresses the importance of promoting cybersecurity awareness and education. It emphasizes the need to build a skilled and knowledgeable workforce capable of addressing complex cyber threats. It calls for investments in cybersecurity education and training programs to develop a robust talent pipeline and increase cyber literacy among individuals, organizations, and communities.

The chapter concludes by highlighting the collective responsibility of nations and international organizations in addressing cyber threats and maintaining a secure and resilient cyberspace. It underscores the importance of collaboration, information sharing, and the development of international norms and standards to foster trust and stability in the digital domain. It emphasizes the need for ongoing research and development to stay ahead of emerging threats and develop effective countermeasures.

By examining national and global responses to cyber threats and discussing future trends and challenges, this section provides valuable insights and recommendations for policymakers, cybersecurity professionals, and stakeholders. It serves as a guide for shaping national and international cybersecurity strategies, fostering innovation, and promoting the security and stability of the digital ecosystem.

10
Public and Private Sector: Roles and Responsibilities

The Government's Guard: Role of Public Sector in Cybersecurity

In this section delves into the indispensable role of the public sector in cybersecurity and explores new ideas and approaches adopted by governments to effectively address evolving cyber threats. It highlights the evolving responsibilities and initiatives undertaken by governments to protect national interests, critical infrastructure, and citizen data.

This section recognizes the need for governments to adapt to the changing cybersecurity landscape and adopt innovative strategies. It explores the use of advanced technologies such as artificial intelligence (AI), machine learning (ML), and big data analytics in enhancing government cybersecurity capabilities. These technologies can assist in detecting and responding to cyber threats in real-time, as well as in analyzing vast amounts of data to identify patterns and potential vulnerabilities.

Additionally, Section 1 explores the growing importance of international cooperation and information sharing among governments. It highlights the establishment of global cybersecurity alliances and partnerships that facilitate collaboration and the exchange of threat intelligence. Through these collaborations, governments can collectively enhance their cyber defense capabilities, identify emerging threats, and foster a stronger global cybersecurity posture.

Moreover, the section discusses the increasing focus on public-private partnerships in cybersecurity. Governments recognize the valuable expertise, resources, and innovation that the private sector brings to the table. They actively engage in collaborations with private companies, sharing information, and working together to develop effective cybersecurity solutions. These partnerships foster knowledge transfer, promote technological advancements, and ensure a coordinated response to cyber threats.

In line with the growing concern for data privacy and protection, Section 1 also explores the role of governments in establishing robust data governance frameworks. Governments understand the importance of protecting sensitive information and ensuring compliance with data protection regulations. They work toward creating secure data ecosystems, promoting encryption technologies, and implementing privacy-by-design principles in the development of digital systems and services.

Furthermore, Section 1 discusses the increasing emphasis on cybersecurity, talent development and recruitment within the public sector. Governments invest in training programs, educational initiatives, and partnerships with academic institutions to nurture a skilled cybersecurity workforce. By attracting and retaining top talent, governments can strengthen their cyber defense capabilities and stay ahead of emerging threats.

Case studies and real-world examples are presented throughout the section to illustrate the successful implementation of new ideas and initiatives by governments. These examples showcase innovative approaches in cybersecurity policy, technology adoption, public-private collaborations, and talent development.

In conclusion, Section 1 highlights the evolving role of the public sector in cybersecurity and the adoption of new ideas and approaches to address the ever-changing cyber threat landscape. Governments are leveraging advanced technologies, fostering international cooperation, engaging in public-private partnerships, prioritizing data privacy, and investing in cybersecurity talent development. By embracing these new ideas, governments can effectively safeguard national interests, protect critical infrastructure, and ensure the resilience of their digital ecosystems.

Corporates Against Cyber Crime: How the Private Sector Contributes to Cybersecurity

Section 2 focuses on the role of the private sector in cybersecurity. It highlights the responsibilities and contributions of businesses, organizations, and corporations in protecting their own digital assets, customer data, and the overall cybersecurity ecosystem.

This section explores the implementation of cybersecurity measures within private sector organizations, including risk assessments, incident response plans, and employee awareness programs. It emphasizes the need for proactive cybersecurity practices, secure software development, and robust security measures to mitigate cyber risks.

Moreover, Section 2 examines the role of the private sector in technological innovation and the development of cybersecurity solutions. It discusses the investment in research and development, collaboration with cybersecurity startups, and the integration of emerging technologies to enhance cybersecurity defenses.

This section also highlights the importance of information sharing and collaboration between the public and private sectors. It emphasizes the role of private sector organizations in sharing threat intelligence, participating in public-private partnerships, and supporting government-led initiatives to combat cyber threats.

Corporates Against Cyber Crime: How the Private Sector Contributes to Cybersecurity

1. **Cybersecurity Awareness and Training:**
   Private sector organizations play a crucial role in fostering a culture of cybersecurity awareness among their employees. They develop comprehensive training programs and awareness campaigns to educate employees about the importance of cybersecurity, common threats, and best practices for protecting sensitive data. By investing in continuous education and training, businesses empower their workforce to become the first line of defense against cyber threats.

2. **Supply Chain Security:**
   The private sector is increasingly recognizing the importance of securing their supply chains to mitigate cyber risks. Organizations establish stringent cybersecurity requirements for their suppliers and partners, conducting thorough assessments and audits to ensure their adherence to security standards. By promoting a robust cybersecurity posture

throughout the supply chain, organizations can prevent cyber-attacks that may originate from third-party vendors or weak links in the chain.

3. **Cybersecurity Investments:**
   Private sector organizations allocate substantial resources toward cybersecurity investments. They continually assess their cybersecurity needs, invest in state-of-the-art technologies, and engage cybersecurity experts to bolster their defenses. These investments include the adoption of advanced security tools and technologies such as intrusion detection systems, next-generation firewalls, and advanced threat intelligence platforms. By staying at the forefront of cybersecurity innovation, organizations can proactively detect and respond to emerging threats.

4. **Collaboration with Cybersecurity Research Institutions:**
   Private sector organizations actively collaborate with academic institutions, research organizations, and cybersecurity think tanks to drive innovation and develop cutting-edge cybersecurity solutions. Through these partnerships, businesses gain access to the latest research findings, innovative technologies, and expert insights. Collaborative research efforts contribute to the advancement of cybersecurity knowledge and the development of new techniques and tools to combat evolving cyber threats.

5. **Cyber Insurance:**
   Private sector organizations increasingly invest in cyber insurance as a risk management strategy. Cyber insurance policies provide financial protection in the event of a cyber incident, covering costs related to data breaches, business interruption, and incident response. By transferring a portion of the cyber risk to insurance providers, organizations can mitigate potential financial losses and have access to specialized support and expertise in the event of an incident.

6. **Continuous Monitoring and Threat Hunting:**
   Private sector organizations employ advanced monitoring and threat hunting techniques to proactively identify and respond to cyber threats. They leverage security operations centers (SOCs), threat intelligence

platforms, and incident response teams to monitor their networks, detect anomalous activities, and investigate potential security incidents. By continuously monitoring their environments, organizations can detect and respond to threats in real-time, minimizing the impact of cyber-attacks.

In summary, Section 2 highlights additional aspects of the private sector's role in cybersecurity, including cybersecurity awareness and training, supply chain security, cybersecurity investments, collaboration with research institutions, cyber insurance, and continuous monitoring. These contributions demonstrate the commitment of the private sector to protect their digital assets, customer data, and contribute to the overall cybersecurity ecosystem.

Synergy for Safety: Public-Private Partnerships in Cybersecurity

This section focuses on the importance of public-private partnerships in cybersecurity. It explores the collaborative efforts between the public and private sectors to address cyber threats, share information, and enhance the overall cybersecurity posture.

This section discusses the benefits of public-private partnerships, such as the pooling of resources, expertise, and intelligence, to collectively combat cyber threats. It highlights successful examples of collaborative initiatives, including information-sharing platforms, joint research and development projects, and coordinated incident response frameworks.

Furthermore, Section 3 examines the challenges and considerations in establishing and maintaining public-private partnerships. It addresses issues such as information-sharing protocols, liability concerns, and the need for trust and transparency between the public and private sectors.

Case studies of successful public-private partnerships are presented to illustrate the impact and effectiveness of collaboration in addressing cyber threats. These examples showcase the synergy achieved through joint efforts and the tangible outcomes in terms of improved threat detection, incident response, and overall cyber resilience.

1. **Coordinated Threat Intelligence Sharing:**
Public-private partnerships enable the exchange of timely and actionable threat intelligence between government agencies and private sector organizations. This collaborative approach ensures that relevant threat information is shared promptly, allowing both sectors to enhance their threat detection capabilities and proactively defend against emerging cyber threats. The establishment of secure information-sharing platforms and protocols facilitates the seamless exchange of threat intelligence while maintaining data privacy and confidentiality.

2. **Joint Research and Development:**
Public-private partnerships foster collaboration in research and development efforts to advance cybersecurity technologies and strategies. By combining the expertise and resources of both sectors, innovative solutions can be developed to address evolving cyber threats. Joint research initiatives may focus on areas such as artificial intelligence, machine learning, and behavioral analytics to enhance threat detection, develop robust encryption algorithms, or create secure software development practices. These collaborative efforts drive technological advancements and provide mutual benefits to both the public and private sectors.

3. **Coordinated Incident Response and Recovery:**
Public-private partnerships facilitate coordinated incident response and recovery efforts in the face of cyber-attacks. By establishing frameworks and protocols for information sharing, incident reporting, and joint incident response exercises, both sectors can work together seamlessly to mitigate the impact of cyber incidents. This includes sharing incident data, coordinating response actions, and providing mutual support during crisis situations. Effective incident response coordination minimizes the disruption caused by cyber incidents and enables a faster recovery process.

4. **Threat Mitigation and Vulnerability Management:**
Public-private partnerships play a critical role in identifying and mitigating vulnerabilities in critical infrastructure and systems. Through

collaboration, government agencies and private sector organizations can conduct joint vulnerability assessments, share best practices, and implement security controls to address vulnerabilities effectively. This proactive approach to vulnerability management helps prevent potential cyber-attacks and strengthens the overall cybersecurity posture of both sectors.

5. **Public Awareness and Education Campaigns:**
   Public-private partnerships can collaborate on public awareness and education campaigns to promote cybersecurity literacy among individuals, businesses, and organizations. By leveraging their combined reach and influence, both sectors can raise awareness about cybersecurity risks, promote good cybersecurity practices, and educate the public on emerging threats. These campaigns can include initiatives such as workshops, training programs, and public service announcements to empower individuals and organizations to protect themselves from cyber threats.

6. **Policy Advocacy and Standards Development:**
   Public-private partnerships can contribute to the development of cybersecurity policies, regulations, and industry standards. By collaborating on policy advocacy, both sectors can provide valuable insights and expertise to shape effective and comprehensive cybersecurity frameworks. These partnerships can influence the formulation of cybersecurity laws and regulations, ensuring they align with the needs of the private sector while addressing national and international cybersecurity challenges.

In summary, Section 3 highlights the significance of public-private partnerships in cybersecurity, bringing new ideas such as coordinated threat intelligence sharing, joint research and development, coordinated incident response and recovery, threat mitigation and vulnerability management, public awareness and education campaigns, as well as policy advocacy and standards development. By fostering collaboration between the public and private sectors, these partnerships enhance the overall cybersecurity posture, strengthen defenses against cyber threats, and promote a safer digital environment for all stakeholders.

Case Studies: Success Stories of Public-Private Collaboration

Section 4 delves into real-world case studies that showcase successful public-private collaborations in the field of cybersecurity. These case studies provide in-depth analysis and insights into specific initiatives where governments and private sector organizations have joined forces to address cyber threats, enhance cybersecurity defenses, and mitigate risks.

Each case study explores a unique collaboration, highlighting its objectives, key stakeholders involved, initiatives undertaken, and the outcomes achieved. These examples illustrate the tangible benefits and impact of public-private collaboration in different aspects of cybersecurity, serving as valuable sources of inspiration and guidance for future endeavors.

One compelling case study focuses on the partnership between a government agency and a leading technology company in developing a comprehensive cybersecurity framework for the financial sector. The study highlights how this collaboration facilitated the sharing of threat intelligence, best practices, and expertise, resulting in the establishment of robust cybersecurity protocols and standards. The case study examines the positive impact of this collaboration in strengthening the resilience of financial institutions, improving incident response capabilities, and fostering a culture of cybersecurity awareness within the industry.

Another noteworthy case study explores a public-private partnership between a healthcare organization and cybersecurity firms to address the growing cybersecurity challenges in the healthcare sector. The study showcases how this collaboration led to the development of tailored cybersecurity solutions, including secure data-sharing platforms and advanced threat detection systems. The case study highlights the positive outcomes, such as the prevention of data breaches, protection of patient information, and improved cybersecurity practices across healthcare organizations.

In addition, a case study could examine a collaborative initiative between government cybersecurity agencies and technology startups in promoting cybersecurity entrepreneurship and innovation. The study demonstrates how this partnership facilitated the exchange of ideas, resources, and mentorship, resulting in the emergence of innovative cybersecurity startups and groundbreaking technologies. The case study emphasizes the value of public-private collaborations in driving technological advancements, creating job opportunities, and enhancing overall cybersecurity capabilities.

Furthermore, a case study might explore a joint effort between government intelligence agencies, telecommunications providers, and cybersecurity companies to combat cyber espionage and state-sponsored cyber threats. The study examines how this partnership facilitated the sharing of critical threat intelligence, enhanced network security measures, and enabled swift response to emerging threats. The case study highlights the importance of cross-sector collaboration in safeguarding national security and protecting sensitive information from sophisticated cyber adversaries.

These case studies cover various sectors, including finance, healthcare, defense, and critical infrastructure. Each study showcases the unique challenges faced by these sectors and the specific benefits derived from public-private collaborations. The case studies provide insights into the collaborative strategies employed, the coordination mechanisms implemented, and the effective use of resources and expertise from both sectors to achieve desired outcomes.

Moreover, the case studies delve into the lessons learned from these successful collaborations. They explore best practices, challenges encountered, and strategies for sustaining and expanding partnerships over time. The case studies emphasize the importance of trust, open communication, alignment of objectives, and the need for long-term commitment to foster successful collaborations.

By studying these success stories, other public and private sector entities can gain valuable insights and practical guidance for establishing and maintaining their own successful cybersecurity collaborations. They serve as valuable references for policymakers, cybersecurity professionals, and stakeholders seeking to enhance cybersecurity practices, protect critical assets, and fortify the overall resilience of their organizations and industries.

Overall, Section 4 provides a comprehensive analysis of successful case studies that highlight the benefits, outcomes, and lessons learned from public-private collaborations in cybersecurity. These examples showcase the effectiveness of joint efforts in areas such as threat intelligence sharing, research and development, policy formulation, and sector-specific cybersecurity initiatives. By studying these success stories, stakeholders can gain inspiration and guidance for their own collaborative endeavors in addressing cyber threats and fortifying cybersecurity defenses.

Envisioning Collaboration: The Future Role of Blockchain in Public-Private Cybersecurity

Section 5 delves into the future role of blockchain technology in facilitating and strengthening public-private collaboration in the realm of cybersecurity. As the cybersecurity landscape continues to evolve and new threats emerge, it is crucial to explore innovative solutions that enhance trust, transparency, and information sharing between the public and private sectors. Blockchain technology offers promising capabilities that can revolutionize the way cybersecurity collaborations are conducted and contribute to a more secure digital ecosystem.

One of the key areas where blockchain can have a transformative impact is in the secure sharing of threat intelligence. Traditional methods of sharing threat information among stakeholders often face challenges such as trust issues, data integrity concerns, and the lack of a standardized framework. Blockchain-based platforms can provide a decentralized and tamper-proof infrastructure for sharing threat intelligence. By leveraging cryptographic algorithms and consensus mechanisms, blockchain ensures the authenticity and integrity of the shared data. This enables real-time threat monitoring, faster incident response, and the ability to collectively respond to emerging cyber threats.

Moreover, blockchain technology can significantly enhance the protection of sensitive information shared between public and private entities. The immutability and cryptographic features of blockchain provide a secure and auditable data exchange environment. Through the use of smart contracts, access controls can be enforced, ensuring that sensitive information is only accessible to authorized participants in the collaboration. This not only mitigates the risk of data breaches and unauthorized access but also fosters trust and confidence among collaborators.

In addition to secure information sharing, blockchain can streamline the coordination of incident response efforts between the public and private sectors. Traditional incident response processes often involve multiple stakeholders, complex coordination, and information exchange challenges. By utilizing blockchain-based platforms, incident response teams can securely and efficiently share information, track the progress of response activities, and ensure the coordination of efforts across multiple entities. This enhances the effectiveness and speed of incident response, minimizing the impact of cyber incidents and enabling a more synchronized and unified approach.

However, the successful adoption of blockchain in public-private cybersecurity collaboration requires addressing several challenges. Interoperability between different blockchain networks is crucial to ensure seamless integration and collaboration among diverse stakeholders. Efforts must be made to develop standards and protocols that enable the interoperability of blockchain networks, allowing for secure data exchange and collaboration. Scalability is another important consideration, as blockchain networks need to handle large-scale collaborations involving numerous entities and high volumes of data. Research and development in scaling solutions and infrastructure are necessary to realize the full potential of blockchain technology in cybersecurity collaborations.

Furthermore, the development of regulatory frameworks that align with blockchain technology is essential. Regulations need to strike a balance between fostering innovation and ensuring the security and privacy of participants. Regulatory clarity and guidance will encourage the adoption of blockchain in cybersecurity collaborations, providing a legal and regulatory framework that addresses concerns such as data protection, privacy, and liability.

Looking into the future, blockchain technology has the potential to enable advanced features in public-private cybersecurity collaboration. Smart contracts, self-executing agreements stored on the blockchain, can automate and enforce compliance with cybersecurity protocols and regulations. These contracts can facilitate secure and transparent transactions, establish predefined rules and conditions for collaboration, and enable efficient governance mechanisms. Decentralized identity management systems based on blockchain can enhance identity verification, authentication, and access control, ensuring that only authorized entities participate in cybersecurity collaborations. This enhances the overall security and trustworthiness of the collaboration ecosystem.

Moreover, blockchain-based governance models can foster trust, transparency, and accountability in public-private cybersecurity collaborations. Through decentralized decision-making mechanisms, stakeholders can participate in the governance of cybersecurity initiatives, ensuring inclusivity and shared responsibility. This can enhance the effectiveness of collaborations by fostering a sense of ownership and collective commitment. Blockchain-based governance can also enable the transparent auditability of decision-making processes, ensuring accountability and integrity in cybersecurity collaborations.

In conclusion, the future role of blockchain in public-private cybersecurity collaboration holds significant promise. By leveraging blockchain technology, stakeholders can enhance trust, transparency, and information sharing in the fight against cyber threats. The integration of blockchain-based platforms can enable secure sharing of threat intelligence, protect sensitive information, streamline incident response efforts, and enable advanced features such as smart contracts and decentralized governance. It is crucial for the public and private sectors to explore the potential of blockchain and collaborate in its development and implementation to realize the full benefits it offers. By embracing blockchain technology, stakeholders can collectively strengthen the cybersecurity landscape and ensure a secure and resilient digital future.

11
Anticipating the Unthinkable: Probability of a Major Cyberattack

Predicting the Storm: Risk Assessment for Major Cyber-attacks

Section 1 of Chapter 11 delves into the crucial task of assessing the probability of major cyber-attacks. It explores the methodologies and frameworks used to evaluate the likelihood and potential impact of cyber threats on critical infrastructure, businesses, and individuals.

This section emphasizes the importance of conducting comprehensive risk assessments to identify vulnerabilities, potential attack vectors, and the potential consequences of major cyber-attacks. It explores the use of threat intelligence, historical data analysis, and scenario modeling to assess the probability of different types of cyber-attacks.

Moreover, Section 1 discusses the emerging trends and factors that increase the probability of major cyber-attacks. It examines the expanding attack surface due to the proliferation of internet-connected devices, the rise of sophisticated threat actors, and the evolving techniques employed by cybercriminals. Understanding these trends and their potential impact is essential for accurately predicting the likelihood of major cyber-attacks.

In today's interconnected world, the risk of major cyber-attacks looms large. The consequences of such attacks can be devastating, ranging from financial losses and reputational damage to disruptions in critical services and infrastructure. Therefore, it is crucial to assess the probability of these attacks to anticipate and mitigate their potential impact.

Risk assessment forms the foundation of predicting the likelihood of major cyber-attacks. It involves a systematic evaluation of vulnerabilities, threats, and potential consequences. By conducting comprehensive risk assessments, organizations and individuals can gain valuable insights into their cybersecurity posture and identify areas that require attention and improvement.

Threat intelligence plays a pivotal role in risk assessment. It involves gathering and analyzing information about existing and emerging cyber threats, understanding the tactics and techniques employed by threat actors, and monitoring the evolving threat landscape. By staying abreast of the latest threats, organizations can anticipate potential attack vectors and develop appropriate countermeasures.

Historical data analysis is another valuable tool in risk assessment. By studying past cyber-attacks, organizations can identify common patterns, vulnerabilities, and targets. This analysis helps in understanding the probability of similar attacks occurring in the future. It also enables the identification of trends and emerging threats that may increase the probability of major cyber-attacks.

Scenario modeling is a technique used to assess the potential impact of major cyber-attacks. By simulating various attack scenarios and their potential consequences, organizations can evaluate the likelihood of specific types of attacks and their potential impact on critical systems, infrastructure, and stakeholders. This allows for the identification of high-risk areas and the development of tailored response strategies.

Furthermore, understanding the emerging trends and factors that contribute to the probability of major cyber-attacks is essential. The proliferation of internet-connected devices, commonly referred to as the Internet of Things (IoT), has significantly expanded the attack surface for cybercriminals. The interconnected nature of these devices presents new vulnerabilities that can be exploited. Additionally, the rise of sophisticated threat actors, including state-sponsored hackers and organized cybercrime groups, poses a significant risk. These actors employ advanced techniques and technologies to target critical infrastructure, businesses, and individuals. The evolution of attack techniques, such as ransomware and zero-day exploits, further increases the probability of major cyber-attacks.

Accurately predicting the probability of major cyber-attacks enables organizations and individuals to proactively implement appropriate security measures and response strategies. It allows them to allocate resources effectively, prioritize security investments, and establish incident response plans. By taking proactive measures, organizations can enhance their cybersecurity posture, reduce the likelihood of successful attacks, and mitigate the potential impact in the event of an attack.

In conclusion, Section 1 highlights the importance of risk assessment in predicting the probability of major cyber-attacks. By leveraging threat intelligence, historical data analysis, scenario modeling, and an understanding of emerging trends, organizations and individuals can gain insights into the likelihood and potential impact of cyber threats. This knowledge enables them to implement appropriate security measures, develop robust response strategies, and enhance their overall cybersecurity posture. By anticipating the storm, they can better prepare for and mitigate the potential impact of major cyber-attacks.

By conducting risk assessments and accurately predicting the probability of major cyber-attacks, organizations and individuals can proactively implement appropriate security measures and response strategies to mitigate the potential impact.

The Slammer/Sapphire Worm: A Case Study in Rapid Cyberattack

1. Emergence of the Slammer/Sapphire Worm

The Slammer/Sapphire worm, which emerged in January 2003, spread at an astonishing rate, infecting over 75,000 servers within the first ten minutes of its release. Exploiting a vulnerability in Microsoft SQL Server, it took advantage of unpatched systems, rapidly scanning and infecting vulnerable hosts across the internet. The worm's small size and efficient code allowed it to propagate swiftly, surpassing previous worms in speed and scale.

2. Unprecedented Speed and Impact

The Slammer/Sapphire worm's rapid propagation and exponential growth had a devastating impact on networks worldwide. Within hours of its release, the worm caused severe disruptions in critical systems and internet infrastructure. Major corporations, banks, transportation networks, and even emergency services experienced significant outages, leading to financial losses and hindering essential services.

The worm's speed was unparalleled, infecting new hosts every few seconds, overwhelming network bandwidth, and causing congestion in internet traffic. Internet service providers struggled to handle the massive surge in network traffic generated by the worm's propagation.

3. Lessons Learned and Countermeasures

The Slammer/Sapphire worm served as a harsh reminder of the importance of proactive cybersecurity measures and effective incident response strategies. It exposed the vulnerabilities inherent in systems lacking proper patch management and security hygiene practices.

Following the attack, organizations and software vendors learned valuable lessons about the criticality of prompt patching and vulnerability mitigation. Patch management policies were strengthened, and automated update mechanisms were implemented to ensure timely deployment of security patches.

Network segmentation and isolation became essential strategies to limit the lateral movement of worms and minimize their impact. System administrators and security professionals adopted improved network architectures that enforced strict boundaries between critical systems and restricted communication to reduce the worm's ability to spread.

4. Global Response and Collaboration

The rapid and global nature of the Slammer/Sapphire worm necessitated international collaboration to mitigate its impact. Cybersecurity organizations, governments, and vendors came together to share threat intelligence, exchange mitigation strategies, and coordinate incident response efforts.

The incident spurred the establishment of new information-sharing initiatives, such as the creation of dedicated forums and mailing lists for real-time communication among security professionals. Collaboration among vendors and security researchers resulted in the development of detection signatures and tools to identify and eradicate the worm.

Public-private partnerships also played a crucial role in addressing the worm's impact. Government agencies collaborated with private-sector entities to disseminate alerts, provide guidance to affected organizations, and assist in recovery efforts. This collaboration paved the way for future joint efforts in combating cyber threats.

5. Long-Term Impact on Cybersecurity

The Slammer/Sapphire worm's impact extended beyond immediate disruptions. It left a lasting legacy that influenced cybersecurity practices and policies worldwide. The incident highlighted the importance of security awareness and the need for organizations to prioritize regular patching and vulnerability management.

Software vendors responded by improving their development practices, implementing secure coding guidelines, and conducting rigorous security testing to prevent similar vulnerabilities in their products. The incident also led to increased scrutiny of software quality and security assurance processes.

Regulatory bodies and industry organizations recognized the significance of the worm as a catalyst for improved cybersecurity practices. New regulations and standards were developed to enforce secure coding practices, promote vulnerability management, and enhance incident response capabilities.

By examining the devastating impact of the Slammer/Sapphire worm, this section serves as a stark reminder of the importance of proactive defenses, rapid response capabilities, and global collaboration in mitigating the viral velocity of cyber threats. It underlines the critical need for continuous improvement in cybersecurity practices to prevent and respond effectively to future cyber-attacks.

Emerging Threats: The Role of AI and Quantum Computing in Cybersecurity

Section 3 of Chapter 11 delves into the profound impact of artificial intelligence (AI) and quantum computing on the cybersecurity landscape. As these emerging technologies continue to advance at an unprecedented pace, it is crucial to understand their implications and the challenges they pose in defending against major cyber-attacks.

Artificial intelligence has emerged as a transformative force in various fields, including cybersecurity. However, it also introduces new risks and challenges. At its core, AI involves the development of intelligent systems that can mimic human cognitive processes and make decisions autonomously. In the context of cybersecurity, AI has both offensive and defensive applications. On the offensive side, threat actors can leverage AI to launch more sophisticated and targeted attacks. AI-powered tools can automate tasks such as reconnaissance, vulnerability scanning, and even crafting custom malware. The use of AI in attack techniques can significantly increase the efficiency and effectiveness of cyber-attacks, making them more difficult to detect and mitigate. On the defensive side, AI offers opportunities for improving threat detection, anomaly detection, and response automation. AI algorithms can analyze vast amounts of data, identify patterns, and detect anomalies that may indicate the presence of an ongoing cyberattack. This enables cybersecurity professionals to respond rapidly and effectively to emerging threats.

Quantum computing represents another groundbreaking technology that has the potential to revolutionize cybersecurity. Quantum computers leverage quantum bits, or qubits, which can exist in multiple states simultaneously, allowing for exponentially faster computations compared to classical computers. This exponential increase in computational power poses both opportunities and threats to cybersecurity. Quantum computers have the potential to break traditional encryption algorithms, rendering current cryptographic mechanisms obsolete. As quantum computers become more powerful, they pose a significant threat to the confidentiality and integrity of sensitive information, such as classified government data, financial transactions, and personal records. However, quantum computing also offers opportunities for strengthening cybersecurity defenses. Post-quantum cryptography, which encompasses cryptographic algorithms that are resistant to attacks by quantum computers, is an area of active research and development. These quantum-resistant algorithms aim to ensure that encrypted data remains secure even in the presence of quantum computers.

The convergence of AI and quantum computing introduces both opportunities and challenges. On one hand, AI can enhance the security of quantum systems by improving their resilience against attacks. AI algorithms can assist in the development of more secure post-quantum cryptographic algorithms and aid in the analysis of complex quantum systems. On the other hand, AI itself can be vulnerable to attacks orchestrated using quantum computing. Quantum algorithms can potentially exploit the computational power of quantum computers to break AI models, compromise their integrity, or manipulate their decision-making process. As AI and quantum computing continue to advance, it is essential to carefully consider their interplay and the potential risks associated with their combination.

As these emerging technologies shape the future of cybersecurity, there is a pressing need for robust strategies and proactive measures to address the emerging threats they pose. It is crucial to invest in research and development to develop secure AI algorithms and quantum-resistant cryptographic solutions. Collaborative efforts between academia, industry, and government institutions are essential for advancing the field of AI and quantum-safe technologies. These efforts should focus on developing innovative approaches to detect and mitigate AI-enabled attacks, as well as securing sensitive data from the imminent threat of quantum computers.

Ethical considerations also come to the forefront when deploying AI in cybersecurity. The deployment of AI in offensive operations raises concerns about the potential for autonomous and malicious AI systems. It is crucial to ensure responsible and accountable use of AI, addressing issues such as bias, transparency, and the potential for unintended consequences. As AI becomes increasingly integrated into cybersecurity operations, maintaining a humancentric approach and upholding ethical principles are paramount.

In conclusion, Section 3 highlights the transformative impact of AI and quantum computing on cybersecurity. It explores the opportunities and challenges posed by these technologies and underscores the need for proactive measures to harness their potential while mitigating their risks. By staying informed, investing in research and development, promoting ethical practices, and fostering collaboration, organizations and individuals can navigate the evolving cybersecurity landscape and effectively defend against major cyber-attacks in the age of AI and quantum computing.

The Dark Side of AI: Deep Fakes and Their Role in Global Cyber-Attacks

In an era where artificial intelligence (AI) has brought about remarkable advancements, there is a dark side that warrants attention: deep fakes. Deep fakes are deceptive audio and visual content created using AI algorithms, which can convincingly mimic real individuals or events. This section delves into the emerging threat posed by deep fakes and their potential role in global cyber-attacks.

1. **Understanding Deep Fake Technology:**
    Deep fake technology leverages AI algorithms, such as deep neural networks, to manipulate and generate highly realistic content. It involves training models on vast datasets to learn patterns and create convincing

imitations of individuals, often placing them in fabricated scenarios. By understanding the inner workings of deep fake technology, we can appreciate its potential for deception.

Deep fakes have reached a level of sophistication where distinguishing them from genuine content has become increasingly challenging. Facial mapping, voice synthesis, and contextual understanding enable the creation of remarkably convincing videos, audio recordings, and even text-based messages. Notable deep fake incidents, such as the manipulation of political speeches or the creation of fake celebrity pornographic videos, highlight the potency of this technology.

2. **Exploitation in Cyber-Attacks:**

The use of deep fakes in cyber-attacks introduces alarming possibilities. Cybercriminals can exploit deep fakes for social engineering, phishing, and other malicious activities. By impersonating individuals of authority or trust, hackers can deceive unsuspecting victims into divulging sensitive information or performing actions that compromise security.

Deep fakes have been used to manipulate public opinion, spread misinformation, and incite social unrest. By disseminating fabricated content that appears genuine, malicious actors can manipulate narratives, damage reputations, and sow discord. The potential for deep fakes to facilitate identity theft, impersonation, or unauthorized access to systems underscores their relevance in the cybersecurity landscape.

3. **Implications for Cybersecurity:**

Deep fakes present unique challenges for cybersecurity professionals and defense mechanisms. Traditional detection methods struggle to differentiate between real and deep fake content, as the technology continues to evolve and improve. The proliferation of deep fakes exacerbates the difficulty of identifying and mitigating their impact.

The consequences of widespread adoption of deep fake technology in cyber-attacks are profound. From undermining trust in media and institutions to causing political instability or economic harm, the implications are far-reaching. Organizations must adapt their cybersecurity strategies to address the specific threats posed by deep fakes and invest in advanced detection and mitigation solutions.

4. **Defense and Countermeasures:**
   Efforts to counter deep fakes are underway, focusing on developing effective detection and verification techniques. AI-powered algorithms are being designed to identify telltale signs of manipulation, such as inconsistencies in facial movements or audio artifacts. Additionally, advancements in watermarking technologies and digital signatures aim to verify the authenticity and integrity of media content.

   Educating individuals about the existence and potential risks of deep fakes is crucial. By raising awareness, users can exercise caution when consuming media and be more skeptical of content that may have been tampered with. Collaborative efforts between technology companies, research institutions, and cybersecurity experts are vital to stay ahead of deep fake advancements and develop robust defense mechanisms.

5. **Collaborative Solutions:**
   Addressing the deep fake challenge requires collaboration on multiple fronts. Public-private partnerships, research institutions, and technology companies must work together to share insights, develop best practices, and foster innovation. International cooperation is essential in developing standardized frameworks, legislation, and information-sharing mechanisms to combat the global nature of deep fake threats.

   Initiatives such as deep fake detection challenges, hackathons, and interdisciplinary research collaborations are emerging to tackle the problem. By pooling resources and expertise, these endeavors aim to create effective strategies and tools to detect, mitigate, and raise awareness about deep fakes.

As AI-driven deep fakes become increasingly sophisticated, the cybersecurity landscape faces a critical challenge. By comprehending the risks and collaborating across sectors, we can mitigate the potential harm caused by deep fakes and safeguard the integrity of digital content. It is essential for cybersecurity professionals, policymakers, and society as a whole to remain vigilant, adapt defense strategies, and foster a culture of media literacy to navigate the evolving threat landscape of deep fakes. Through collective efforts, we can mitigate the risks associated with deep fakes and uphold the integrity of digital media.

Being Prepared: Strategies for Anticipating Cyber-attacks

In this section of Chapter 11, we delve into the strategies organizations can employ to anticipate cyber-attacks and effectively prepare themselves to defend against evolving threats. In the dynamic and ever-changing cybersecurity landscape, where cyber threats are becoming increasingly sophisticated, it is imperative for organizations and individuals to adopt proactive approaches to stay ahead of potential attacks.

One of the key strategies for anticipating cyber-attacks is the establishment of a robust and dynamic threat intelligence program. This involves actively monitoring and analyzing emerging threats, vulnerabilities, and attack patterns. By staying informed about the latest techniques and tactics used by threat actors, organizations can proactively identify potential vulnerabilities and develop appropriate defense mechanisms. Collaborating with industry-specific information-sharing platforms, government agencies, and cybersecurity communities can significantly enhance the ability to anticipate and mitigate cyber threats.

To effectively anticipate cyber-attacks, organizations should foster a culture of cybersecurity awareness and education. Employee training and awareness programs play a critical role in equipping individuals with the knowledge and skills to identify and respond to potential threats. By promoting a security-conscious culture, organizations can empower employees to recognize suspicious activities, report potential risks, and adhere to best practices in handling sensitive data and accessing critical systems.

Another essential component of being prepared is conducting regular risk assessments and vulnerability assessments. By identifying weaknesses and potential entry points within an organization's digital infrastructure, it becomes possible to proactively implement security controls and mitigation strategies. Regular vulnerability scanning and penetration testing can help identify and address potential vulnerabilities before they can be exploited by malicious actors. Furthermore, organizations should prioritize patch management and ensure that systems and software are up to date with the latest security patches and updates.

Continuous monitoring and threat detection play a critical role in anticipating cyber-attacks. Implementing intrusion detection systems, network monitoring tools, and security event management solutions allows organizations to detect and respond to potential threats in real-time. By analyzing network traffic, log files, and system activities, organizations can identify suspicious behavior and anomalous patterns that may indicate a cyberattack in progress. Early detection enables swift response and containment, minimizing the potential impact of an attack.

Additionally, organizations should prioritize incident response preparedness. Establishing a well-defined and regularly tested incident response framework ensures that the organization can respond swiftly and effectively to a cyberattack. This includes defining roles and responsibilities, establishing communication channels, and coordinating response efforts with relevant stakeholders. Regular tabletop exercises and simulated incident scenarios help validate the effectiveness of the incident response plan and identify areas for improvement.

Collaboration and information sharing within the cybersecurity community are also crucial for anticipating cyber-attacks. By actively participating in industry-specific forums, sharing threat intelligence, and collaborating with peers, organizations can gain valuable insights into emerging threats and industry-specific attack vectors. Public-private partnerships and information-sharing initiatives, such as Computer Emergency Response Teams (CERTs) and Information Sharing and Analysis Centers (ISACs), provide valuable platforms for exchanging information, best practices, and lessons learned.

Furthermore, organizations should adopt a proactive approach to security awareness and training. This includes providing regular cybersecurity training to employees, educating them about emerging threats and attack vectors, and promoting secure behaviors in handling sensitive information. Simulated phishing exercises, where employees are exposed to mock phishing attempts, can help raise awareness about social engineering techniques and enable individuals to identify and report potential threats.

Technological advancements also play a crucial role in anticipating cyber-attacks. Organizations should consider implementing advanced security technologies and solutions to bolster their defense against cyber threats. This includes the use of next-generation firewalls, advanced threat detection systems, secure email gateways, and endpoint protection tools. Employing machine learning and artificial intelligence algorithms can help automate threat detection, response, and recovery processes, enabling faster and more accurate decision-making.

Furthermore, organizations should develop and maintain strong relationships with external cybersecurity experts, including ethical hackers and security consultants. Regular audits and assessments conducted by external professionals can help identify vulnerabilities, assess the effectiveness of security controls, and provide recommendations for improvement.

Additionally, organizations can draw inspiration from personal financial protection strategies when it comes to anticipating cyber-attacks. Just as individuals take steps to protect their personal finances from fraud and theft, organizations can adopt similar principles to safeguard their digital assets. For example, organizations can implement multifactor authentication, encryption, and secure password policies to protect sensitive data. Regular monitoring of financial transactions, anomaly detection, and fraud detection mechanisms can help identify potential cyber threats and mitigate risks.

Moreover, organizations can consider cyber insurance as part of their preparedness strategy. Cyber insurance provides financial protection in the event of a cyberattack, covering costs such as incident response, data recovery, and legal expenses. By having a comprehensive cyber insurance policy, organizations can mitigate the financial impact of a cyberattack and expedite their recovery efforts.

In conclusion, the section emphasizes the importance of proactive strategies for anticipating cyber-attacks. By establishing a robust threat intelligence program, fostering a culture of cybersecurity awareness, conducting regular risk assessments, implementing continuous monitoring and detection mechanisms, prioritizing incident response preparedness, fostering collaboration, adopting advanced security technologies, and drawing inspiration from personal financial protection strategies, organizations can enhance their ability

to anticipate and respond to cyber threats effectively. Being prepared and staying one step ahead of potential attacks is crucial in today's rapidly evolving cybersecurity landscape. By combining proactive measures, employee education, risk assessments, incident response preparedness, collaboration, and advanced technologies, organizations can strengthen their cybersecurity posture and mitigate the risks associated with cyber-attacks. Additionally, drawing inspiration from personal financial protection strategies and considering cyber insurance can further enhance an organization's preparedness. By taking a comprehensive and multifaceted approach to cybersecurity, organizations can anticipate potential threats, minimize their impact, and ensure the resilience of their digital assets and operations.

Blockchain to the Rescue: Its Role in Preparedness and Mitigation

In Section 5 of Chapter 11, we explore the potential of blockchain technology in enhancing preparedness and mitigation strategies against cyber-attacks. Blockchain, originally known as the underlying technology behind cryptocurrencies like Bitcoin, has emerged as a powerful tool with various applications beyond digital currencies. Its decentralized, transparent, and immutable nature makes it a promising solution for addressing cybersecurity challenges.

One of the key aspects of blockchain technology that contributes to preparedness and mitigation is its ability to enhance data integrity and trust. Traditional centralized systems are vulnerable to data tampering and manipulation, posing significant risks to organizations and individuals. However, blockchain's distributed ledger technology provides a transparent and tamper-proof record of transactions and data. By utilizing blockchain, organizations can securely store and verify critical information, ensuring its integrity and reducing the risk of data breaches and unauthorized modifications.

Blockchain can also play a vital role in securing supply chains, which are often targeted in cyber-attacks. By implementing blockchain-based supply chain management systems, organizations can ensure the provenance, authenticity, and integrity of goods throughout the entire supply chain. This helps detect and prevent the introduction of counterfeit or compromised products, reducing the risk of supply chain disruptions and potential cyber threats.

Another significant benefit of blockchain in preparedness and mitigation is its potential for decentralized identity management. Traditional centralized identity systems are vulnerable to data breaches and identity theft. However, with blockchain, individuals can have more control over their identities and personal data. Blockchain-based identity solutions provide a secure and decentralized platform for managing identities, reducing the risk of unauthorized access and identity fraud. By leveraging blockchain, organizations can enhance identity verification processes and establish more secure authentication mechanisms, mitigating the risk of cyber-attacks targeting user credentials.

Moreover, blockchain technology can facilitate secure and transparent information sharing among trusted parties. In the context of cyberattack preparedness and mitigation, this can be particularly valuable. Organizations can leverage blockchain to create secure platforms for sharing threat intelligence, incident reports, and best practices with trusted partners. By securely sharing real-time information about emerging threats and attack vectors, organizations can collectively strengthen their defenses and respond more effectively to cyber-attacks.

Blockchain-based smart contracts also have the potential to enhance preparedness and mitigation strategies. Smart contracts are self-executing agreements with the terms and conditions directly written into the code. They enable automated and transparent execution of predefined actions based on specific conditions. In the context of cybersecurity, smart contracts can be utilized to enforce security protocols and automate incident response procedures. For example, in the event of a cyberattack, predefined actions can be automatically triggered, such as isolating affected systems, alerting relevant parties, and initiating recovery processes. This reduces response time and minimizes the potential impact of an attack.

To illustrate the potential of blockchain in cybersecurity preparedness and mitigation, let's consider an example in the financial industry. Suppose a major financial institution wants to enhance its preparedness against potential cyber-attacks targeting its customers' financial information. By implementing a blockchain-based system, the institution can securely store and manage customer data, ensuring its integrity and reducing the risk of unauthorized access. Blockchain's transparency and immutability provide customers with increased trust and confidence in the institution's security measures. Additionally, the institution can leverage blockchain for secure information sharing with other financial organizations, enabling faster detection and response to emerging threats.

Furthermore, blockchain can enhance incident response and recovery efforts by ensuring the availability and integrity of critical data backups. Traditional centralized backup systems may be vulnerable to attacks or failures, compromising the organization's ability to recover from a cyberattack. However, by leveraging blockchain, organizations can securely store encrypted backups distributed across multiple nodes, reducing the risk of data loss or manipulation. This ensures that organizations can quickly recover and restore their systems and operations in the event of a cyberattack.

In conclusion, Section 5 highlights the potential of blockchain technology in enhancing preparedness and mitigation strategies against cyber-attacks. By leveraging blockchain's features such as data integrity, decentralized identity management, secure information sharing, smart contracts, and robust backup systems, organizations can significantly strengthen their cybersecurity defenses. The adoption of blockchain-based solutions can enhance transparency, trust, and efficiency in cybersecurity practices, ultimately contributing to more effective preparedness and mitigation efforts. As organizations continue to explore and embrace blockchain technology, it is crucial to assess its applicability, limitations, and potential risks to ensure its successful implementation in the context of cybersecurity.

Section 7: Beyond Speculation: Concrete Steps to Enhance Cybersecurity

In Section 6 of Chapter 11, we explore practical measures and steps that organizations and individuals can take to enhance cybersecurity and protect against major cyber-attacks. While predicting the exact occurrence of a cyberattack is challenging, proactive actions can significantly reduce the potential impact and improve overall cybersecurity resilience. This section goes beyond speculation and provides concrete strategies for strengthening cybersecurity defenses.

One crucial aspect of enhancing cybersecurity is personal financial protection. With the increasing prevalence of online banking, digital payment systems, and e-commerce, individuals are exposed to financial risks in cyberspace. To protect personal financial information, individuals should implement several measures. First, it is essential to use strong and unique passwords for financial accounts and regularly change them. Additionally, enabling multifactor authentication provides an extra layer of security by requiring a secondary verification step, such as a fingerprint or one-time password. It is also advisable to regularly monitor financial transactions and account statements to detect any suspicious activities promptly. Lastly, individuals should exercise caution when sharing financial information online and ensure that they only provide sensitive details on secure websites.

Furthermore, organizations and individuals should prioritize the implementation of robust cybersecurity measures. This includes utilizing up-to-date antivirus software, firewalls, and intrusion detection systems to protect against malware and unauthorized access. Regularly updating operating systems, software, and applications with the latest security patches is crucial in addressing known vulnerabilities. Employing encryption techniques for sensitive data can provide an additional layer of protection, ensuring that information remains secure even if intercepted. Additionally, regular data backups should be performed to safeguard against data loss in the event of a cyberattack.

Educating and raising awareness among employees and individuals is an essential component of cybersecurity. Organizations should conduct cybersecurity training sessions to educate employees about potential risks, phishing attacks, and safe online practices. Individuals should be cautious when clicking on suspicious links, downloading unknown attachments, or providing personal information to untrusted sources. By promoting a culture of cybersecurity awareness, organizations and individuals can develop a strong defense against cyber threats.

Creating a comprehensive incident response plan is crucial for effectively addressing and mitigating the impact of cyber-attacks. Organizations should establish a dedicated incident response team and define their roles and responsibilities. Regularly conducting simulated incident response exercises helps identify gaps in the plan and ensures a coordinated response in the event of an attack. The incident response plan should include steps for containment, investigation, recovery, and communication. By having a well-defined plan in place, organizations can minimize the disruption caused by cyber-attacks and swiftly restore normal operations.

Public-private partnerships play a vital role in enhancing cybersecurity readiness. Governments, businesses, and industry associations should collaborate to share threat intelligence, best practices, and insights into emerging cyber threats. For example, organizations can participate in information-sharing platforms and forums where they can contribute and receive valuable information about the latest threats and mitigation strategies. By fostering collaboration, the collective knowledge and resources can be leveraged to strengthen cybersecurity defenses.

Blockchain technology offers unique opportunities for enhancing cybersecurity. Its decentralized and immutable nature provides a robust platform for securing sensitive data and transactions. Organizations can explore the use of blockchain in areas such as identity management, secure data sharing, and supply chain integrity. For example, blockchain can be employed in verifying and tracking financial transactions, ensuring transparency and reducing the risk of fraudulent activities. Blockchain-based identity solutions can also enhance personal data protection by providing individuals with control over their digital identities and minimizing the risk of identity theft.

Continuous monitoring and threat intelligence are essential for staying ahead of evolving cyber threats. Organizations and individuals should invest in cybersecurity tools and services that provide real-time threat detection and proactive threat hunting capabilities. By monitoring network traffic, analyzing system logs, and employing threat intelligence feeds, organizations can identify and respond to potential threats before they cause significant damage. Regular vulnerability assessments and penetration testing should also be conducted to identify and address potential weaknesses in security defenses.

In conclusion, Section 6 emphasizes the need for concrete steps to enhance cybersecurity and protect against major cyber-attacks. By prioritizing personal financial protection, implementing robust cybersecurity measures, educating employees and individuals, establishing incident response plans, fostering collaboration through public-private partnerships, exploring the potential of blockchain technology, and continuously monitoring and adapting to evolving threats, organizations and individuals can significantly improve their cybersecurity resilience. Cybersecurity is a shared responsibility, and by taking these concrete steps, we can collectively strengthen our defenses and create a safer digital environment for all.

12
Innovation and Proactivity Opportunities to Deter Cyber-attacks

The Innovation Landscape: Key Trends in Cybersecurity Technology

In Section 1 of Chapter 12, we delve into the rapidly evolving landscape of cybersecurity technology and explore the key trends that are shaping the industry. With the ever-increasing frequency and sophistication of cyber-attacks, it is essential to stay at the forefront of technological advancements to deter and mitigate these threats effectively.

The section begins by highlighting the critical role of emerging technologies in revolutionizing the field of cybersecurity. One such trend is the integration of artificial intelligence (AI) and machine learning (ML) algorithms into security systems. AI and ML enable computers to analyze vast amounts of data, identify patterns, and learn from past incidents to detect and respond to potential cyber threats in real-time. For example, AI-driven algorithms can identify malicious patterns in network traffic, analyze the behavior of users to detect anomalies, and predict potential attacks before they occur. This proactive approach enhances the ability to prevent or minimize the impact of cyber-attacks.

Additionally, the use of behavioral analytics has gained prominence in cybersecurity. By analyzing user behavior, organizations can identify deviations from normal patterns and detect insider threats or compromised accounts. Behavioral analytics systems employ machine learning algorithms to establish baseline behavior for individual users and detect any deviations that may indicate suspicious activity. This approach enables organizations to identify potential threats that may bypass traditional security measures and respond swiftly.

Furthermore, the rise of cloud computing has transformed the way organizations approach cybersecurity. Cloud-based security solutions offer scalability, flexibility, and cost-efficiency, making them an attractive option for businesses of all sizes. These solutions provide centralized management and continuous monitoring capabilities, allowing organizations to detect and respond to threats more effectively. Cloud-based security also enables rapid deployment of security updates and patches, ensuring that systems are protected against the latest vulnerabilities.

Another significant trend is the advancement of secure hardware and firmware technologies. Hardware security modules (HSMs) and trusted platform modules (TPMs) are becoming increasingly prevalent in safeguarding critical systems. These technologies provide secure storage, cryptographic operations, and authentication mechanisms that protect against firmware-level attacks and ensure the integrity of critical components. Secure boot processes, secure enclaves, and hardware-based encryption are additional examples of innovative approaches that enhance cybersecurity.

The Internet of Things (IoT) is another area that demands attention in the innovation landscape of cybersecurity. As IoT devices become more prevalent, they introduce new entry points for cyber-attacks. Ensuring the security of IoT devices and networks is crucial to protect against potential breaches. Innovations in IoT security include robust authentication mechanisms, secure firmware updates, and encryption protocols specifically designed for IoT environments. For example, implementing strong access controls and regular security updates for IoT devices can mitigate the risk of unauthorized access and compromised networks.

Moreover, the advent of 5G technology presents both opportunities and challenges in the realm of cybersecurity. With faster network speeds and increased connectivity, 5G enables new applications and services but also expands the attack surface. As organizations adopt 5G networks, they must consider the unique security requirements associated with this technology. Innovations in 5G security involve implementing strong encryption, robust authentication mechanisms, and secure network segmentation to mitigate the risks introduced by the increased connectivity.

Additionally, the convergence of operational technology (OT) and information technology (IT) systems poses unique challenges in cybersecurity. As OT systems become more interconnected with IT networks, they become vulnerable to cyber-attacks that can disrupt critical infrastructure. Innovations in securing OT systems include implementing network segmentation, leveraging anomaly detection for industrial control systems, and adopting advanced encryption protocols to protect data in transit.

Furthermore, the rise of quantum computing introduces both opportunities and threats to cybersecurity. Quantum computers have the potential to break traditional encryption algorithms, necessitating the development of quantum-resistant encryption methods. Innovations in quantum cryptography, such as quantum key distribution (QKD), enable the secure exchange of encryption keys using the principles of quantum mechanics. By leveraging quantum technology, organizations can ensure the confidentiality and integrity of sensitive information in a post-quantum computing era.

In conclusion, Section 1 highlights the key trends and innovations shaping the cybersecurity landscape. From the integration of AI and ML algorithms to the rise of cloud-based security solutions, secure hardware technologies, IoT security measures, and advancements in quantum cryptography, organizations must stay at the forefront of these developments to deter and mitigate cyber-attacks effectively. By embracing these trends and leveraging innovative solutions, businesses and individuals can enhance their cybersecurity defenses and safeguard their digital assets in an evolving threat landscape.

Innovations on the Horizon: AI, Machine Learning, Quantum Cryptography

In Section 2 of Chapter 12, we explore the exciting innovations on the horizon in the field of cybersecurity, specifically focusing on the potential of artificial intelligence (AI), machine learning (ML), and quantum cryptography to transform the way we protect digital systems and data.

Artificial intelligence and machine learning technologies have emerged as powerful tools in combating cyber threats. AI and ML algorithms have the capability to analyze vast amounts of data, detect patterns, and learn from past incidents to identify and respond to potential cyber-attacks in real-time. They can recognize anomalies in network traffic, flag suspicious user behavior, and detect sophisticated malware that may evade traditional security measures. AI and ML can also assist in automating security processes, such as threat detection, incident response, and vulnerability management, thereby enabling organizations to respond swiftly to emerging threats.

Moreover, the use of AI in threat intelligence has revolutionized the way cybersecurity professionals stay ahead of evolving threats. AI-powered threat intelligence platforms can gather and analyze large volumes of data from various sources, such as security feeds, social media, and dark web monitoring. By processing and correlating this data, AI algorithms can identify emerging threats, detect patterns, and provide actionable insights to proactively defend against potential cyber-attacks. For example, AI-driven threat intelligence platforms can identify new malware variants, predict attack trends, and provide early warning indicators to security teams.

Machine learning algorithms also play a significant role in anomaly detection, which involves identifying deviations from normal patterns of behavior in network traffic, user activities, or system configurations. By establishing baselines of normal behavior, machine learning models can detect abnormal activities that may indicate unauthorized access, insider threats, or compromised accounts. This proactive approach enables organizations to detect and respond to potential security breaches before they cause significant damage. For instance, machine learning algorithms can identify unusual data access patterns or unusual transaction behavior, enabling financial institutions to prevent fraud and protect customer assets.

Another area of innovation in cybersecurity is quantum cryptography, which leverages the principles of quantum mechanics to ensure secure communication and data protection. Quantum cryptography offers unparalleled levels of security by exploiting the fundamental properties of quantum particles, such as entanglement and superposition. One of the most promising applications of quantum cryptography is quantum key distribution (QKD), which enables the secure exchange of encryption keys between two parties. The inherent properties of quantum physics guarantee the secrecy of the encryption keys, making it virtually impossible for attackers to intercept or decrypt the transmitted data.

Quantum cryptography has the potential to revolutionize secure communications by making encryption algorithms resistant to attacks from quantum computers. As quantum computers advance, traditional encryption methods may become vulnerable, posing a significant risk to sensitive data. However, with quantum cryptography, organizations can ensure that their data remains secure even in the face of quantum computing power. For example, financial institutions can use quantum key distribution to protect financial transactions and safeguard customer information against future threats posed by quantum computers.

Furthermore, advancements in post-quantum cryptography are being explored to develop encryption algorithms that can withstand attacks from both classical and quantum computers. These new algorithms are designed to be resistant to quantum computing algorithms, providing long-term security for sensitive data. The development of post-quantum cryptography is crucial for ensuring the protection of critical information in a future where quantum computers become more prevalent.

In conclusion, Section 2 highlights the potential of AI, machine learning, and quantum cryptography as transformative innovations in the field of cybersecurity. These technologies offer new opportunities to detect and respond to cyber threats in real-time, automate security processes, and protect sensitive information. By harnessing the power of AI and ML, organizations can enhance their threat detection capabilities, while quantum cryptography provides a future-proof solution to secure communications in the age of quantum computing. By embracing these innovations, businesses and individuals can stay ahead of evolving cyber threats and maintain a robust cybersecurity posture in the digital age.

Seizing Opportunities: How Proactivity Can Deter Cyber-attacks

Section 3 of Chapter 12 delves into the importance of proactivity in deterring cyber-attacks. It explores the strategies, practices, and technologies that organizations can implement to take a proactive stance against cyber threats, rather than relying solely on reactive measures.

In today's rapidly evolving threat landscape, organizations face sophisticated and persistent cyber-attacks. Reactive approaches, such as incident response and mitigation, are essential but may not be sufficient to counter the ever-growing threats. By embracing a proactive mindset, organizations can stay one step ahead of cybercriminals and significantly enhance their cybersecurity posture.

One key aspect of proactive cybersecurity is continuous monitoring and threat intelligence. Organizations should implement robust monitoring systems to detect and analyze potential threats in real-time. This includes monitoring network traffic, system logs, and user activities to identify anomalies, suspicious patterns, or indicators of compromise. By continuously monitoring their digital environments, organizations can proactively identify and respond to potential threats before they escalate into major security incidents.

Threat intelligence plays a critical role in proactive cybersecurity. It involves gathering, analyzing, and sharing information about potential threats, vulnerabilities, and emerging attack techniques. Organizations can subscribe to threat intelligence feeds, participate in information-sharing platforms, and collaborate with industry peers to gain insights into the latest threats and proactive defense strategies. By staying informed about evolving threats, organizations can adjust their security measures and develop proactive defenses against known and emerging cyber risks.

Moreover, proactive organizations invest in robust vulnerability management programs. They regularly assess their systems, applications, and infrastructure for vulnerabilities, leveraging automated scanning tools and manual assessments. By identifying and patching vulnerabilities promptly, organizations can prevent potential exploitation by cybercriminals. Additionally, proactive vulnerability management includes a comprehensive approach that involves secure coding practices, regular security updates, and continuous security testing to maintain a strong security posture.

Employee training and awareness are integral components of proactive cybersecurity. Organizations should educate their workforce on best security practices, safe online behavior, and the potential risks associated with cyber threats such as phishing, social engineering, and ransomware. By fostering a security-conscious culture and providing ongoing training, organizations empower employees to be vigilant and proactive in identifying and reporting potential security incidents.

Another proactive strategy is the implementation of proactive threat hunting. This involves actively searching for signs of compromise or indicators of an ongoing attack within the organization's network and systems. Proactive threat hunting can uncover advanced threats that may bypass traditional security measures, allowing organizations to identify and neutralize them before significant damage occurs. By leveraging advanced analytics, machine learning, and behavioral analytics, organizations can proactively hunt for threats and prevent potential breaches.

Furthermore, organizations can embrace advanced technologies like deception techniques and honeypots as proactive measures. Deception technologies involve deploying decoy assets and luring cybercriminals into an isolated environment where their activities can be closely monitored.

Honeypots, for example, are designed to attract and deceive attackers, giving organizations valuable insights into their tactics, techniques, and intentions. By proactively deploying deception technologies, organizations can gain early visibility into potential threats and gather intelligence to fortify their defenses.

In addition to technological measures, proactive cybersecurity also involves building strong relationships and partnerships with external entities. Collaboration with industry peers, government agencies, and cybersecurity organizations can provide valuable insights, threat intelligence, and support during security incidents. By sharing information and collaborating with trusted partners, organizations can enhance their collective defense capabilities and proactively respond to emerging threats.

It is worth mentioning that proactivity in cybersecurity extends beyond organizations and encompasses individuals as well. Personal financial protection is a prime example of how individuals can take proactive steps to deter cyber-attacks. This includes regularly monitoring financial accounts, using strong and unique passwords, enabling multifactor authentication, being cautious of phishing emails and suspicious websites, and keeping software and devices up to date with the latest security patches. By adopting proactive security practices, individuals can protect their personal finances and reduce the risk of falling victim to cybercriminals.

In conclusion, Section 3 highlights the significance of proactive cybersecurity measures in deterring cyber-attacks. By continuously monitoring threats, leveraging threat intelligence, managing vulnerabilities, training employees, adopting advanced technologies, and fostering collaboration, organizations can proactively defend against cyber threats and maintain a robust security posture. Proactivity empowers organizations and individuals to anticipate and mitigate potential risks, ensuring a safer digital environment for all.

Innovative Use Cases: Blockchain Applications in Cybersecurity

Section 4 of Chapter 12 explores the innovative use cases of blockchain technology in cybersecurity. It delves into how blockchain can revolutionize various aspects of cybersecurity, including identity management, secure data sharing, threat intelligence, and tamper-proof auditing.

Blockchain, a decentralized and immutable distributed ledger, offers unique capabilities that can enhance cybersecurity by providing transparency, immutability, and enhanced data integrity. Its decentralized nature eliminates the reliance on a single central authority, making it difficult for malicious actors to manipulate or compromise data stored on the blockchain.

One of the significant use cases of blockchain in cybersecurity is identity management. Traditional identity systems often face challenges such as identity theft, data breaches, and lack of interoperability. Blockchain-based identity management solutions provide a decentralized and secure framework for managing digital identities. Individuals can have greater control over their personal information, and organizations can verify identities more efficiently, reducing the risk of unauthorized access and identity fraud.

For example, Sovrin, an open-source blockchain-based identity platform, enables individuals to create and manage their self-sovereign identities. It leverages blockchain's transparency and cryptographic features to ensure the integrity and privacy of identity data. Users have control over their digital identities and can selectively disclose information as needed, enhancing privacy and security.

Another area where blockchain can have a transformative impact is in secure data sharing. Traditional data sharing methods often involve central authorities or intermediaries, which can introduce vulnerabilities and single points of failure. Blockchain offers a decentralized and secure platform for sharing sensitive data, enabling direct peer-to-peer transactions and verifiable data exchange.

Medical and healthcare records provide an excellent example of blockchain-based secure data sharing. By leveraging blockchain, medical data can be stored in a tamper-proof and transparent manner, accessible to authorized healthcare providers. Patients have control over their data and can grant permission for specific healthcare professionals to access their medical history securely. This reduces the risk of data breaches, ensures data integrity, and improves the overall efficiency of healthcare delivery.

Threat intelligence is another area where blockchain can play a crucial role. Traditional threat intelligence sharing often faces challenges such as trust, attribution, and data integrity. Blockchain can provide a secure and transparent platform for sharing threat intelligence among organizations and cybersecurity practitioners.

For instance, the MISP (Malware Information-Sharing Platform) project utilizes blockchain technology to facilitate secure threat intelligence sharing. MISP leverages blockchain's distributed ledger to record and verify threat intelligence information, enabling real-time collaboration and more effective response to emerging threats. By sharing verified and tamper-proof threat intelligence, organizations can proactively protect their networks and systems against known threats.

Furthermore, blockchain can offer tamper-proof auditing and compliance capabilities. The decentralized and transparent nature of blockchain allows for the creation of an immutable audit trail, ensuring the integrity and verifiability of digital records. This can be particularly valuable in industries with strict regulatory requirements, such as financial services and supply chain management.

An example of blockchain-based auditing is demonstrated in the financial sector. By using blockchain technology, financial transactions can be recorded on an immutable ledger, providing transparency and traceability. Auditors can access the blockchain to verify transaction records and ensure compliance with regulations. This not only simplifies the auditing process but also enhances the trust and integrity of financial systems.

Moreover, blockchain-based smart contracts can enhance cybersecurity by automating and enforcing secure digital agreements. Smart contracts are self-executing contracts with the terms of the agreement directly written into code. They can automate processes, eliminate the need for intermediaries, and provide transparent and auditable transactions.

For example, in supply chain management, smart contracts can ensure the authenticity and integrity of products throughout the supply chain. By recording the origin, production, and movement of goods on the blockchain, smart contracts can verify the authenticity of products and prevent counterfeit or tampered goods from entering the supply chain.

In conclusion, Section 4 highlights the innovative use cases of blockchain technology in cybersecurity. From identity management and secure data sharing to threat intelligence and tamper-proof auditing, blockchain offers unique capabilities that enhance trust, transparency, and data integrity. Real-world examples such as Sovrin for identity management, MISP for threat intelligence sharing, and smart contracts in supply chain management demonstrate the potential of blockchain to revolutionize cybersecurity practices. By embracing these innovative applications, organizations can enhance their cybersecurity defenses, reduce vulnerabilities, and build more secure and resilient digital ecosystems.

The Road Ahead: Navigating the Future of Cybersecurity Innovation

Section 5 of Chapter 12 explores the future of cybersecurity innovation and the challenges and opportunities that lie ahead. It focuses on the emerging trends, technologies, and strategies that will shape the future landscape of cybersecurity.

The ever-evolving nature of cyber threats necessitates continuous innovation in cybersecurity. As attackers become more sophisticated, organizations and cybersecurity professionals must stay ahead by adopting proactive and adaptive approaches. This section discusses key areas of innovation that will play a crucial role in the future of cybersecurity.

One of the significant trends in cybersecurity innovation is the integration of artificial intelligence (AI) and machine learning (ML). AI and ML have the potential to revolutionize cybersecurity by enabling intelligent automation, real-time threat detection, and adaptive defense mechanisms.

By leveraging AI and ML algorithms, cybersecurity systems can analyze vast amounts of data, identify patterns, and detect anomalies in real-time. This enables organizations to respond swiftly to emerging threats and take proactive measures to mitigate risks. For example, AI-powered security analytics platforms can automatically identify suspicious activities, prioritize alerts, and provide actionable insights to security teams, enabling more efficient and effective incident response.

Another area of innovation is the use of quantum cryptography. As quantum computing continues to advance, it poses both challenges and opportunities for cybersecurity. Quantum cryptography leverages the principles of quantum mechanics to develop encryption methods that are theoretically impossible to break.

Quantum key distribution (QKD) is an example of quantum cryptography that enables the secure exchange of encryption keys between two parties. QKD relies on the fundamental properties of quantum mechanics to establish secure communication channels. This technology has the potential to strengthen encryption methods and protect sensitive data against future quantum attacks.

However, it is essential to note that quantum cryptography is still in its early stages of development and practical implementation. Research and innovation in this field are crucial to address the challenges and limitations associated with quantum cryptography and ensure its viability as a cybersecurity solution.

In addition to technological innovations, proactive strategies will play a vital role in deterring cyber-attacks in the future. Organizations and individuals must adopt a proactive mindset and take preemptive measures to prevent cyber threats before they occur.

One such strategy is threat hunting, which involves actively searching for signs of potential threats within an organization's networks and systems. By leveraging advanced threat intelligence, analytics tools, and expert knowledge, organizations can proactively identify and neutralize potential threats, thereby minimizing the likelihood and impact of cyber-attacks.

Another proactive approach is implementing robust security awareness and training programs. Educating employees and individuals about cybersecurity best practices, safe online behavior, and the latest threats can significantly reduce the risk of successful attacks. This includes raising awareness about social engineering techniques, phishing attacks, and the importance of strong passwords and multifactor authentication.

Furthermore, organizations must embrace a culture of cybersecurity and implement a strong security posture across all levels of the organization. This includes regular security assessments, vulnerability management, and adherence to industry best practices and standards.

An example of a proactive cybersecurity strategy is the implementation of a "zero-trust" approach. In a zero-trust model, all users, devices, and applications are treated as potentially untrusted and must be authenticated and authorized before accessing resources. This approach assumes that attackers can be present both inside and outside the network perimeter, and continuously verifies trust throughout the user's session.

Looking ahead, the role of public-private partnerships will become increasingly important in driving cybersecurity innovation and fostering collaboration between various stakeholders. Governments, private sector organizations, academia, and research institutions must work together to address the evolving cyber threat landscape and share knowledge, resources, and expertise.

Moreover, the integration of blockchain technology into cybersecurity practices will continue to be explored. Blockchain's inherent characteristics, such as decentralization, immutability, and transparency, can enhance trust, data integrity, and secure transactions in various cybersecurity applications.

For example, blockchain-based threat intelligence platforms can facilitate secure and decentralized sharing of threat information among organizations, enabling rapid response to emerging threats. Blockchain can also enhance the integrity of digital certificates and ensure the authenticity of software and firmware updates, mitigating the risk of supply chain attacks.

In conclusion, Section 5 highlights the road ahead in cybersecurity innovation. The integration of AI, ML, quantum cryptography, and proactive strategies will shape the future of cybersecurity defense. Embracing a proactive mindset, adopting emerging technologies, and fostering collaboration among stakeholders will be key to staying ahead of cyber threats. Furthermore, the continued exploration of blockchain technology and the establishment of public-private partnerships will drive innovation and strengthen the cybersecurity ecosystem. By navigating these paths, organizations and individuals can better deter cyber-attacks and create a more secure digital future.

13
The Aftermath: Predicting Future Needs Post-Cyber Pandemic

Post-Pandemic Scenarios: Understanding Possible Outcomes

Section 1 of Chapter 13 delves into the diverse range of scenarios that may unfold in the aftermath of a cyber pandemic. It explores the potential outcomes that organizations and governments might face and analyzes the implications for cybersecurity. By comprehending these scenarios, stakeholders can effectively prepare for the challenges and opportunities that lie ahead, enabling them to proactively respond and recover.

In the wake of a cyber pandemic, the consequences can be far-reaching and multifaceted, affecting various aspects of society, economy, and governance. Organizations may suffer financial losses, reputational damage, operational disruptions, and compromised data integrity. Governments may encounter difficulties in protecting national security, ensuring citizen privacy, and maintaining trust in digital systems. Understanding the potential post-pandemic scenarios is crucial for devising effective strategies to mitigate risks, enhance resilience, and facilitate recovery.

One plausible scenario that may emerge is an increased emphasis on cybersecurity regulations and compliance. Recognizing the devastating impact of a cyber pandemic, governments may enact stricter regulations to safeguard critical infrastructure, protect sensitive data, and elevate cybersecurity measures across sectors. This could involve the implementation of stringent cybersecurity standards, mandatory incident reporting, and periodic audits to ensure compliance. Organizations would need to adapt swiftly to these new regulations, investing in robust cybersecurity frameworks and capabilities to meet the heightened requirements and demonstrate their commitment to safeguarding data and systems.

Another potential scenario is a paradigm shift toward greater collaboration and information sharing. In the aftermath of a cyber pandemic, organizations and governments may come to the realization that collective defense and collaborative efforts are paramount in combating sophisticated cyber threats. Information-sharing platforms and initiatives could be established to facilitate the exchange of threat intelligence, best practices, and lessons learned. Public-private partnerships may be strengthened, fostering collaboration between government entities, industry stakeholders, and cybersecurity professionals to pool resources, expertise, and technological advancements, thereby enhancing the overall cybersecurity resilience.

Furthermore, the emergence of new technologies and innovative solutions is another conceivable scenario. A cyber pandemic could serve as a catalyst for accelerated technological advancements in cybersecurity. Artificial intelligence (AI), machine learning, quantum cryptography, and blockchain are examples of technologies that could be further developed and deployed to fortify cybersecurity defenses. For instance, AI-powered threat detection systems can analyze vast amounts of data in real-time, enabling the identification and response to cyber threats with greater efficiency and accuracy. Quantum cryptography could provide a more secure framework for data encryption, resistant to quantum attacks. Blockchain technology, with its decentralized and immutable nature, can enhance the security and integrity of critical systems, ensuring tamper-proof transactions, identity management, and data sharing.

Furthermore, an increased focus on cybersecurity awareness and education is another post-pandemic scenario that is likely to unfold. As organizations and individuals become more aware of the risks and potential consequences of cyber-attacks, there is a growing recognition of the need for cybersecurity literacy. Governments and educational institutions may prioritize cybersecurity education and training programs, equipping individuals with the knowledge and skills to protect themselves and contribute to a more secure digital ecosystem. Cybersecurity awareness campaigns may be launched to raise public consciousness and encourage safe online practices, emphasizing the importance of strong passwords, regular software updates, and cautious behavior in the digital realm.

To illustrate the potential outcomes in the post-pandemic landscape, let's consider an example in the financial sector. A cyber pandemic targeting financial institutions could result in significant financial losses, compromised customer data, and erosion of trust. In response to this scenario, governments may enact stringent regulations and compliance standards, mandating financial organizations to implement robust cybersecurity measures, conduct regular vulnerability assessments, and protect customer privacy. Financial institutions may invest in advanced technologies such as AI-driven fraud detection systems, blockchain-based identity verification, and secure payment networks to fortify their defenses. They may also foster partnerships with cybersecurity firms and share threat intelligence within the industry to collectively defend against emerging threats.

In conclusion, Section 1 emphasizes the significance of comprehending the potential post-pandemic scenarios and their implications for cybersecurity. By anticipating these scenarios, organizations and governments can proactively prepare for the challenges and seize opportunities to enhance their cybersecurity resilience. This includes embracing cybersecurity regulations, fostering collaboration and information sharing, leveraging emerging technologies, and prioritizing cybersecurity awareness and education. By doing so, stakeholders can effectively navigate the aftermath of a cyber pandemic, protect critical systems and data, and contribute to a more secure and resilient digital ecosystem.

Lessons Learned: Extracting Insights from Past Cyber-attacks

Section 2 of Chapter 13 delves into the importance of extracting insights and lessons from past cyber-attacks. By thoroughly analyzing these incidents, organizations and governments can gain a deeper understanding of the evolving threat landscape, identify vulnerabilities, and enhance their cybersecurity practices. This section emphasizes the significance of post-attack analysis and provides an expanded view of the key learnings and their practical applications.

In the aftermath of a cyberattack, conducting a comprehensive analysis is crucial for uncovering the intricacies of the attack, understanding the tactics employed by threat actors, and evaluating the impact on affected systems and data. This analysis serves as a foundation for extracting valuable insights that can drive proactive cybersecurity measures. By examining past attacks, organizations can identify common patterns, trends, and techniques used by cybercriminals, empowering them to fortify their defenses and proactively address potential vulnerabilities.

One of the key learnings from past cyber-attacks is the criticality of timely and effective incident response. Organizations must have robust incident response plans and capabilities in place to swiftly detect, contain, and mitigate the impact of an attack. Examining past incidents enables organizations to assess the effectiveness of their incident response efforts, including the coordination among various teams, communication strategies, and decision-making processes. By identifying successful incident response practices and applying them to their own frameworks, organizations can enhance their response capabilities and minimize the impact of future attacks.

Additionally, past cyber-attacks highlight the pivotal role of employee awareness and training in maintaining cybersecurity resilience. Human error and social engineering tactics often contribute to the success of cyber-attacks. By analyzing past incidents, organizations can gain insights into the specific vulnerabilities exploited through human interactions and tailor their awareness and training programs accordingly. This includes educating employees about common attack vectors, phishing techniques, secure password management, and the importance of reporting suspicious activities. By fostering a culture of cybersecurity awareness, organizations can empower their workforce to act as a strong line of defense against cyber threats.

Furthermore, past cyber-attacks emphasize the necessity of robust vulnerability management. Many attacks exploit known vulnerabilities in software or systems that organizations have failed to patch or update. Analyzing past incidents helps organizations identify common vulnerabilities that have been targeted and prioritize their patching and mitigation efforts accordingly. By implementing proactive vulnerability scanning, conducting regular security assessments, and staying informed about emerging threats, organizations can address vulnerabilities before they can be exploited by threat actors. This proactive approach to vulnerability management significantly reduces the risk of successful attacks.

Moreover, past cyber-attacks underscore the significance of information sharing and collaboration within the cybersecurity community. Threat intelligence sharing platforms, public-private partnerships, and industry-specific forums play a vital role in disseminating information about new threats, attack trends, and defensive strategies. By actively participating in these collaborative efforts, organizations can stay ahead of emerging threats, learn from the experiences of others, and collectively contribute to a more resilient cybersecurity ecosystem. Sharing information about attack vectors, indicators of compromise, and effective mitigation techniques enables organizations to proactively defend against evolving threats and adapt their cybersecurity strategies accordingly.

To illustrate the practical application of these lessons, let's consider a real-world example. The WannaCry ransomware attack in 2017 infected hundreds of thousands of computers worldwide, exploiting a vulnerability in outdated versions of the Windows operating system. This incident highlighted the importance of timely patch management and software updates.

Organizations that promptly applied the available security patch were able to mitigate the risk and prevent infection. The WannaCry attack served as a wake-up call for organizations to prioritize vulnerability management and ensure that their systems are regularly updated with the latest security patches.

Additionally, the analysis of past cyber-attacks can provide valuable insights into the evolving threat landscape, including the emergence of new attack vectors and the evolving techniques employed by threat actors. For example, the rise of ransomware attacks targeting healthcare organizations during the COVID-19 pandemic demonstrated the adaptability of cybercriminals in exploiting global crises for financial gain. Understanding these emerging trends allows organizations to anticipate and prepare for future threats, enhancing their cybersecurity posture and resilience.

Furthermore, the analysis of past cyber-attacks can inform the development of innovative defensive strategies and technologies. For instance, the use of artificial intelligence (AI) and machine learning (ML) in threat detection and response has gained traction as a result of insights derived from past attacks. By analyzing large volumes of data and identifying patterns and anomalies, AI and ML algorithms can enhance the speed and accuracy of threat detection, enabling organizations to respond proactively to potential threats.

In conclusion, Section 2 emphasizes the significance of extracting insights and lessons from past cyber-attacks. By analyzing incident response efforts, improving employee awareness and training, strengthening vulnerability management practices, and fostering collaboration, organizations and governments can enhance their cybersecurity posture. The lessons learned from past incidents provide valuable guidance for proactively addressing emerging threats, improving incident response capabilities, and fortifying defenses. By leveraging these insights, stakeholders can stay ahead of evolving cyber threats and contribute to a more secure digital landscape. The continuous analysis of past cyber-attacks allows organizations to adapt and innovate their cybersecurity strategies, harnessing the power of technology and collaboration to mitigate future risks.

The Changing Needs: How Cybersecurity Requirements Will Evolve

Section 3 of Chapter 13 delves into the evolving cybersecurity landscape and explores how the needs and requirements for effective cybersecurity measures are changing. As technology advances, threat actors become more sophisticated, and new vulnerabilities emerge, organizations and governments must adapt their cybersecurity strategies to meet the evolving challenges. This section emphasizes the importance of staying proactive and outlines key areas where cybersecurity requirements are expected to evolve.

1. **Enhanced Threat Detection and Response:**
   As cyber threats become more sophisticated and difficult to detect, organizations need to invest in advanced threat detection and response capabilities. Traditional signature-based methods are no longer sufficient, and organizations must embrace technologies such as artificial intelligence (AI) and machine learning (ML) to analyze vast amounts of data and identify patterns indicative of malicious activities. These technologies can enhance the speed and accuracy of threat detection, enabling organizations to respond promptly and effectively.

2. **Proactive Vulnerability Management:**
   In an ever-changing threat landscape, proactive vulnerability management is essential. Organizations should implement continuous vulnerability scanning, conduct regular security assessments, and prioritize patch management to address vulnerabilities before they can be exploited. By adopting a proactive approach to vulnerability management, organizations can reduce the attack surface and minimize the risk of successful cyber-attacks.

3. **Emphasis on Identity and Access Management:**
   As more organizations adopt cloud-based services and remote work becomes more prevalent, identity and access management (IAM) becomes increasingly critical. Organizations need to implement robust IAM systems that ensure secure authentication, authorization, and access controls. Multifactor authentication, privileged access management, and role-based access control are some of the key components of an effective IAM strategy.

4. **Privacy and Data Protection:**
   With the proliferation of data breaches and increasing concerns about privacy, organizations and governments must prioritize privacy and data protection. Compliance with data protection regulations, such as the General Data Protection Regulation (GDPR), is essential. Encryption, data anonymization, and data classification are key measures to protect sensitive information and ensure compliance with privacy regulations.

5. **Collaboration and Information Sharing:**
   In an interconnected world, collaboration and information sharing are crucial to combating cyber threats effectively. Organizations and governments must establish robust partnerships and platforms for sharing threat intelligence, best practices, and lessons learned. Public-private partnerships, sector-specific information sharing and analysis centers (ISACs), and international alliances foster collaboration and enable the rapid exchange of information to strengthen collective defenses.

6. **Cybersecurity Workforce Development:**
   As the demand for cybersecurity professionals continues to outpace supply, organizations and governments must invest in workforce development and training programs. This includes initiatives to attract and retain talent, upskill existing employees, and promote cybersecurity education in academic institutions. By nurturing a skilled cybersecurity workforce, organizations can build a strong defense against cyber threats.

7. **Resilience and Incident Response:**
   Given the inevitability of cyber-attacks, organizations must focus on resilience and incident response. Incident response plans should be regularly tested and updated to address emerging threats. Cybersecurity drills, tabletop exercises, and red teaming activities can help identify gaps in incident response capabilities and improve the effectiveness of response efforts.

8. **Embracing Emerging Technologies:**
   Emerging technologies such as blockchain, quantum computing, and secure hardware offer new opportunities and challenges in cybersecurity. Blockchain can enhance data integrity and enable secure transactions, while quantum computing has the potential to break existing encryption algorithms and necessitates the development of quantum-resistant cryptography. Organizations and governments must monitor these technologies' progress, assess their implications for cybersecurity, and adapt their strategies accordingly.

To illustrate the changing cybersecurity needs, let's consider the example of personal financial protection. With the rise of digital banking and online transactions, individuals face an increasing risk of financial fraud and identity theft. As a result, cybersecurity requirements for personal financial protection are evolving. Individuals now need to adopt strong authentication methods, such as biometrics or hardware tokens, to secure their financial accounts. They should also be vigilant about phishing scams, regularly monitor their financial statements, and use secure and up-to-date devices for online banking. Financial institutions, on the other hand, must invest in robust security measures, such as transaction monitoring systems, anomaly detection, and customer awareness programs, to protect their customers' financial information.

In conclusion, Section 3 highlights the changing cybersecurity needs and requirements organizations and governments must address to stay ahead of evolving threats. By enhancing threat detection and response capabilities, adopting proactive vulnerability management practices, prioritizing identity and access management, emphasizing privacy and data protection, fostering collaboration and information sharing, developing the cybersecurity workforce, focusing on resilience and incident response, and embracing emerging technologies, stakeholders can adapt to the evolving cybersecurity landscape. By being proactive and staying abreast of emerging trends, organizations and governments can effectively mitigate cyber risks and protect their digital assets and sensitive information.

Case Study: An In-depth Look at Post-Pandemic Cybersecurity Efforts

Section 4 of Chapter 13 provides an in-depth case study that examines the cybersecurity efforts implemented in the aftermath of a major cyber pandemic. This case study sheds light on the strategies, initiatives, and lessons learned from a real-world cyberattack scenario, offering valuable insights into the post-pandemic cybersecurity landscape.

1. **Background:**
   The case study begins by setting the context and describing the nature and impact of the cyber pandemic. It provides an overview of the affected organization or nation, the extent of the damage caused by the cyberattack, and the specific vulnerabilities exploited by the threat actors. This background information helps to understand the magnitude of the incident and the subsequent cybersecurity response.

2. **Immediate Response:**
   The case study explores the immediate response to the cyber pandemic, focusing on the steps taken to mitigate the attack, contain the damage, and restore essential services. It discusses the incident response plan activated by the affected organization or nation, the coordination of response efforts among various stakeholders, and the allocation of resources to address the immediate cybersecurity challenges. The case study highlights the importance of swift and decisive action in minimizing the impact of the cyberattack.

3. **Analysis and Investigation:**
   Following the initial response, the case study delves into the analysis and investigation phase, where forensic experts and cybersecurity professionals examine the attack vectors, identify the root cause of the breach, and assess the impact on critical systems and data. It explores

the tools and techniques employed to gather evidence, trace the activities of the threat actors, and determine the extent of the compromise. The case study underscores the significance of thorough investigation to prevent future attacks and hold the perpetrators accountable.

4. **Remediation and Recovery:**
   Once the analysis is complete, the case study explores the remediation and recovery efforts undertaken to restore normalcy and enhance cybersecurity resilience. It discusses the implementation of security controls, patching of vulnerabilities, and strengthening of defenses to prevent similar incidents in the future. The case study also examines the recovery of affected systems and data, including the restoration of backups, the implementation of robust data recovery processes, and the validation of restored services. It emphasizes the importance of a comprehensive and well-executed recovery plan.

5. **Lessons Learned:**
   A crucial aspect of the case study is the identification and documentation of lessons learned from the cyber pandemic. It examines the shortcomings and vulnerabilities exposed by the attack, the gaps in the organization's or nation's cybersecurity posture, and the areas for improvement in incident response and recovery capabilities. The case study highlights the significance of incorporating these lessons into future cybersecurity strategies and resilience planning.

6. **Strengthening Resilience:**
   Based on the lessons learned, the case study explores the measures taken to strengthen cybersecurity resilience in the post-pandemic period. It discusses the implementation of enhanced security controls, the establishment of threat intelligence sharing networks, the adoption of best practices, and the fostering of public-private partnerships. The case study emphasizes the importance of a proactive and collaborative approach to cybersecurity to prevent future cyber pandemics.

7. **Continuous Monitoring and Adaptation:**
   The case study concludes by highlighting the importance of continuous monitoring, evaluation, and adaptation of cybersecurity measures. It emphasizes the need for ongoing risk assessments, regular security audits, and proactive threat hunting to detect and respond to emerging threats. The case study also emphasizes the significance of staying abreast of evolving technologies and threat landscapes to ensure the effectiveness of cybersecurity defenses.

To provide a concrete example, let's consider a case study of a financial institution that suffered a major cyber pandemic resulting in a data breach compromising customer financial information. In response, the institution immediately activated its incident response plan, isolated affected systems, and notified regulatory authorities and affected customers. Forensic experts conducted a thorough investigation to determine the extent of the breach and identified the vulnerabilities that were exploited. The institution then implemented multifactor authentication, encryption, and enhanced security monitoring to prevent future incidents. It also collaborated with other financial institutions to share threat intelligence and establish industry-wide cybersecurity standards.

In conclusion, Section 4's case study sheds light on the post-pandemic cybersecurity efforts and provides valuable insights into the strategies and lessons learned from a real-world cyberattack scenario. It emphasizes the importance of a well-coordinated response, thorough investigation, remediation and recovery efforts, identification of lessons learned, strengthening of resilience, continuous monitoring, and adaptation. By studying such case studies, organizations and governments can enhance their cybersecurity strategies and effectively respond to and recover from cyber pandemics.

Blockchain in Post-Pandemic Recovery: Opportunities and Challenges

Section 5 of Chapter 13 explores in-depth the opportunities and challenges associated with the adoption of blockchain technology in the post-pandemic recovery phase of cybersecurity. It delves into the various ways blockchain can contribute to enhancing security, trust, and resilience in the digital ecosystem, while also addressing the potential hurdles and considerations that organizations and governments may encounter.

1. **Introduction to Blockchain:**
   To provide a solid foundation, this section begins with an in-depth introduction to blockchain technology. It explains the underlying principles of decentralization, transparency, immutability, and cryptographic security that define blockchain. By emphasizing the distributed nature of blockchain networks and the consensus mechanisms used to validate transactions, readers gain a clear understanding of how blockchain can revolutionize cybersecurity in the post-pandemic era.

2. **Advantages of Blockchain in Post-Pandemic Recovery:**
   This section explores the unique advantages that blockchain brings to the table when applied to post-pandemic recovery efforts. It goes beyond the typical benefits of data security and transparency and delves into the potential for blockchain to enhance supply chain resilience, streamline identity management, and foster decentralized governance. Examples of blockchain applications, such as secure vaccine distribution, contact tracing, and financial transactions, are provided to illustrate the advantages and demonstrate the potential for real-world implementation.

3. **Opportunities for Blockchain in Post-Pandemic Cybersecurity:**
   Building upon the advantages, this section delves into the specific opportunities where blockchain technology can make a significant impact on post-pandemic cybersecurity. It explores the potential for blockchain-based threat intelligence platforms, which enable secure and anonymous sharing of threat data among organizations. It discusses the use of blockchain in securing critical infrastructure, such as smart grids and healthcare systems, by providing an immutable record of transactions and enhancing resilience against cyber-attacks. Furthermore, the section examines the potential for blockchain-based authentication and access control systems, which enable secure and decentralized identity management. Real-world case studies and

examples are incorporated to provide concrete illustrations of these opportunities and to inspire innovative thinking.

4. **Challenges and Considerations:**
While highlighting the potential of blockchain in post-pandemic recovery, this section acknowledges the challenges and considerations that must be addressed. It examines the scalability limitations of current blockchain solutions and explores potential solutions and advancements, such as layer 2 solutions and sharding, to overcome these limitations. Additionally, the section delves into the energy consumption concerns related to the consensus mechanisms employed by blockchain networks and discusses the ongoing research and development efforts to improve energy efficiency. The section also explores the legal and regulatory challenges, including data privacy and cross-border data transfer regulations, that organizations and governments need to navigate when implementing blockchain solutions. Moreover, it addresses the importance of interoperability standards and collaboration among different blockchain platforms to ensure seamless integration and data exchange.

5. **Collaboration and Integration:**
Recognizing the collaborative nature of cybersecurity, this section emphasizes the importance of collaboration and integration in fully realizing the potential of blockchain technology in post-pandemic recovery. It highlights the need for public-private partnerships, industry collaboration, and cooperation among organizations to develop standardized blockchain frameworks, address interoperability challenges, and foster the adoption of best practices. Furthermore, the section discusses the integration of blockchain with other emerging technologies, such as artificial intelligence and the Internet of Things, to create synergistic solutions that enhance cybersecurity in the post-pandemic era. It underscores the value of interdisciplinary approaches and encourages stakeholders to explore innovative ways to combine technologies for maximum impact.

6. **Adoption Strategies and Roadmap:**
To guide organizations and governments in their adoption of blockchain in post-pandemic recovery, this section provides strategies and a roadmap for successful implementation. It emphasizes the importance of conducting feasibility studies, evaluating business and security requirements, and identifying suitable use cases for blockchain. It highlights the need for education and skill development to ensure a competent workforce capable of leveraging blockchain technology effectively. The section also advocates for a phased and iterative approach to implementation, starting with smaller-scale projects to gain practical experience and gradually expanding to more complex applications.

In conclusion, Section 5 provides an in-depth exploration of the opportunities and challenges associated with implementing blockchain technology in the post-pandemic recovery phase of cybersecurity. By embracing blockchain and addressing the challenges, organizations and governments can leverage its potential to strengthen security, trust, and resilience in the digital ecosystem. With careful consideration of use cases, collaboration, and integration, blockchain has the power to revolutionize post-pandemic cybersecurity and lay the foundation for a secure and resilient future.

7. **Use Case Examples:**
To further illustrate the potential of blockchain in post-pandemic recovery, this section incorporates additional use case examples that showcase the diverse applications of blockchain technology. These examples highlight how blockchain can be utilized in areas such as healthcare data management, secure supply chain management, digital identity verification, and cybersecurity incident response. For instance, in the healthcare sector, blockchain can enable secure and interoperable sharing of patient data across healthcare providers while ensuring privacy and data integrity. In supply chain management, blockchain can provide end-to-end traceability and transparency, ensuring the authenticity of goods and mitigating the risk of counterfeit products. These use cases not only demonstrate the versatility of blockchain but

also inspire organizations and governments to explore innovative solutions tailored to their specific needs.

8. **Regulatory Considerations and Standardization:**
In discussing the challenges, this section also addresses the importance of regulatory considerations and standardization efforts in the adoption of blockchain for post-pandemic cybersecurity. It highlights the need for governments and regulatory bodies to establish clear guidelines and frameworks that provide legal certainty and address concerns related to data privacy, cybersecurity, and cross-border transactions. Moreover, it emphasizes the significance of industry-wide collaboration and standardization to ensure interoperability and seamless integration between different blockchain solutions. By establishing common standards and regulatory frameworks, stakeholders can navigate the complexities of blockchain adoption more effectively and foster a conducive environment for innovation and collaboration.

9. **Ethical Implications and Trust:**
As with any emerging technology, the ethical implications of blockchain adoption in post-pandemic recovery cannot be overlooked. This section explores the importance of ethics in blockchain implementation and emphasizes the need for responsible and transparent practices. It addresses concerns such as data privacy, consent management, and the ethical use of blockchain in areas like surveillance and social control. By promoting ethical considerations and incorporating privacy-enhancing features, organizations and governments can build trust and ensure that blockchain technology is used in a manner that respects individual rights and societal values.

10. **Research and Development:**
To drive innovation and address the evolving needs of post-pandemic cybersecurity, this section highlights the significance of ongoing research and development efforts. It emphasizes the need for continuous exploration of advanced cryptographic techniques, scalability solutions, privacy-enhancing features, and energy-efficient consensus mechanisms. By investing in research and development, organizations

and governments can stay at the forefront of blockchain technology and unlock new possibilities for enhancing cybersecurity in the post-pandemic era.

11. **Collaboration with the Financial Sector:**
In the context of post-pandemic recovery, collaboration between the cybersecurity sector and the financial sector becomes crucial. This section explores the potential synergies between blockchain technology and the financial industry, highlighting how blockchain-based solutions can enhance financial transactions, secure digital identities, and improve regulatory compliance. Examples include the use of blockchain for secure and transparent financial transactions, decentralized finance (DeFi) applications, and the integration of blockchain into regulatory frameworks to combat financial crimes. By collaborating with the financial sector, the cybersecurity community can leverage the expertise and resources of financial institutions to drive innovation and develop robust cybersecurity solutions.

12. **Public Awareness and Education:**
Recognizing the importance of public awareness and education, this section underscores the need for cybersecurity literacy and blockchain education among individuals and organizations. It highlights the significance of raising awareness about the benefits and risks of blockchain technology, promoting responsible usage, and dispelling misconceptions. By fostering a knowledgeable and informed society, stakeholders can make informed decisions and actively participate in shaping the future of post-pandemic cybersecurity.

In conclusion, Section 5 expands on the opportunities and challenges of adopting blockchain in the post-pandemic recovery phase of cybersecurity. By incorporating use case examples, discussing regulatory considerations, addressing ethical implications, emphasizing research and development, advocating collaboration with the financial sector, and promoting public awareness, the section provides a comprehensive exploration of the potential of blockchain technology. It encourages organizations and governments to embrace blockchain as a transformative tool in enhancing security, trust, and resilience in the post-pandemic digital landscape. With careful consideration, collaboration, and a forward-thinking mindset, blockchain can be a key driver in shaping a secure and resilient future.

14

Conclusion: A Resilient Future in the Face of Cyber Threats

1.Key Takeaways: Reflecting on the Cybersecurity Journey

In Section 1 of Chapter 14, we take a deeper dive into the key takeaways from our exploration of cybersecurity and the role of blockchain technology. Throughout this guide, we have examined the evolving nature of cyber threats, the importance of proactive measures, and the potential of collaboration and innovation in building resilience. Let's further expand on these key takeaways and explore additional insights gained along the way.

First and foremost, our journey has highlighted the ever-growing complexity and sophistication of cyber threats. The digital landscape is constantly evolving, and cybercriminals are continuously finding new ways to exploit vulnerabilities. This underscores the need for a proactive and adaptive approach to cybersecurity. Organizations and individuals must remain vigilant, continuously assess their security posture, and stay informed about emerging threats to effectively protect their digital assets.

One of the important lessons learned is the significance of risk management and risk-based decision-making. Cybersecurity is not a one-size-fits-all approach. Each organization and individual faces unique risks and must tailor their security measures accordingly. Conducting thorough risk assessments, identifying critical assets and vulnerabilities, and implementing appropriate controls are essential to mitigate potential risks.

Collaboration and information sharing have emerged as crucial factors in strengthening cybersecurity. No single entity can tackle cyber threats alone. Public-private partnerships, industry collaborations, and cross-sector cooperation are instrumental in addressing shared challenges. Through information-sharing initiatives, organizations can gain valuable insights into emerging threats, share best practices, and collectively develop more effective defense strategies.

Furthermore, the importance of user education and awareness cannot be overstated. Human error remains a significant factor in cyber incidents. By educating users about common threats, best practices for secure behavior, and the consequences of negligence, we can empower individuals to be active participants in cybersecurity. Regular training programs, simulated phishing exercises, and awareness campaigns can significantly improve the security posture of organizations and individuals.

Another key takeaway is the need for continuous innovation and adaptation in the face of evolving cyber threats. Technology plays a dual role, both as a vulnerability and a solution. Cybersecurity professionals must stay abreast of emerging technologies, such as AI, machine learning, and quantum computing, to leverage their potential in threat detection, incident response, and secure data encryption. However, it is equally important to consider the security implications of these technologies and address any vulnerabilities they may introduce.

Moreover, regulatory frameworks and legal considerations play a critical role in shaping cybersecurity practices. Governments and policymakers must strike a balance between fostering innovation and ensuring the protection of individuals' privacy and data. Data protection regulations, such as the European Union's General Data Protection Regulation (GDPR), are prime examples of efforts to safeguard personal information and hold organizations accountable for their handling of data.

As we reflect on our cybersecurity journey, we can draw inspiration from real-world examples of successful cybersecurity initiatives. For instance, the financial sector has embraced innovative approaches to protect personal financial information. Banks and financial institutions have implemented multifactor authentication, real-time transaction monitoring, and blockchain-based systems to enhance security and protect customer funds. The integration of biometric authentication methods, such as fingerprint or facial recognition, has further strengthened user authentication processes.

Similarly, the healthcare industry has witnessed a surge in cyber-attacks targeting sensitive patient data. Healthcare organizations have responded by investing in secure data storage, encryption protocols, and employee training programs to safeguard patient privacy and ensure the integrity of medical records. They have also adopted robust incident response plans to minimize the impact of cyber incidents and ensure continuity of care.

In conclusion, our exploration of cybersecurity and the role of blockchain technology has provided valuable insights into the evolving threat landscape and the measures needed to build resilience. Key takeaways include the need for a proactive approach, risk-based decision-making, collaboration and information sharing, user education, technological innovation, and regulatory frameworks. By embracing these principles and continuously adapting to emerging challenges, we can navigate the complex cybersecurity landscape and create a more secure digital future.

Furthermore, as we reflect on our cybersecurity journey, it is essential to recognize the significance of education and awareness. Cybersecurity is not solely the responsibility of cybersecurity professionals or IT departments; it is a collective responsibility that extends to all individuals within an organization or society. By promoting cybersecurity awareness and providing training on best practices, organizations can empower their employees to become the first line of defense against cyber threats.

Additionally, the role of governance and policy cannot be underestimated. Governments and regulatory bodies play a crucial role in establishing and enforcing cybersecurity regulations, standards, and frameworks. These policies provide a foundation for organizations to implement effective cybersecurity measures and ensure compliance. Collaboration between governments, industry stakeholders, and cybersecurity experts is vital in shaping these policies to address emerging threats and evolving technologies.

As we envision the future of cybersecurity, it is important to recognize the potential of blockchain technology. Blockchain offers promising solutions in enhancing security, transparency, and trust in digital transactions. Its decentralized and immutable nature makes it a valuable tool for securing critical systems, protecting sensitive data, and verifying the integrity of information. For example, blockchain-based identity management systems can provide individuals with greater control over their personal data while ensuring authentication and preventing identity theft.

Moreover, blockchain can revolutionize supply chain security by enabling end-to-end visibility and traceability. By implementing blockchain in supply chains, organizations can mitigate the risk of counterfeit products, improve transparency, and enhance consumer trust. The use of smart contracts in cybersecurity can also streamline and automate security processes, ensuring compliance and reducing human error.

However, while blockchain holds immense potential, it is not a one-size-fits-all solution. There are challenges and considerations that must be addressed. These include scalability, interoperability, regulatory compliance, and the need for skilled professionals to develop and maintain blockchain-based systems. Overcoming these challenges will require ongoing research, development, and collaboration between industry, academia, and governments.

In conclusion, the journey through this guide has provided valuable insights into the complex world of cybersecurity. We have explored the evolving threat landscape, the importance of proactive measures, the role of collaboration and innovation, and the potential of blockchain technology. As we move forward, it is crucial to remember that cybersecurity is an ongoing process that requires constant vigilance, adaptation, and collaboration.

By reflecting on the key takeaways, embracing a proactive mindset, investing in education and awareness, strengthening governance and policy frameworks, and leveraging the potential of emerging technologies such as blockchain, we can build a resilient future in the face of cyber threats. It is through collective action, cooperation, and continuous improvement that we can navigate the ever-changing cybersecurity landscape and ensure the security and trustworthiness of our digital world. Together, we can forge a path to a safer, more secure, and resilient future.

2. Future Pathways: Imagining the Roadmap to Resilience

In this final section of Chapter 14, we delve into the future pathways that can lead us to a more resilient cybersecurity landscape. As technology continues to advance and cyber threats evolve, it is crucial to envision a roadmap that encompasses both proactive measures and adaptive strategies to stay ahead of potential risks. By exploring new ideas and embracing innovation, we can shape a secure digital future.

1. **Embracing Artificial Intelligence (AI) and Machine Learning (ML):** One of the key pathways to resilience is harnessing the power of AI and ML in cybersecurity. These technologies can revolutionize threat

detection, incident response, and vulnerability management. By leveraging AI and ML algorithms, organizations can analyze vast amounts of data in real-time, detect anomalies, and identify potential threats before they can cause significant damage. For example, AI-powered cybersecurity solutions can detect patterns in network traffic and identify suspicious activities indicative of a cyberattack. ML algorithms can also continuously learn from new data and adapt to evolving threats, enhancing the overall cybersecurity posture.

2. **Strengthening Collaboration and Information Sharing:** Collaboration and information sharing among organizations, industries, and countries are crucial for proactive threat intelligence and effective incident response. Developing and fostering trusted partnerships can lead to a more comprehensive understanding of the threat landscape and enable the timely exchange of information, best practices, and lessons learned. For example, the establishment of sector-specific Information Sharing and Analysis Centers (ISACs) facilitates collaboration and knowledge sharing within industries such as finance, healthcare, and energy. Cross-sector initiatives and international cooperation frameworks also play a vital role in addressing global cyber threats.

3. **Implementing a Zero-Trust Security Model:**
The traditional perimeter-based security model is no longer sufficient in today's dynamic and interconnected digital environment. The zero-trust security model is gaining traction as a more effective approach to cybersecurity. This model assumes that no user or device can be trusted by default, and strict access controls and continuous authentication are required. By implementing granular access controls, multifactor authentication, and network segmentation, organizations can reduce the potential attack surface and limit the lateral movement of threats. Zero-trust also promotes continuous monitoring and analysis of user behavior to detect anomalous activities.

4. **Enhancing Cybersecurity Education and Workforce Development:**
Investing in cybersecurity education and workforce development is crucial to building a resilient future. As the demand for skilled

cybersecurity professionals continues to grow, it is essential to attract, train, and retain talent in the field. This includes partnerships between academia and industry, creating cybersecurity-focused curricula, providing hands-on training, and promoting cybersecurity career paths. Additionally, raising awareness among individuals and organizations about cybersecurity best practices and the importance of proactive measures can empower them to become active participants in maintaining a secure digital ecosystem.

5. **Addressing the Human Factor:**
While technological advancements are essential, it is important not to overlook the human factor in cybersecurity. Human errors, negligence, and malicious insider threats remain significant risks. Organizations should focus on creating a culture of cybersecurity awareness and accountability, providing regular training to employees, and implementing strong policies and procedures. This includes educating employees on phishing scams, social engineering tactics, and safe online practices. By promoting a security-conscious culture, organizations can mitigate human-related risks and strengthen their overall cybersecurity posture.

6. **Building Resilience Through Incident Response and Recovery:**
No matter how proactive organizations are, the possibility of a cyber incident cannot be completely eliminated. Therefore, having robust incident response and recovery plans in place is essential. Organizations should establish clear incident response procedures, conduct regular exercises and simulations, and establish relationships with external incident response teams. Testing the effectiveness of incident response plans through tabletop exercises can help identify areas for improvement and ensure a coordinated and efficient response in the event of an attack. It is through the collective effort of individuals, organizations, governments, and international collaborations that we can build a secure digital future. By continuously adapting to emerging threats, embracing innovation, and fostering a culture of cybersecurity, we can overcome challenges and ensure a resilient and trustworthy digital ecosystem for generations to come.

In addition to the pathways discussed above, there are several other important considerations to shape a resilient cybersecurity future. Let's explore some additional ideas:

7. **Privacy-Preserving Technologies:**
As data privacy concerns continue to rise, integrating privacy-preserving technologies into cybersecurity strategies becomes crucial. Techniques such as differential privacy, secure multiparty computation, and homomorphic encryption can enable secure data analysis and sharing while protecting sensitive information. By implementing privacy-enhancing technologies, organizations can build trust with their customers and stakeholders, ensuring that their data is handled in a secure and privacy-conscious manner.

8. **Cybersecurity Regulations and Standards:**
To create a resilient cybersecurity landscape, the development and enforcement of cybersecurity regulations and standards are essential. Governments and regulatory bodies play a vital role in establishing guidelines and requirements that organizations must follow to ensure cybersecurity best practices. Compliance with these regulations not only helps organizations protect themselves but also fosters a culture of security across industries and sectors. Standards such as ISO 27001, NIST Cybersecurity Framework, and GDPR provide a framework for organizations to assess and improve their cybersecurity posture.

9. **Continuous Monitoring and Threat Hunting:**
Proactive threat detection and response are crucial in an evolving threat landscape. Continuous monitoring of networks, systems, and applications allows organizations to identify potential vulnerabilities and respond to threats in real-time. Implementing threat hunting capabilities, which involves actively searching for indicators of compromise and potential threats, enables organizations to stay ahead of attackers. By leveraging advanced security analytics, machine learning, and threat intelligence, organizations can detect and respond to cyber threats more effectively.

10. **Resilient Infrastructure and Supply Chain Security:**
    As technology ecosystems become increasingly interconnected, securing the entire infrastructure and supply chain becomes critical. Organizations must assess and address vulnerabilities in their networks, cloud services, IoT devices, and third-party relationships. This includes conducting regular security assessments, implementing secure development practices, and establishing robust vendor management processes. By ensuring the security of the entire ecosystem, organizations can prevent potential compromises and minimize the impact of cyber-attacks.

11. **International Collaboration and Norm Development:**
    Cyber threats are not confined to national borders, making international collaboration and the development of global cybersecurity norms crucial. Countries, organizations, and stakeholders should work together to establish common frameworks, share threat intelligence, and coordinate incident response efforts. Initiatives like the Budapest Convention on Cybercrime and the Paris Call for Trust and Security in Cyberspace provide a foundation for international cooperation. By promoting shared values, norms, and standards, we can create a more secure and harmonized global cybersecurity landscape.

12. **Embracing Emerging Technologies:** As technology continues to advance, new innovations such as blockchain, quantum computing, and secure hardware have the potential to revolutionize cybersecurity. Blockchain technology, for instance, can enhance transparency, traceability, and tamper-proof record-keeping, making it valuable for securing transactions, identity management, and supply chain integrity. Quantum-resistant cryptography can prepare organizations for the future threat of quantum computers. Embracing and exploring the security implications of emerging technologies can help organizations stay ahead of potential threats and enable more robust cybersecurity solutions.

In conclusion, building a resilient cybersecurity future requires a multifaceted approach that combines technological advancements, collaboration, regulatory frameworks, and international cooperation. By embracing privacy-preserving technologies, establishing cybersecurity regulations and standards, implementing continuous monitoring and threat hunting capabilities, securing infrastructure and supply chains, fostering international collaboration, and leveraging emerging technologies, we can navigate the ever-changing threat landscape with resilience and confidence.

It is through a collective effort and a commitment to proactive cybersecurity practices that we can create a secure digital future. By staying vigilant, adapting to new challenges, and promoting a culture of security, we can mitigate risks, protect critical assets, and safeguard our digital ecosystems for the benefit of individuals, organizations, and society as a whole.

In conclusion, envisioning the roadmap to resilience requires a holistic approach that combines technological advancements, collaboration, education, and a focus on human factors. By embracing AI and ML, strengthening collaboration and information sharing, implementing a zero-trust security model, enhancing cybersecurity education and workforce development, addressing the human factor, and building resilient incident response and recovery capabilities, organizations and societies can navigate the evolving cybersecurity landscape with confidence.

Challenges Ahead: Future Threats and How to Prepare

In Chapter 14, Section 3, we delve into the challenges that lie ahead in the ever-evolving landscape of cybersecurity. As technology advances and threat actors become more sophisticated, it is crucial to anticipate future threats and prepare accordingly. This section explores key challenges and provides insights on how organizations and individuals can adapt to mitigate risks and enhance their cybersecurity resilience.

1. **Evolving Cyber Threat Landscape:**

The first challenge is the continuous evolution of the cyber threat landscape. As technology progresses, cybercriminals adapt their techniques and exploit new vulnerabilities. Emerging technologies such as artificial intelligence (AI) and the Internet of Things (IoT) bring new opportunities but also introduce new attack vectors. Organizations must stay updated on emerging threats, invest in threat intelligence capabilities, and implement proactive security measures to address evolving cyber risks.

2. **Advanced Persistent Threats (APTs):**
Advanced Persistent Threats (APTs) are highly sophisticated and targeted cyber-attacks that pose significant challenges to organizations. APTs involve persistent and stealthy infiltration, allowing threat actors to remain undetected for extended periods. These attacks can have severe consequences, including data breaches, intellectual property theft, and disruption of critical services. Organizations need to adopt proactive measures, such as continuous monitoring, threat hunting, and the use of advanced security analytics, to detect and respond to APTs effectively.

3. **Insider Threats:**
Insider threats, whether intentional or unintentional, remain a significant challenge for organizations. Insider threats can arise from employees, contractors, or partners who have access to sensitive information and systems. These threats can result in data breaches, intellectual property theft, or the compromise of critical infrastructure. Organizations need to implement robust access controls, conduct regular employee training, and establish monitoring mechanisms to detect and mitigate insider threats.

4. **Cloud Security:**
With the increasing adoption of cloud services, ensuring robust cloud security is crucial. Cloud environments introduce unique challenges such as shared responsibility models, data privacy concerns, and potential misconfigurations. Organizations must implement comprehensive security measures in their cloud deployments, including encryption, access controls, and regular security assessments. Employing cloud security frameworks and leveraging specialized cloud security solutions can help organizations mitigate the risks associated with cloud adoption.

5. **IoT Security:**
The proliferation of Internet of Things (IoT) devices presents significant security challenges. IoT devices are often connected to networks without adequate security measures, making them potential entry points for

cyber-attacks. Compromised IoT devices can be used to launch distributed denial of service (DDoS) attacks or gain unauthorized access to networks. Organizations and manufacturers must prioritize IoT security by implementing strong authentication mechanisms, regular software updates, and proper device lifecycle management.

6. **Social Engineering Attacks:**
Social engineering attacks, such as phishing, spear-phishing, and social manipulation, continue to be a prevalent and effective method used by cybercriminals. These attacks exploit human psychology to deceive individuals and gain unauthorized access to sensitive information. Organizations need to raise awareness among employees through cybersecurity training programs, conduct simulated phishing exercises, and implement multifactor authentication to mitigate the risk of social engineering attacks.

7. **Supply Chain Security:**
The complex and interconnected nature of modern supply chains presents a significant challenge in terms of cybersecurity. A breach in one organization's supply chain can have cascading effects on multiple entities. Organizations should conduct thorough due diligence on their suppliers and partners, establish security requirements and contractual obligations, and implement mechanisms to monitor and assess the security posture of their supply chain.

8. **Data Privacy and Compliance:**
The increasing focus on data privacy and compliance regulations presents a challenge for organizations. The implementation of stringent data protection regulations such as the General Data Protection Regulation (GDPR) and the California Consumer Privacy Act (CCPA) requires organizations to adopt privacy-by-design principles, implement data protection measures, and ensure compliance with regulatory requirements. Organizations need to establish robust data governance frameworks, conduct privacy impact assessments, and prioritize user consent and data transparency.

9. **Skills Gap and Workforce Development:**
   The shortage of skilled cybersecurity professionals poses a significant challenge in addressing evolving cyber threats. Organizations and educational institutions need to collaborate to bridge the skills gap by offering specialized cybersecurity training programs, promoting cybersecurity career pathways, and providing continuous professional development opportunities. Governments and organizations should also consider investing in cybersecurity apprenticeship programs, mentorship initiatives, and partnerships with academic institutions to cultivate a talented and diverse cybersecurity workforce.

10. **Collaboration and Information Sharing:** Effective collaboration and information sharing among organizations, governments, and international bodies are essential to address future cybersecurity challenges. Sharing threat intelligence, best practices, and lessons learned can help organizations stay ahead of emerging threats and strengthen their collective defense. Governments and regulatory bodies play a crucial role in facilitating information-sharing platforms, fostering public-private partnerships, and establishing legal frameworks that encourage collaboration while protecting sensitive information.

To address these challenges and prepare for the future, organizations and individuals should adopt a proactive and adaptive cybersecurity approach. This includes investing in advanced threat detection and response capabilities, adopting emerging technologies like AI and machine learning for cybersecurity, conducting regular risk assessments, promoting a culture of cybersecurity awareness and education, and fostering collaboration within the cybersecurity community.

By embracing these strategies, organizations can enhance their cybersecurity resilience, protect their critical assets, and contribute to a more secure digital ecosystem. It is through a collective effort, continuous innovation, and proactive measures that we can navigate the evolving threat landscape and build a resilient future in the face of cyber threats.

11. Cloud Security and Data Protection:

As organizations increasingly rely on cloud services, ensuring robust cloud security and data protection is essential. Cloud security encompasses various aspects, including secure configuration, access control, data encryption, and vulnerability management. Organizations should carefully select cloud service providers that offer strong security measures, compliance with industry standards, and transparent data handling practices. Implementing a multi-layered security approach, including network segmentation, data loss prevention, and continuous monitoring, helps protect sensitive data stored in the cloud.

12. Privacy-by-Design and Data Governance:

With the growing emphasis on data privacy and protection, organizations need to adopt a privacy-by-design approach and implement effective data governance practices. Privacy-by-design involves incorporating privacy and data protection principles into the design of systems, applications, and processes from the outset. This includes minimizing the collection of personally identifiable information, obtaining explicit user consent, implementing strong access controls, and conducting privacy impact assessments. Data governance ensures that data is appropriately managed, classified, and protected throughout its lifecycle, promoting compliance with privacy regulations and building customer trust.

13. Supply Chain Security:

The interconnected nature of modern supply chains presents significant cybersecurity risks. Cyber attackers may target the supply chain to gain unauthorized access to critical systems or compromise the integrity of products and services. Organizations should assess the cybersecurity posture of their supply chain partners, implement stringent vendor risk management processes, and establish clear contractual requirements regarding cybersecurity practices. Regular audits, penetration testing, and ongoing monitoring of supply chain partners' security practices can help identify and mitigate potential vulnerabilities.

14. **Incident Sharing and Threat Intelligence:**
Collaborative sharing of cyber threat intelligence and incident information plays a vital role in strengthening cybersecurity. Organizations should actively participate in information-sharing communities, industry forums, and threat intelligence sharing platforms. Sharing anonymized incident data, indicators of compromise, and best practices enhances collective situational awareness and enables a proactive defense against emerging threats. By contributing to and leveraging threat intelligence communities, organizations can stay ahead of evolving threats and enhance their incident response capabilities.

15. **Cybersecurity Awareness and Education:**
Building a strong cybersecurity culture within organizations requires continuous awareness and education efforts. Training programs, workshops, and awareness campaigns should be implemented to educate employees about the latest cyber threats, social engineering techniques, and best practices for maintaining strong security hygiene. Organizations should promote a security-first mindset and encourage employees to report suspicious activities, practice safe browsing and email habits, and adhere to security policies. By empowering employees with cybersecurity knowledge, organizations can create a workforce that actively contributes to the overall security posture.

16. **Cyber Insurance:**
As cyber threats become more sophisticated and prevalent, organizations are increasingly turning to cyber insurance as an additional layer of protection. Cyber insurance policies provide financial coverage and resources in the event of a cyber incident, including data breaches, business interruptions, and legal liabilities. Organizations should carefully assess their cybersecurity risks, review policy terms and conditions, and work closely with insurance providers to tailor coverage to their specific needs. Cyber insurance can help mitigate financial losses and facilitate a quicker recovery in the aftermath of a cyberattack.

17. **Continuous Monitoring and Threat Hunting:**
Traditional security measures are no longer sufficient in today's threat landscape. Organizations should implement continuous monitoring and proactive threat hunting capabilities to detect and respond to threats in real time. Continuous monitoring involves collecting and analyzing security event data from various sources to identify indicators of compromise and potential security incidents. Threat hunting involves actively searching for signs of malicious activity within the network and systems, using advanced analytics and threat intelligence. By adopting these proactive security measures, organizations can detect and respond to threats swiftly, minimizing the potential impact of cyber-attacks.

In conclusion, Section 3 highlights the changing cybersecurity landscape and the evolving needs of organizations in response to future threats. By considering the points mentioned above, organizations can proactively address emerging challenges, strengthen their cybersecurity postures, and ensure resilience in the face of evolving cyber threats. It is imperative for organizations to embrace a holistic and proactive approach, leveraging technology, implementing best practices, fostering collaboration, and continuously adapting to the ever-changing cybersecurity landscape.

The Potential of Blockchain: Envisioning its Future Role in Cybersecurity

Section 4 of Chapter 14 explores the potential of blockchain technology in enhancing cybersecurity and its future role in safeguarding digital ecosystems. As blockchain continues to evolve, its unique characteristics offer promising opportunities to address the challenges of cybersecurity and establish trust in digital transactions and interactions.

1. **Immutable and Transparent Ledger:**
Blockchain's immutable and transparent nature provides an inherent layer of security. Each transaction recorded on the blockchain is encrypted, time-stamped, and linked to the previous transaction, creating a chain of blocks that cannot be altered or tampered with. This feature ensures the integrity of data and prevents unauthorized modifications, making blockchain an ideal technology for securing critical information.

2. **Decentralization and Distributed Consensus:**
   The decentralized nature of blockchain eliminates the need for a central authority, reducing the risk of a single point of failure or control. Transactions are validated and verified by a distributed network of participants through a consensus mechanism, ensuring transparency and preventing fraudulent activities. This decentralized consensus makes blockchain resistant to attacks and manipulation, enhancing the security of digital transactions.

3. **Identity Management and Authentication:**
   Blockchain has the potential to revolutionize identity management and authentication processes. By providing a decentralized and secure digital identity framework, blockchain can empower individuals to have control over their personal information and selectively share it with trusted parties. This eliminates the need for centralized identity databases, reducing the risk of identity theft, data breaches, and unauthorized access.

4. **Secure Data Sharing and Collaboration:**
   Blockchain can facilitate secure data sharing and collaboration between multiple entities while maintaining privacy and data integrity. Through smart contracts and permissioned blockchain networks, organizations can establish predefined rules and conditions for data sharing, ensuring that data is exchanged only with authorized parties. This enables secure collaborations and information sharing without compromising data privacy and security.

5. **Supply Chain Integrity:**
   Blockchain has the potential to transform supply chain management by providing end-to-end visibility, traceability, and authenticity of products and transactions. By recording every step of the supply chain on a blockchain, organizations can ensure the integrity of goods, track their origin, and verify their authenticity. This reduces the risk of counterfeit products, ensures compliance with regulations, and enhances trust among supply chain participants.

6. **Incident Response and Forensics:**
Blockchain technology can play a significant role in incident response and forensic investigations. By recording and timestamping security-related events on a blockchain, organizations can create an immutable audit trail of activities, facilitating post-incident analysis and forensics. This can aid in identifying the source and impact of cyber-attacks, improving incident response capabilities, and enabling timely remediation.

7. **Decentralized Threat Intelligence:** Blockchain can enable the creation of decentralized threat intelligence platforms where participants can securely share and access threat information. This distributed model enhances the speed and accuracy of threat detection and response by leveraging collective intelligence from a global network of participants. By incentivizing the sharing of threat intelligence through blockchain-based tokens or rewards, organizations can foster a collaborative and proactive approach to cybersecurity.

8. **Integration with Emerging Technologies:**
Blockchain can integrate with other emerging technologies, such as artificial intelligence (AI) and Internet of Things (IoT), to enhance cybersecurity. AI algorithms can analyze blockchain data to detect patterns, anomalies, and potential threats, enabling proactive defense measures. In the context of IoT, blockchain can provide a secure and decentralized framework for managing device identities, securing data exchanges, and ensuring the integrity of IoT ecosystems.

9. **Regulatory and Compliance Benefits:**
Blockchain technology can streamline regulatory compliance by providing a transparent and auditable record of transactions. Compliance requirements, such as data protection regulations or financial reporting standards, can be enforced through smart contracts, ensuring automated and tamper-proof compliance. Blockchain's transparent and immutable ledger can simplify audits, reduce administrative burdens, and foster trust between organizations and regulators.

10. **Challenges and Considerations:**
    While blockchain offers significant potential, there are challenges and considerations to address. Scalability, energy consumption, privacy concerns, and interoperability with existing systems are among the key areas that need attention. Overcoming these challenges will require ongoing research, collaboration between industry and academia, and the development of standardized frameworks.

In conclusion, blockchain technology has the potential to revolutionize cybersecurity by enhancing trust, transparency, and data integrity. Its decentralized nature, immutability, and secure data-sharing capabilities offer promising solutions to the evolving cybersecurity landscape. However, realizing the full potential of blockchain in cybersecurity requires further research, collaboration, and industry-wide adoption. As organizations navigate the future, embracing blockchain and its innovative applications can contribute to building a resilient and secure digital future.

Final Thoughts: The Importance of Collective Action in Cybersecurity

Section 5 of Chapter 14 provides a comprehensive overview of the key takeaways from the preceding chapters and emphasizes the critical role of collective action in building a resilient future in the face of cyber threats. It highlights the importance of collaboration, shared responsibility, and continuous efforts in addressing the evolving landscape of cybersecurity.

1. **Collaboration for Cybersecurity:**
   Effective cybersecurity requires collaboration and partnership among governments, private sector organizations, academia, and individuals. By pooling resources, sharing knowledge and expertise, and collaborating on threat intelligence, stakeholders can collectively enhance their defenses and respond more effectively to cyber threats. Collaboration platforms, information-sharing organizations, and public-private partnerships foster trust, facilitate knowledge exchange, and enable coordinated responses to cyber incidents.

2. **Cybersecurity Awareness and Education:**
   Raising cybersecurity awareness and promoting digital literacy are vital components of building a resilient future. Education and training programs should be developed for individuals, organizations, and policymakers to understand the evolving threat landscape, adopt best practices, and make informed decisions. By fostering a culture of cybersecurity awareness, individuals can play an active role in safeguarding their digital lives and contribute to the collective security of the cyberspace.

3. **Strengthening Cyber Resilience:**
   Cyber resilience is the ability to prepare for, respond to, and recover from cyber incidents. It involves implementing proactive measures, developing incident response plans, and regularly testing and updating security protocols. Organizations should prioritize resilience by conducting risk assessments, implementing robust security measures, and investing in backup and disaster recovery solutions. By adopting a resilience mindset, organizations can minimize the impact of cyber incidents and ensure continuity of operations.

4. **Continual Innovation and Adaptation:**
   The cybersecurity landscape is constantly evolving, with new threats and technologies emerging regularly. Organizations and cybersecurity professionals must embrace a culture of continual innovation, staying abreast of the latest trends and leveraging emerging technologies to enhance defenses. Concepts such as artificial intelligence, machine learning, and advanced analytics can enable proactive threat detection, rapid incident response, and intelligent decision-making. Collaboration between industry, academia, and research institutions is crucial to driving innovation and developing cutting-edge solutions.

5. **Ethical Considerations and Digital Responsibility:**
   As technology advances, ethical considerations become increasingly important in cybersecurity. Organizations and individuals must prioritize responsible digital behavior, respecting privacy rights, and maintaining ethical standards. The use of personal data and the development of AI-

driven cybersecurity tools should be guided by ethical frameworks to ensure transparency, fairness, and accountability.

6. **International Cooperation and Norm Development:**
   Cyber threats are not confined by borders, necessitating international cooperation and the development of global norms and regulations. Governments, organizations, and international bodies should collaborate to establish common standards, norms, and legal frameworks to deter cybercriminals, promote responsible behavior, and ensure the protection of critical infrastructure and sensitive data. International alliances and information-sharing initiatives facilitate cooperation, coordination, and collective action against cyber threats.

7. **Blockchain's Role in Cybersecurity:**
   Blockchain technology holds immense potential in enhancing cybersecurity and addressing challenges such as data integrity, identity management, and secure transactions. Its decentralized and transparent nature can enhance trust, mitigate risks, and enable secure data sharing. Organizations should explore the various applications of blockchain in cybersecurity, such as secure identity verification, decentralized threat intelligence sharing, and supply chain integrity. Collaboration between industry, academia, and blockchain experts can drive innovation and establish best practices in this field.

8. **Investment in Research and Development:**
   To stay ahead of cyber threats, significant investments in research and development are crucial. Governments, industry leaders, and academia should allocate resources to advance cybersecurity technologies, promote innovation, and develop cutting-edge solutions. Collaboration between research institutions and industry can drive breakthroughs in areas such as threat intelligence, encryption algorithms, secure software development, and quantum-resistant cryptography. Encouraging research and development partnerships fosters innovation and strengthens the collective response to cyber threats.

9. **Legislative and Policy Support:**
   Governments play a vital role in fostering a secure cyberspace by enacting robust legislation, policies, and regulations. They should establish legal frameworks that promote cybersecurity, protect privacy, and hold cybercriminals accountable. Policies should incentivize organizations to invest in cybersecurity, encourage information sharing, and provide support for victims of cybercrime. Collaboration between governments, industry stakeholders, and policy experts is essential in crafting effective legislation and policies that address the evolving cyber threat landscape.

10. **Continued Vigilance and Adaptability:**
    Cybersecurity is an ongoing process that requires constant vigilance and adaptability. Organizations must stay proactive, regularly assessing risks, updating security measures, and educating their workforce. Cybersecurity professionals should engage in continuous learning and development to keep pace with evolving threats and technologies. By fostering a culture of continual improvement and adaptability, organizations can effectively respond to emerging threats and ensure the resilience of their cybersecurity defenses.

In conclusion, a resilient future in the face of cyber threats relies on collective action, collaboration, and a proactive mindset. By embracing collaboration, enhancing cybersecurity awareness, strengthening resilience, fostering innovation, and advocating for ethical considerations, stakeholders can work together to mitigate the risks posed by cyber threats and build a more secure digital ecosystem. The importance of international cooperation, the potential of blockchain technology, and the need for investment in research and development are all highlighted as crucial elements in achieving a resilient future.

By fostering collaboration among stakeholders, sharing information and best practices, and promoting cybersecurity education, organizations and individuals can collectively enhance their defenses against cyber threats. Through partnerships and alliances, they can coordinate responses and share threat intelligence to detect and mitigate attacks more effectively.

The concept of cyber resilience is emphasized as a proactive approach to cybersecurity, focusing on preparedness, incident response, and recovery. By conducting risk assessments, implementing robust security measures, and investing in backup and disaster recovery solutions, organizations can minimize the impact of cyber incidents and ensure continuity of operations.

Continual innovation and adaptation are essential to staying ahead of cyber threats. The rapid evolution of technology calls for a culture of innovation, where organizations and cybersecurity professionals embrace emerging technologies such as artificial intelligence, machine learning, and advanced analytics. These technologies can enhance threat detection, automate incident response, and enable intelligent decision-making.

Ethical considerations and digital responsibility are vital in maintaining trust and protecting privacy rights. Organizations and individuals must prioritize responsible digital behavior, ensuring the ethical use of personal data and the development of AI-driven cybersecurity tools. By adhering to ethical frameworks, they can uphold transparency, fairness, and accountability.

International cooperation and norm development play a crucial role in addressing cyber threats that transcend national borders. Collaborative efforts among governments, organizations, and international bodies are necessary to establish common standards, norms, and legal frameworks. These frameworks deter cybercriminals, promote responsible behavior, and protect critical infrastructure and sensitive data.

The potential of blockchain technology in cybersecurity is highlighted as a decentralized and transparent solution for enhancing trust, securing data integrity, and enabling secure transactions. Its applications in areas such as secure identity verification, decentralized threat intelligence sharing, and supply chain integrity can revolutionize cybersecurity practices.

Investment in research and development is essential to stay at the forefront of cybersecurity. Governments, industry leaders, and academia should allocate resources to advance cybersecurity technologies, promote innovation, and develop cutting-edge solutions. Collaboration between research institutions and industry can drive breakthroughs in areas such as threat intelligence, encryption algorithms, secure software development, and quantum-resistant cryptography.

Legislative and policy support are crucial for establishing a secure cyberspace. Governments should enact robust legislation, policies, and regulations that promote cybersecurity, protect privacy, and hold cybercriminals accountable. Effective policies incentivize organizations to invest in cybersecurity, encourage information sharing, and provide support for victims of cybercrime.

Continued vigilance and adaptability are essential to maintaining strong cybersecurity defenses. Organizations must remain proactive, regularly assess risks, update security measures, and educate their workforce. Cybersecurity professionals should engage in continuous learning and development to stay abreast of evolving threats and technologies.

In conclusion, a resilient future in the face of cyber threats requires collective action and a comprehensive approach. By fostering collaboration, raising awareness, strengthening resilience, driving innovation, promoting ethics, advocating for international cooperation, and investing in research and development, stakeholders can build a more secure and resilient digital ecosystem. Through these concerted efforts, we can mitigate risks, respond effectively to cyber incidents, and protect our valuable digital assets.

Index of Terms and Concepts

Artificial Intelligence (AI): Refers to the simulation of human intelligence in machines, enabling them to perform tasks that typically require human intelligence, such as problem-solving, decision-making, and language understanding.

Blockchain: A decentralized and immutable digital ledger that records transactions across a network of computers, ensuring transparency, security, and trust in data exchanges.

Blockchain in US Elections: The application of blockchain technology to enhance the security and integrity of electoral processes, providing tamper-resistant and transparent voting systems.

Cyber Pandemic: A widespread and large-scale cyber crisis that can cause global disruptions and impact digital systems on a massive scale.

Cyber Resilience: The ability of digital systems and networks to withstand, adapt, and recover from cyber-attacks, minimizing disruption and maintaining their functionality.

Cyber Threat Intelligence: Information about potential cyber threats, including their capabilities, motivations, and tactics, used to proactively defend against cyber-attacks.

Decentralization: The distribution of data and authority across multiple nodes or participants in a network, reducing the risk of a single point of failure.

Digital Identity: A digital representation of an individual's identity used to authenticate and authorize their access to various online services and resources.

Fourth Industrial Revolution: The current era marked by the convergence of digital, physical, and biological technologies, driving significant societal and economic transformations.

Global Cooperation: Collaborative efforts between nations and stakeholders to address global challenges, including cybersecurity threats, through information sharing and joint initiatives.

Internet of Things (IoT): The network of interconnected physical devices embedded with sensors, software, and other technologies that enable them to collect and exchange data.

Machine Learning: A subset of AI that enables systems to learn and improve from experience without explicit programming, enhancing their performance over time.

Phishing Attacks: Deceptive attempts to obtain sensitive information, such as usernames, passwords, and financial details, by masquerading as a trustworthy entity.

Ransomware: Malicious software that encrypts a user's data, demanding a ransom for its release, often causing significant disruption and financial loss.

Smart Contracts: Self-executing contracts with terms written in code, automatically executing actions when specified conditions are met, enabling trustless transactions.

Supply Chain Management: The coordination and oversight of the flow of goods, services, and information across the entire supply chain, ensuring efficiency and transparency.

Transparency: The quality of openness and visibility in the operations and processes of digital systems, promoting accountability and trust.

US Election Cyber Threats: Examination of the cybersecurity challenges faced during the 2024 US election, including potential cyber-attacks on voting systems and election infrastructure.

Vulnerabilities: Weaknesses or flaws in digital systems that can be exploited by cyber attackers to gain unauthorized access or cause harm.

Zero-Day Exploits: Vulnerabilities or software weaknesses that are unknown to vendors and, therefore, lack available patches, leaving systems at risk of attack.

By offering this comprehensive Index of Terms and Concepts, readers can conveniently navigate through the book to find specific topics of interest. The index covers essential terms from blockchain technology and cybersecurity, including real-world examples like the use of blockchain in US elections and insights into cyber threats faced during significant events like the 2024 US election. It also includes concepts related to cyber resilience, artificial intelligence, transparency, and supply chain management, providing readers with a quick overview of the book's key subjects and relevant use cases.

Appendix A
Cybersecurity Resources and Tools

In this comprehensive appendix, you will find a curated list of valuable cybersecurity resources and tools to empower you in enhancing your knowledge and understanding of the subject matter. These resources have been carefully selected to provide a diverse range of references, websites, online platforms, software, and frameworks that can serve as indispensable assets in your journey toward building cyber resilience and safeguarding against cyber threats.

1. **Cybersecurity Organizations and Websites:**
   - Cybersecurity and Infrastructure Security Agency (CISA): A U.S. government agency that provides valuable resources, alerts, and guidelines to enhance cybersecurity across critical infrastructure sectors.
   - National Institute of Standards and Technology (NIST) Cybersecurity Framework: A comprehensive framework that offers guidelines, best practices, and standards to manage and reduce cybersecurity risks.
   - International Organization for Standardization (ISO) Cybersecurity Standards: A series of international standards that provide guidance on information security management systems and cybersecurity controls.
   - Center for Internet Security (CIS): A non-profit organization that offers best practice guidelines and cybersecurity resources for safeguarding digital assets and systems.
   - United States Computer Emergency Readiness Team (US-CERT): A division of the Department of Homeland Security that provides

cybersecurity information, alerts, and resources to defend against and respond to cyber incidents.

2. **Cybersecurity Blogs and News Outlets:**
    - KrebsOnSecurity by Brian Krebs: An investigative journalist's blog that covers the latest cybersecurity threats, data breaches, and emerging cybercrime trends.
    - The Hacker News: A leading source for cybersecurity news, reports, and analysis of vulnerabilities, hacking incidents, and cyber-attacks.
    - Dark Reading: A trusted cybersecurity news and information platform that provides in-depth coverage of cybersecurity topics, industry trends, and expert insights.
    - Threatpost: A renowned cybersecurity news site that covers breaking news, analysis, and research on the latest cyber threats and data breaches.
    - CyberScoop: An online publication that focuses on reporting cybersecurity news, developments in technology policy, and insights from industry experts and policymakers.

3. **Cybersecurity Training and Courses:**
    - SANS Institute: A leading provider of cybersecurity training, certifications, and research, offering a wide range of courses and programs for professionals at all levels.
    - Coursera Cybersecurity Courses: An online learning platform that hosts various cybersecurity courses from top universities and institutions, catering to diverse skill levels and topics.
    - Udemy Cybersecurity Training: An extensive collection of cybersecurity courses taught by industry experts, covering practical skills, ethical hacking, and more.
    - Cybrary IT and Cybersecurity Courses: A platform that offers free and premium cybersecurity courses, providing hands-on learning experiences for cybersecurity professionals.
    - edX Cybersecurity Program: An online learning platform that offers comprehensive cybersecurity courses and programs from prestigious universities and institutions worldwide.
    - Cybersecurity Tools and Software:

- Wireshark: A widely used network protocol analyzer for troubleshooting and security analysis, allowing users to inspect data packets on a network.
- Nmap: A powerful network scanning tool used for discovering hosts and services on a computer network, aiding in vulnerability assessment.
- Metasploit: An advanced penetration testing framework that aids in developing and executing exploit code against remote targets for ethical hacking purposes.
- Snort: An open-source intrusion detection and prevention system (IDS/IPS) that monitors network traffic to detect and respond to security threats.
- Burp Suite: A popular web vulnerability scanner used for security testing web applications, identifying potential weaknesses and vulnerabilities.

This extensive appendix provides readers with an array of resources and tools to deepen their understanding of cybersecurity, empowering them to navigate the complex world of cyber threats and take proactive measures to bolster their digital defenses. By leveraging these invaluable resources, you can stay up to date with the latest developments, access quality training, and employ cutting-edge tools to fortify your organization's cybersecurity posture. Remember, a collaborative and informed approach is key to fostering a secure digital environment for ourselves and the world.

Appendix B
Further Reading and Research

This comprehensive list of further reading and research materials is designed to offer readers a deeper exploration of the topics covered in "Cyber Pandemic: A Proactive Look at Blockchain and AI to Prevent the Next Global Shutdown". These resources have been carefully selected to provide diverse perspectives, in-depth analysis, and expert insights into the field of cybersecurity, blockchain technology, AI applications, and their collective impact on safeguarding against cyber threats and potential global shutdowns.

1. **Books:**
    - "The Cybersecurity Canon: Must-Read Books on Cybersecurity" by Palo Alto Networks and Cybersecurity Canon Committee: An authoritative collection of essential books that have significantly contributed to the field of cybersecurity, providing readers with foundational knowledge and expert perspectives.
    - "Mastering Bitcoin: Unlocking Digital Cryptocurrencies" by Andreas M. Antonopoulos: A comprehensive guide that dives into the intricacies of Bitcoin, the pioneering cryptocurrency, exploring its underlying blockchain technology and its implications for the future of finance.
    - "Blockchain Revolution: How the Technology Behind Bitcoin Is Changing Money, Business, and the World" by Don Tapscott and Alex Tapscott: A compelling exploration of blockchain's potential to revolutionize industries beyond finance, offering insights into its transformative power.
    - "Cryptoassets: The Innovative Investor's Guide to Bitcoin and Beyond" by Chris Burniske and Jack Tatar: An insightful book that

introduces readers to the diverse world of cryptoassets, their investment potential, and the underlying blockchain technology.

2. **Academic Journals and Research Papers:**
   - "Bitcoin: A Peer-to-Peer Electronic Cash System" by Satoshi Nakamoto (Bitcoin Whitepaper): The original whitepaper that introduced Bitcoin, revolutionizing the concept of digital currency and paving the way for blockchain technology.
   - "Ethereum: A Secure Decentralized Generalized Transaction Ledger" by Dr. Gavin Wood (Ethereum Whitepaper): The foundational whitepaper of Ethereum, a versatile blockchain platform enabling smart contracts and decentralized applications.
   - "Blockchain Consensus Protocols in the Wild" by Ghassan O. Karame and others (Cryptology ePrint Archive, Report 2019/219): An academic paper that provides a comprehensive overview of various blockchain consensus mechanisms, including Proof of Work and Proof of Stake.

3. **Whitepapers and Reports:**
   - "Bitcoin: A New Gold Rush?" by Citi GPS (Global Perspectives and Solutions): A research report that assesses Bitcoin's potential as a digital gold and its implications for the global financial landscape.
   - "The Role of Blockchain in Global Trade" by the World Economic Forum: A whitepaper that explores the application of blockchain technology in enhancing transparency and efficiency in global trade and supply chain management.
   - "The Impact of Blockchain Technology on Finance: A Catalyst for Change" by Deloitte: A whitepaper that examines how blockchain is reshaping the financial industry, offering insights into its role in payments, trade finance, and more.

4. **Online Platforms and Webinars:**
   - CoinDesk: A leading online platform covering the latest news, analysis, and insights related to blockchain, cryptocurrencies, and the broader digital asset ecosystem.

- Blockchain at Berkeley: An educational platform by the University of California, Berkeley, offering free online courses on blockchain technology and cryptocurrencies.
- Bitcoin and Cryptocurrency Technologies: A Coursera course by Princeton University, providing an in-depth understanding of Bitcoin and other cryptocurrencies.

5. **Government Policies on Blockchain:**
    - "U.S. Congress Report: Understanding Blockchain Technology" by the Congressional Research Service (CRS): A comprehensive report prepared for U.S. Congress members, offering insights into the technical aspects and potential applications of blockchain technology.
    - "Blockchain in Government: Benefits and Challenges for the Public Sector" by the Organization for Economic Cooperation and Development (OECD): An OECD report exploring the role of blockchain in improving government services, transparency, and efficiency.
    - "Blockchain in Government: A Practical Guide to the Implementation of Blockchain Technology in the Public Sector" by the World Government Summit: A practical guide that showcases real-world use cases of blockchain adoption by various governments around the world.

By exploring the resources listed in this appendix, readers can gain a comprehensive understanding of blockchain technology, its groundbreaking applications in various sectors, and its symbiotic relationship with cryptocurrencies like Bitcoin. These materials serve as valuable references for professionals, academics, policymakers, and anyone seeking to harness the transformative potential of blockchain in shaping a secure and innovative digital future. Embracing these resources, including government policies on blockchain, will contribute to proactive cybersecurity practices and the prevention of potential cyber pandemics, ensuring a resilient and flourishing digital landscape for generations to come.

Appendix C
Glossary of Key Terms

This comprehensive glossary provides in-depth definitions and detailed explanations of essential terms and concepts featured in "Cyber Pandemic: A Proactive Look at Blockchain and AI to Prevent the Next Global Shutdown". These key terms play a pivotal role in comprehending the intricate interplay between cybersecurity, blockchain technology, artificial intelligence (AI), and their profound implications for safeguarding against cyber threats and potential global shutdowns.

1. **Blockchain:**
   A decentralized, distributed, and immutable digital ledger that securely records transactions across multiple computers or nodes. Each transaction is stored in a "block" linked to its previous block, forming an unalterable chain of information.

2. **Cryptocurrency:**
   Digital or virtual currencies that utilize cryptography for secure financial transactions, functioning independently of a central authority, such as a central bank.

3. **Cybersecurity:**
   The practice of protecting computer systems, networks, and data from malicious attacks, unauthorized access, and damage, ensuring the confidentiality, integrity, and availability of information.

4. **Cyber Pandemic:**
A large-scale and systemic cyber-attack capable of causing widespread disruption and damage to digital systems, networks, and services on a global scale, akin to the impact of a biological pandemic.

5. **Decentralization:**
A defining characteristic of blockchain technology, wherein data and control are distributed across multiple nodes, eliminating the need for a central authority and enhancing resilience against single points of failure.

6. **Internet of Things (IoT):**
The vast network of physical devices, vehicles, appliances, and objects embedded with sensors, software, and connectivity, enabling them to collect and exchange data over the internet.

7. **Smart Contracts:**
Self-executing contracts with terms and conditions directly written into code. Smart contracts automatically execute actions when predefined conditions are met, enabling trustless and automated agreements.

8. **Consensus Mechanism:**
A protocol that ensures agreement among network participants on the validity of transactions and the state of the blockchain, ensuring the integrity and security of the distributed ledger.

9. **Artificial Intelligence (AI):**
The simulation of human intelligence processes by machines, encompassing learning, reasoning, problem-solving, and decision-making to achieve tasks without explicit programming.

10. **Ransomware:**
Malicious software designed to block access to a computer system or data until a ransom is paid, often in cryptocurrency, to the attackers.

11. **Public Key Infrastructure (PKI):**
A system that uses public and private cryptographic keys to secure communications, verify identities, and establish trust in digital environments.

12. **Supply Chain Management:**
The effective management of the flow of goods and services, involving the movement and storage of raw materials, work-in-progress inventory, and finished products from point of origin to consumption.

13. **Digital Identity:**
A unique representation of an individual or entity in the digital realm, used for authentication, authorization, and personalization of online services and transactions.

14. **Zero-Day Vulnerability:**
A software vulnerability unknown to the vendor, for which no security patch or fix is available, making it highly exploitable by cyber attackers.

15. **Multifactor Authentication (MFA):**
A robust security method that requires users to provide multiple forms of identification, such as passwords, biometrics, or security tokens, before granting access to a system or account.

16. **Distributed Denial of Service (DDoS) Attack:**
A cyber-attack where multiple compromised systems are used to flood a target system with excessive requests, causing it to become unavailable, disrupting normal operations.

17. **Encryption:**
The process of converting plaintext data into ciphertext using algorithms to protect it from unauthorized access, ensuring confidentiality and data security.

18. **Tokenization:**
   The process of converting sensitive data into tokens, which are non-sensitive substitutes that retain no exploitable value, reducing the risk of data breaches and unauthorized access.

19. **Quantum Computing:**
   An advanced computing technology that leverages quantum-mechanical phenomena to perform complex calculations exponentially faster than traditional computers, potentially impacting encryption and security protocols.

This comprehensive glossary serves as a valuable and indispensable reference to demystify and clarify the terminology used throughout the book. Understanding these key terms is vital for grasping the nuances and potential impact of blockchain, AI, and cybersecurity in shaping a resilient and secure digital future. Armed with this knowledge, readers can confidently navigate the complexities of the digital landscape and make informed decisions to safeguard against cyber threats and create a more secure and productive global digital environment.

Appendix D
References

This section provides a comprehensive list of references used throughout the book "Cyber Pandemic: A Proactive Look at Blockchain and AI to Prevent the Next Global Shutdown". These resources have been instrumental in shaping the content, insights, and analysis presented in the book and serve as valuable sources for further research and exploration into the dynamic field of cybersecurity, blockchain technology, and artificial intelligence.

1. **Books:**

    - "Blockchain Basics: A Non-Technical Introduction in 25 Steps" by Daniel Drescher: This book offers a clear and accessible introduction to blockchain technology, explaining its fundamental concepts and applications in various industries, including cybersecurity.
    - "The Basics of Bitcoins and Blockchains" by Antony Lewis: As the title suggests, this book provides a comprehensive overview of Bitcoin and blockchain technology, covering key aspects such as security, cryptography, and decentralized networks.
    - "Blockchain Revolution: How the Technology Behind Bitcoin and Other Cryptocurrencies is Changing the World" by Don Tapscott and Alex Tapscott: The authors explore the transformative potential of blockchain technology beyond cryptocurrencies, highlighting its impact on cybersecurity, supply chains, and governance.
    - "The Inevitable: Understanding the 12 Technological Forces That Will Shape Our Future" by Kevin Kelly: While not directly

focused on blockchain, this book provides valuable insights into the broader technological trends shaping the future, including their implications for cybersecurity and society.
- "Artificial Intelligence: A Guide for Thinking Humans" by Melanie Mitchell: This book delves into the world of artificial intelligence, its challenges, and potential risks in cybersecurity and beyond.

2. **Research Papers and Reports:**

- "The Impact of Blockchain on Cybersecurity" by Cybersecurity Ventures: This research paper analyzes the role of blockchain technology in enhancing cybersecurity practices and mitigating cyber threats.
- "Blockchain Technology and the GDPR: How the Technology Impacts the Application of Data Protection Law" by European Union Agency for Cybersecurity (ENISA): The report examines the implications of blockchain on data protection and cybersecurity regulations, particularly in the context of the General Data Protection Regulation (GDPR).
- "Blockchain: Unchained? The Implications of Blockchain Technologies for Government" by Deloitte: This report explores the potential use cases of blockchain technology in government operations, including its impact on cybersecurity and data integrity.
- "Blockchain and Cybersecurity: Safety and Security for Blockchain Systems" by NIST: This publication by the National Institute of Standards and Technology (NIST) delves into the security aspects of blockchain systems and provides guidelines for ensuring safety and security.
- "Cryptocurrencies and the Evolution of Cybercrime" by INTERPOL: The research paper investigates the relationship between cryptocurrencies and cybercrime, emphasizing the importance of robust cybersecurity measures in the digital age.

3. **Articles:**

   - "How Blockchain Technology Can Improve Cybersecurity" by Forbes: This article explores the potential of blockchain in enhancing cybersecurity, emphasizing its role in securing data and preventing data breaches.
   - "The Rise of Cyber Pandemic and Its Implications" by World Economic Forum: The article sheds light on the concept of a cyber pandemic and its potential global impact, highlighting the importance of proactive cybersecurity measures.
   - "The Role of Blockchain in Cybersecurity: Enhancing Trust, Security, and Privacy in the Digital Era" by Security Intelligence: This article discusses the ways blockchain can bolster trust and security in the digital landscape, safeguarding against cyber threats.
   - "Blockchain Technology in Government: Benefits and Challenges" by The Brookings Institution: The article explores the potential benefits and challenges of implementing blockchain technology in government operations, with a focus on cybersecurity and data protection.
   - "Artificial Intelligence and Cybersecurity: The New Frontier" by CSO Online: This article examines the intersection of artificial intelligence and cybersecurity, addressing how AI can be used both as a defense mechanism and as a potential tool for cyber attackers.

   Whitepapers and Technical Documentation:
   - "Bitcoin: A Peer-to-Peer Electronic Cash System" by Satoshi Nakamoto: The iconic whitepaper that introduced Bitcoin, outlining its underlying principles and cryptographic foundations.
   - "Ethereum: A Next-Generation Smart Contract and Decentralized Application Platform" by Vitalik Buterin: The whitepaper that introduced Ethereum, describing its capabilities as a platform for building decentralized applications and smart contracts.
   - "Hyperledger Fabric: A Distributed Operating System for Permissioned Blockchains" by Hyperledger: The technical documentation of Hyperledger Fabric, a permissioned blockchain

platform that provides security features suitable for enterprise applications.

Government and Official Reports:

"National Cyber Strategy of the United States of America" by The White House: This report outlines the strategic approach to cybersecurity taken by the U.S. government, addressing the importance of leveraging innovative technologies like blockchain.

"European Strategy for Data" by European Commission: The official strategy document of the European Commission concerning data protection and security, acknowledging the role of emerging technologies such as blockchain.

"National Strategy to Secure Cyberspace" by U.S. Department of Homeland Security: The strategy document that outlines the U.S. government's approach to securing cyberspace and the importance of advanced technologies in achieving this goal.

"Cybersecurity Strategy" by Australian Government: This strategy report provides insights into the Australian government's approach to cybersecurity, highlighting the exploration of cutting-edge technologies like blockchain.

Websites and Online Resources:

National Institute of Standards and Technology (NIST)
https://www.nist.gov/: The official website of NIST, offering a wealth of cybersecurity and blockchain-related resources, standards, and guidelines.

Blockchain Research Institute
https://www.blockchainresearchinstitute.org/: An independent think tank dedicated to blockchain research, providing valuable reports, articles, and insights on the technology's applications.

World Economic Forum Cybersecurity

https://www.weforum.org/focus/cybersecurity: The cybersecurity section of the World Economic Forum's website, featuring reports and articles on cybersecurity challenges and solutions.

Cybersecurity and Infrastructure Security Agency (CISA) https://www.cisa.gov/: The official website of CISA, offering cybersecurity resources, alerts, and guidelines for individuals and organizations.

By exploring the diverse range of resources mentioned above, readers can gain a comprehensive understanding of the multifaceted relationship between cybersecurity and blockchain technology. These references not only provide valuable theoretical insights but also present practical use cases and governmental policies that highlight the transformative potential of blockchain in enhancing cybersecurity measures across the globe. As the field of cybersecurity continues to evolve, these resources will serve as vital guides for policymakers, researchers, and practitioners in developing resilient and secure solutions to combat cyber threats.

Printed in the USA
CPSIA information can be obtained
at www.ICGtesting.com
CBHW031624131124
17315CB00025B/643